LIB/LEND/002

UNIVERSITY OF

WITHDRAWN

D1336079

WP 0880177 0

Women in Western
Political Philosophy

Also by Ellen Kennedy

Carl Schmitt: The Crisis of Parliamentary Democracy
(The MIT Press, 1985)

Also by Susan Mendus

Aspects of Toleration (Methuen, 1985)

Women in Western Political Philosophy
Kant to Nietzsche

Edited by

Ellen Kennedy
Lecturer in Politics
University of York

and

Susan Mendus
Lecturer in Philosophy and
Morrell Fellow in Toleration, University of York

UNIVERSITY OF WOLVERHAMPTON
LIBRARY

Acc No. 880177

CLASS

CONTROL
0710807317

305.
4201

DATE
12 DEC 1995

SITE
DY

WOM

WHEATSHEAF BOOKS

First published in Great Britain in 1987 by
WHEATSHEAF BOOKS LTD
A MEMBER OF THE HARVESTER PRESS PUBLISHING GROUP
Publisher: John Spiers
16 Ship Street, Brighton, Sussex

© Ellen Kennedy and Susan Mendus, 1987

British Library Cataloguing in Publication Data
Women in western political philosophy:
   Kant to Nietzsche
   1. Women—Social conditions
   2. Political science—History
   I. Kennedy, Ellen   II. Mendus, Susan
   305.4'2'01   HQ1122

   ISBN 0-7108-0731-7
   ISBN 0-7108-0726-0 Pbk

Typeset in Times Roman 11pt by
Graham Burn Productions
Printed and bound in Great Britain by
Biddles Ltd, Guildford and King's Lynn

All rights reserved

THE HARVESTER PRESS PUBLISHING GROUP
The Harvester Group comprises Harvester Press Ltd (chiefly
publishing literature, fiction, philosophy, psychology, and
science and trade books); Harvester Press Microform
Publications Ltd (publishing in microform previously
unpublished archives, scarce printed sources, and indexes to
these collections); Wheatsheaf Books Ltd (chiefly publishing in
economics, international politics, sociology, women's studies
and related social sciences).

Contents

Acknowledgements   vi

Introduction   1
1. Kant: An Honest but Narrow-Minded Bourgeois?
    Susan Mendus   21
2. Virtue and Commerce: Women in the Making of
    Adam Smith's Political Economy
    Jane Rendall   44
3. Rousseau's Two Concepts of Citizenship
    Margaret Canovan   78
4. Humboldt and the Romantics: Neither Hausfrau
    nor Citoyenne
    Ursula Vogel   106
5. Women and the Hegelian State
    Joanna Hodge   127
6. Utilitarianism and Feminism
    Lea Campos Boralevi   159
7. Nietzsche: Women as Untermensch
    Ellen Kennedy   179

Bibliography   202
Index   211

Acknowledgements

The final editing work on this book was done during the early part of my period as Morrell Fellow in Toleration at the University of York. I am grateful to the trustees of the C. and J.B. Morrell Trust for their generosity in funding my research.

Thanks are due to Mrs Jacqueline Morgan for her exemplary typing, and to Edward Elgar of Wheatsheaf Books who has been a most patient and sympathetic editor.

Susan Mendus

Introduction

Ellen Kennedy and Susan Mendus

The essays collected in this volume focus on some of the most influential political philosophers writing in the period from the Enlightenment to the late nineteenth century. Their work spans an age that witnessed dramatic changes in the way people thought about themselves and their government, a period in which the rights we take for granted today were first declared and fought for in the great revolutions of eighteenth century America and France. Seen against the backdrop of political thought from Plato and Aristotle through the Middle Ages and into the Renaissance, political philosophy in this period developed a remarkable conception of politics and the state: a theory of individual rights and personal freedoms which liberalism in the nineteenth century strove to realize.

Two concepts were essential to this view of politics. The first was a notion of human equality derived from natural law theory that was asserted typically in the American Declaration of Independence, the French Declaration of the Rights of Man and by successive liberal assemblies and constitutions throughout the nineteenth century and into the twentieth. However differently the idea of 'the rights of man' was expressed in the various political cultures of Western Europe and North America, however gradually or suddenly it appeared in the various nation-states here, it was and remains the central normative conception of modern political thought. Even where it has been augmented or transformed by socialist ideas and institutions, this essential conception of Western liberalism has preserved its place on the agenda of political consciousness and action today. The second characteristic of political philosophy in this period was its concern with the definition of the scope and powers of public authority. Whereas political thought in the preceding two centuries, and much political practice in Europe and England, had emphasized the sovereign power of the state as a factor independent of social life and in principle unrestrained, philosophers from Locke onwards asserted the primacy of individual freedom. In the late eighteenth century Montesquieu and Kant developed a theory of the state in which a normative individualism became the criterion of public power. Those institutional safeguards and checks on governmental power now familiar in the liberal notion of the state—division of powers, rule of law, checks and balances—were intended to protect individual freedom against arbitrary transgressions and the encroachment of the state.

Suffrage rights and legal equality were the formal prerequisites for a political system on this model. But even in America and Europe, these rights were only gradually extended to encompass the whole of the adult population. Successive barriers to full citizenship had to be overcome before everyone was entitled to the rights and freedoms characteristic of modern liberal democracy. For much of the period from the late eighteenth to the early twentieth century, most of the populations of America and Europe did not enjoy these rights.

This central problem in modern political thought did not, as Gierke observed a hundred years ago, appear suddenly in the history of European philosophy. Aspects of what Gierke called the 'ancient-modern' were already evident in the later middle ages and these grew together with the dissolution of medieval social life and the emergence of natural rights theories. Towards the end of the middle ages the conceptions of a sovereign state and a sovereign individual ('state absolutism' and 'individualism', as Gierke called them) increasingly became the central axioms of social, constitutional and political thought in Europe.[1] Thereafter all principled political debate and opposition focused on the relations between these two.

If the middle ages were a melting pot of ancient and modern, European politics concentrated its distillations in increasingly powerful doses during the next century. By 1500

absolute monarchy had become, or was rapidly becoming, the prevailing type of government in western Europe. Everywhere there was an enormous wreckage of medieval institutions. [Absolute monarchy] overturned feudal constitutionalism and the free city-states on which medieval civilisation had largely depended ... the Church itself, the most characteristic of all medieval institutions, itself fell prey to it, or to the social forms on which it depended.[2]

The complicated network of rights and duties in a land-locked agricultural society gave way to social and political institutions more suited to the interests of men, of money, and of initiative. The nation and the king, not the city and the emperor pope, were the new political factors in Europe. During the sixteenth and seventeenth centuries Jean Bodin and Thomas Hobbes asserted a concept of sovereignty that took no heed of the restraints feudal social life had imposed on the state. Within the new European nation-states, too, the question of a central political authority seemed to Hobbes and the other absolutists, in the wake of the Reformation and religious wars, a more pressing problem than individual rights.

Of all the groups excluded from full citizenship, none was more stubbornly barred than women, nor were philosophical arguments for exclusion from the vote and from legal equality so patently self-contradictory and archaic in any other case. In almost all respects the theories of Adam Smith and Hegel, of Kant and Mill, of Rousseau and Nietzsche are poles apart, but in their treatment of women, these otherwise diverse philosophers present a surprisingly united front. In the articles below, several themes recur throughout: the assumption that women's biological nature dictates and justifies her lack of political status; the belief that woman's psychological nature is gentle, submissive, emotional, irrational; the insistence on confining women to hearth and home; the assertion that women are suited to rearing citizens but not to being citizens themselves—all these views are either explicitly or implicitly adopted by philosophers otherwise completely at odds in their moral and political philosophy.

While progressive thinkers offered powerful arguments for the extension of political rights to more and more of the male population, Mary Wollstonecraft's plea that the philosophical justification for political equality applied just as well to women as to men, fell on deaf ears: 'consider ... whether, when men contend for their freedom, and to be allowed to judge for themselves respecting their own happiness, it be not inconsistent and unjust to subjugate women, even though you firmly believe that you are acting in the manner best calculated to promote their happiness?'[3] Not until the women's suffrage movement gained momentum in the mid nineteenth century—and then in combination with demands for the emancipation of slaves by American abolitionists and for the enfranchisement of the working classes in England—were the arguments for including women within the general claims of liberty and equality taken seriously by any major political philosopher. So powerful was the political and cultural resistance to John Stuart Mill's argument (and to proposals for women's suffrage from legislators and other publicists in America and Europe) that women did not receive the minimal right of citizenship in a democracy, the right to vote, until after the First World War.

It is usual in much teaching of political philosophy and theory to overlook aspects of a philosopher's argument which strike us today as irrelevant to our understanding of political life, or as simply mistaken. Aristotle's views on slavery or Rousseau's conception of democracy are good examples; taken too seriously, these aspects of Aristotle's or Rousseau's arguments would, it seems, make their whole political philosophy appear unfruitful for contemporary concerns and problems. What is true of these specific aspects of two major philosophers in the usual curriculum of political theory is also true of the entire range of political philosophy when women are mentioned. Because contemporary political thought assumes the political equality of both sexes and much contemporary social legislation tries to achieve a modicum of economic and material equality between women and men, both the substance and linguistic style of political philosophy in this regard tends to be passed by without much analysis of its implications. But when the particularities of male and female are taken into consideration, when the reader reads gender-specific references as written, not transforming them into neutral denotations, then, as the essays below make clear, a radically different way of approaching these texts opens up.

Each of the philosophers dealt with here must, we assume, be read in that way. An historical, and with it political, interpretation of what they thought and intended cannot be dispensed with except at the risk of missing a genuine theoretical tension. Although there is a uniformity of attitude towards women evident in all the philosophers concerned—with the exception of the Utilitarians—we have not tried to produce a single explanation for this uniformity. Rather, each author offers an explanation for each philosopher individually, while trying to look beyond her own subject towards the shared assumptions that generate such a surprising degree of agreement among such otherwise diverse thinkers over such a long span of time. The essays have been organized, then, along the dimensions of two aspects of modern political philosophy: the distinction between public and private spheres of life, and the argument about human nature. In both cases, as we shall see, very different criteria were applied in the analysis of women's place and role in the first category, and in the second in the determination of her nature and its implications for women's political status.

THE PUBLIC–PRIVATE DISTINCTION

As Margaret Canovan comments in her essay on Rousseau, the public–private distinction is one which seems natural to us now: we are well used to separating public roles from private interests and political offices from personal lives.

But as Jane Rendall points out in her essay on Adam Smith, it is a distinction born of the commercial nature of modern society. The Ancient Greek model of citizenship that influenced both Adam Smith and Rousseau, recognized no such separation of private from public realms, nor did the Greeks distinguish between public and private morality or between offical roles and personal interests. In the words of Thucydides; 'Here each individual is interested not only in his own affairs, but in the affairs of the state as well . . . we do not say that a man who takes no interest in politics is a man who minds his own business; we say that he has no business here at all.⁴ Comparing this with the views of a modern British politician, we can see quite clearly, if crudely, some of the differences which divide the ancient from the modern conception of citizenship: 'we do not want a busy, bustling society in which everyone is politically active and fussing around in an interfering and responsible manner, and herding us all into participating groups'.⁵

While the public–private distinction is familiar to us, it was wholly alien to earlier societies in which political and private life were largely indistinguishable. That conception of the state, which leaves no room for a distinct sphere of private life, has been widely condemned as totalitarian and, as Margaret Canovan points out, it is a model which is deeply unattractive to us now, implying as it does the complete absorption of the individual in public life to the exclusion of all else.

The modern conception, and the liberal political institutions mentioned above that accompanied it, aimed at securing an arena of political and economic activity from regulation, and it thus freed private individuals from the constraints and financial duties imposed by absolutist states. Although it has been an important institutional safeguard in modern societies against 'totalitarian' developments, the division of public and private, with its inherent political and moral values, has worked to women's disadvantage historically. Once the private realm had been separated theoretically from the public, we find theorists anxious to confine women within the private, domestic sphere. The public–private distinction becomes another version of the male–female distinction. The justification for this is given in terms both of woman's biological nature and her (supposed) psychological character—of which more later.

Jane Rendall points out that the public–private distinction separates not only two realms of activity but also two areas of morality. With its advent, the private realm became associated with virtue, whereas the public realm was associated with rights. These differences between, on the one hand, 'the sweet, the gentle, the amiable' and, on the other, 'the great, the awful, the respectable', were then interpreted as differences between female and male: the rejection of absolutism and the unity of social and political spheres was bought at the price of confining women to the domestic, private realm. Virtue was relocated within the family, and even though education in the virtues was considered a necessary prerequisite for aspiring citizens, the educators themselves were nevertheless deemed unworthy of citizenship in their own right.

Jane Rendall's and Margaret Canovan's articles discuss these differences between the ancient and modern conceptions of citizenship and consider their implications for modern feminism. The consequences of our own acceptance of a public–private distinction are also weighed by several other contributors, who point to the fact that women's confinement to the domestic realm depends on an assumption about the homogeneity of woman's life quite distinct from the fragmentation of man's life. Where a public–private distinction is accepted, then philosophers have uniformly construed man as occupying both a public and private role. For him there is a balance to be struck between the demands of public office and personal life. On the other hand, woman has only a single, private role to fulfil, and this means that for her there are no choices to be made, no balance to be struck, as the essays on Hegel, Adam Smith, Rousseau, and the Romantics point out. In all these writers the supposed homogeneity, simplicity and integrity of woman's life is placed in stark contrast to the disunity and fragmentation of man's life. Thus Joanna Hodge notes that, for Hegel, 'there is no question but that women are destined to give birth to children, to look after them and to manage the household. 'Hegel supposes' she says 'that women never confront choices, nor make decisions'. Similarly, Jane Rendall remarks that Adam Smith urged the necessity for men to strike a balance between 'the soft, the gentle, the amiable' and 'the great, the awful, the respectable', but observes that for women only one side of the balance was relevant. There was little suggestion that women might acquire the virtues of public life. Even in the writings of the Romantics, a strange asymmetry exists between men's capacity to cross traditionally female boundaries and the capacity of women to cross male boundaries, and Ursula Vogel draws our attention to the fact that Schlegel's attitude to sexual roles is rather less radical than may at first appear: 'However much we emphasize the flexibility of the concepts used to convey a contrast of original disposition, woman's sexual nature remains associated with the inner life. Moreover, it is in an indirect way realigned with domesticity'. The evaluation is of course different in the different writers. The Romantics and, to some extent Rousseau, elevate the private realm above the public and laud the integration of domestic life as against the fragmentation which political existence brings with it. By contrast, Nietzsche sees political life as being of supreme importance and the introduction of women as a threat guaranteed to wreak havoc within the state. For him, 'it is doubtful whether women can be just all . . . because they are so much more interested in persons than in things, and because they carry their personalized way of loving and hating, of taking sides for and against, with them'.

This quotation from Ellen Kennedy's essay on Nietzsche leads us on to a second point about the consequences of adhering to a public–private distinction in political theory. So far, we have seen the growth of the distinction in contrast to a republican or Spartan conception of citizenship. We have seen too that theorists appealing to the distinction usually associated women with the private side and men with the public. This in turn leads to the assumption of homogeneity in woman's life, for whereas men are constantly faced with choices between their public and private existences, there are no such choices for women, whose sole existence is within the domestic sphere. Now, with Nietzsche's assertion that women are concerned with loving and hating, we find an attempted justification of woman's exclusively domestic role. This is that women are particularistic in their thinking and attitudes and are therefore unsuited to public life, which necessarily involves universal responses to situations. There is almost unanimous agreement amongst political theorists on this facet of woman's character. It occurs not only in Nietzsche but also in Hegel, who warns us that, 'when women hold the helm of government, the state is at once in jeopardy, because women regulate their actions not by demands of universality, but by arbitrary inclinations and opinions'. Almost indistinguishable is Kant's claim that 'woman should reign and man should rule; because inclination reigns and reason rules', and similarly Margaret Canovan reminds us of the suggestion that Rousseau regards women as a subversive influence precisely because he sees the demands of love and family bonds as antagonistic to the demands of justice and universality.

The utilitarians, especially Jeremy Bentham and John Stuart Mill, are the most outstanding exception to this general view. In contrast to all the other philosophers discussed here, Bentham and Mill supported the cause of women's enfranchisement and regarded 'this one-half of the human race' as morally equal to men. Lea Boralevi's article rightly stresses the emancipatory character of utilitarian principles and points to the fact that its empirical approach to social life and the emphasis philosophical radicalism placed on social reform provided the theoretical and practical basis for changes in women's social and political status which were only realized in the twentieth century. While utilitarian philosophers continued to accept the public–private division characteristic of liberal thought in general—a distinction contemporary socialists including William Thompson, Robert Owen and Charles Fourier minimized—Lea Boralevi demonstrates that this distinction, when combined with the 'moral arithmetic' of utilitarianism, did not necessarily work to women's disadvantage but could provide a very modern liberal feminist perspective: 'compensatory discrimination is part of a pragmatism which takes into account existing situations and tries to cope with them in the short run, tries to alleviate the suffering produced by oppression'.

The reason why utilitarians took up such a liberating position with respect to women's situation in their own age can ultimately be accounted for, as Lea Boralevi shows, in terms of the radically different view of human nature—and with it women's nature—which they held. This is the second theme that runs through these essays and will be described below in greater detail. For now it is enough to note that utilitarianism, at least in the form given it by Bentham and J.S. Mill, can readily be seen to have broken with an earlier view of women shared by Rousseau, Kant and the Romantics and which Nietzsche returned to at the end of the nineteenth century. According to this view the confinement of women to the private sphere is justified by reference to woman's particularistic, emotional, non-universal nature. Since she knows only the bonds of love and friendship, she will be a dangerous person in political life, prepared, perhaps, to sacrifice the wider public interest to some personal tie or private preference. By contrast, men will recognize the wider interest and will not be guided by mere emotion and sentimentality. Thus the public–private distinction is also construed as a distinction between the rational and the emotional; the universal and the particular; the reflective and the intuitional, women being associated with the latter elements and men with the former. What began as a distinction between rights and virtues in Adam Smith and his predecessors, has been transformed into a distinction between male and female realms, and then into a distinction between rational and irrational spheres. Why are women assigned to the private, irrational, emotional, particularistic side of the dichotomy? To answer that question we need to consider the assumptions about woman's nature which emerge in the philosophers we are dealing with and which are discussed in the essays in this volume.

WOMAN'S NATURE

In most of the philosophers we have been considering, the arguments for confining women to hearth and home are rooted in a particular conception of woman's nature. We have already seen something of what this amounts to: woman is construed as a slave to her passions, capable only of emotional responses to the situations she finds herself in and entirely consumed by her unreflective attitudes of love and hate. Schlegel goes so far as to assert that, 'Love is, so to speak, a woman's calling: she is unable to experience it as only a partial interest'. However, in addition to this emotional, non-rational facet of woman's character, many philosophers also point to woman's 'natural' subservience and submissiveness. Nietzsche tells us that women are natural servants: 'women want to serve and find their happiness in this', he says. And similarly Rousseau asserts that women are 'fitted by nature to please and be subjected'. Of course, in the case of Rousseau this is mere wishful thinking. Rousseau knew well that women are not so, and yet the myth of female docility remains strangely powerful. We do not here attempt to explain why it remains powerful. What is important is not that the view is false, or partial, but that it is often illegitimately employed to reinforce itself. Woman's supposed nature as emotional, passive and subservient is first given as the reason for denying her access to political life, and then her lack of experience in political life is used to justify her continued exclusion from political life. As Joanna Hodge puts it, 'women are prevented from disputing the arrangements through which women are disadvantaged'. More generally, the situation can be described as follows: woman's (supposed) nature is used to justify her social status, and then her actual social status is used as a disqualification for any other status. This series of manoeuvres, which systematically traps woman in an inferior social and political position, might be dismissed as no more than unthinking prejudice of a kind commonly found in the eighteenth and nineteenth centuries. But such an explanation seems inadequate for at least two reasons: first, the philosophers we are considering here are original thinkers, known for their willingness and ability to criticize the received opinion of the day; second, and more important, many of them are in other contexts anxious to urge the importance of distinguishing between socially relative facts and immutable truths about human nature.

Although its empirical basis and reformist intention made utilitarian philosophy a particularly sharp analytical weapon against socially received prejudice, Bentham and Mill were not the only philosophers concerned with the distinction between causes and contingencies in society. All the philosophers discussed here were aware of the difficulty involved in distinguishing what was necessary and immutable from accidental and various aspects of the world we live in. So, for example, Margaret Canovan points out with respect to Rousseau, 'to identify human nature, he said, we need to lay aside all the accretions and corruptions of centuries of social life. But when he wrote about women he continually committed that very error that he had himself identified'. The same error is repeated in other writers: Kant's whole political philosophy has been interpreted as a careful analysis of the distinction between what actually is the case in eighteenth-century German society and what ought ideally to be the case. Yet in his treatment of women, Kant never makes the distinction between social convention and eternal truth, apparently believing that woman's social condition is a true reflection of her inherent nature. Even Mill does not escape with honour, urging both that human nature cannot easily be disentangled from social convention and that woman's nature is intuitive and unreflective. In Hegel the problem is even more acute, for as Joanna Hodge points out, 'while Hegel seeks to draw conclusions for all time about women and men and the differences between them, the conceptions of the family and of property with which he works are historically specific'.

Thus we find either a refusal to recognize the differences between the historically specific and the eternal and immutable, or a recognition of these differences at the theoretical level, but a refusal to implement them at the practical level, in looking at woman's nature and woman's social condition.

This refusal to distinguish between the immutable and the socially relative raises a more general question concerning the importance of woman's actual (if historically relative) economic and social circumstances. If, as has been suggested, views about woman's nature are employed to justify her exclusively domestic role, and her domestic preoccupations are then used to reinforce views about her nature as submissive, particularistic and emotional, still we need to ask what is the importance of woman's domestic role. Some commentators have seen the economic and social dependence of women as quite distinct from her political emancipation, whilst others have urged that the domestic role allotted to women is a way of guaranteeing political inferiority. If this latter view is correct, then political equality for women cannot be attained independently of economic and social emancipation. There is evidence that this was the view implicit in some of the philosophers considered here, at least in the negative sense that confining women to the home was seen as a method of subverting their political aspirations. Thus in Nietzsche we find the explicit suggestion that the 'cure' for a woman who wants equal rights with men is to 'give her a child'. This suggestion is an important recognition of the difficulties inherent in generating political equality whilst woman's social condition is that of domestic confinement. Nietzsche thought pregnancy the cure; modern feminists, on the other hand, see pregnancy, childrearing and domesticity generally as the barriers to political equality. For them, emancipation can never be anything other than a sham as long as women are identified with their private work of childrearing. Both Margaret Canovan and Joanna Hodge remark upon the difficulties inherent in urging political equality, whilst recognizing the wide social differences between woman's role and man's. This brings us to a final question arising from the papers gathered here: what lessons can feminism learn from these philosophers? More importantly, perhaps, what should the feminist response be to the unsympathetic, stereotyped and misogynistic attitudes prevalent in the history of modern political theory?

THE FEMINIST RESPONSE

The modern distinction between public and private spheres has been employed in such a way that women are construed as occupying only the private realm, as we have seen, while men are assumed to span both, their lives having both a public, political identity and a private personal one. The public–private split thus becomes a male–female distinction and woman's existence within the private realm is justified by her nature. Woman's biological function as a childbearer does not have to be distinguished, according to this view, from her social role as mother and home-maker. Moreover, this social function is seen as one which encourages certain character traits already thought to be inherent in woman's psychological nature: woman is by nature submissive, emotional, particularistic. For her, life and love are identical and inseparable. This inherent psychological trait is encouraged and developed by her role as childrearer, making her incapable of the rationality and universality required in those who are to wield political power. Woman's initial exclusion from political life is thus reinforced by her social role and her social role reinforces, in turn, her inherent nature.

Contemporary feminism offers two general responses to this dilemma. One view, shared by most of the contributors to this collection, asserts that women's exclusion from the political realm works to her disadvantage. Exclusion from citizenship and from full legal equality, the authors agree, served to enhance male power and to keep women passive and subservient throughout the period in which the philosophers discussed here were writing—at least in terms of their vision of women's place in society. According to this view, political life is a superior arena of activity, and the challenge of a feminist politics is to fight for recognition of women on equal terms with men. From this argument follow all the specific legislative proposals for affirmative action on behalf of women, for equal pay and equal access to the goods and benefits of modern society. Politics takes on a value greater than 'private' pursuits, not because, as the Ancient Greeks supposed, it is only the public realm that offers an opportunity for the full realization of humanity, but because the political processes of modern democratic states allocate those values which are most in demand and most sought after.

But this view, as radical and socialist-feminists have pointed out, entails the acceptance of values dominant in the political sphere as it now exists and these are, so they assert, necessarily 'male' values. From this perspective, Nietzsche's vision of a state inhabited by *Übermenschen* motivated by their will to dominate and to exercise power, far from challenging the political and moral values which liberal political philosophers had held, reinforces them and magnifies their status. Nietzsche's ideal state is not only a cold vision of human relationships after the death of god, but a resigned acceptance that this is the only world really possible. Political Romanticism, as Ursula Vogel's essay shows, took a very different view, and one more compatible with the values and perspective of a second strand of modern feminism. By contrast with liberal feminism, whose vision of political emancipation 'allows women only the freedom to become like men; romantic sociability, on the other hand, envisages a situation where they can express and develop their specifically feminine qualities which will liberate men too from the fetters of conventional roles'.

This view combines two features of contemporary feminism. It implies first that the scope of politics is limited and that there are distinct restrictions on what can be attained by its methods. But the Romantic view, in common with much contemporary feminism, also recognizes that many of those traits characteristically associated with women are valuable and important in themselves.

But while the Romantics disdained politics as an arena of decisions taken according to the calculus of power, and in this respect foreshadowed the unpolitical stance taken by some contemporary feminists, the affirmation of feminine virtues and values need not necessarily lead to a devaluation of the political. On the contrary, contemporary feminists argue for the introduction of feminist values and women's influence into the political sphere precisely because the decisions taken there are so important. This view urges the incorporation of the emotional, the particular, the individual within a conception of the political and alongside the rational and universal aspects stressed by some of those philosophers discussed here.

Of course this insistence on seeing the political realm as something other than the realm of the universal and 'rational' is not exclusively a feminist insistence. Recent political and moral philosophy generally has found something lacking in what Stuart Hampshire describes as 'rational computational morality' of the sort associated with political thinking since the Enlightenment. Referring to American policy-makers during the Vietnam War, Hampshire remarks that:

They thought that their opponents in the USA were sentimental and guided only by their unreflective emotions, while they, the policy-makers, were computing consequences with precision and objectivity, using quasi-quantitative methods . . . they had the minimum of natural feeling for, and perception of, the peculiar mechanical brutality and unfeelingness of their conduct of the war.[6]

Hampshire's argument is not a feminist demand: but it is one closely related to feminist issues and thinking and could be seen as a call, in common with much contemporary anti-war sentiment, for the instatement of 'female' qualities and values within a world too much dominated by 'male' attitudes and virtues. It is a plea for the re-evaluation of emotion, especially for a recognition of the importance of love and sympathy—the characteristics of feminine nature according to much modern philosophy—and thus for the reform of political practice in accordance with these.

Another strain in contemporary feminism, and in the 'alternative' movements associated with it historically and ideologically, rejects the sphere of the political altogether. Instead of emphasizing the importance of the state and political power, this kind of feminism stresses its ultimate irrelevance to individual life. The key assumption in this form of feminist argument is profoundly anti-liberal: it asserts the final impotence of the individual to shape or determine events beyond the very restricted borders of his or her own life, and it challenges the meaning, even the importance, of all those rights and freedoms which political philosophy in the period after the Enlightenment put at the top of the agenda, however political philosophers thought about them. Like their Romantic precursors, this school of feminist (and alternative-pacifist) thought takes seriously, as Ursula Vogel notes with respect to the Romantics themselves 'as matters of common human concern, only those political events which [have] a direct impact upon the personal relationships among individuals'.

These, then, are two familiar feminist responses to the evaluation of women present in political philosophy: either to accept the importance of politics, but argue for its 'feminization', or to reject the importance of politics and emphasize instead the importance of the personal. The former strategy aims to undermine the public–private distinction (and its associates) by urging the introduction of the traditionally private values into the public realm. The latter, by contrast, accepts the public–private distinction but urges a reassessment of the comparative values of public and private, with the private now taking priority over the public, individuality taking precedence over universality, and emotion taking precedence over rationality.

A third strategy, one that dominated the political struggle for women's emancipation from the late eighteenth century onwards, is more closely associated with the demands of classical liberalism than either of the views discussed above. The movement for women's suffrage and for 'admission, in law and in fact, to equality in all rights, political, civil, and social, with the male citizens of the community' which prompted J.S. Mill to write *The Subjection of Women*, was an extension of liberal demands. He recognized, as did the suffragettes of the mid nineteenth century, that the 'truths held to be self-evident' by the American Declaration of Independence did not apply to one sex alone. Mill rejected 'the aristocracy of sex' and the power of men over women in law and political practice as the last tyranny of otherwise civilized nations. Neither Mill nor his predecessors, Mary Wollenstonecraft and Condorcet, rejected the public–private distinction as such. Rather, they argued that women's emancipation would be achieved by resisting the interpretation of public–private as a male–female division, or as the distinction between the emotional and rational, the universal and the particular.

While all these versions of a feminist philosophy and politics have enjoyed a certain success and popular influence, their power to persuade, and their appropriateness depends on the particular situation in which women find themselves. It would be absurd to suppose that Arab women today would be wrong to take up the position and make the demands of women in Western Europe and America a century ago. Where the fundamental rights and freedoms of citizenship have not been achieved, those have to be fought and argued for first. Where, by contrast, those rights have been attained and the political struggle has moved on to some other arena—economic security and social equality, for example—a feminist politics must articulate demands appropriate to that level of political development. Whether, as certain versions of feminist pacifism imply, the power relations that have always characterized politics and the organization of state power can be explained purely in terms of masculine values and instincts is a question whose answer would take us too far afield. Certainly, though, this perspective seems to reintroduce, however unwittingly, exactly that distinction of natures and their connection to politics which liberal feminism has been most at pains to deny or at least to reduce.

A final word should go to a tradition of political thought deliberately not represented here. By excluding Marx and the Marxist critique, we were uncomfortably aware of drawing a line around one of the most powerful and influential analyses of the tradition of political philosophy we *did* choose to look at in these essays. Moreover, as we noted in the paragraph above, the transfer of political conflict from issues of legal and political equality to the arena of social and economic life went hand in hand with the success of liberalism: the Marxist critique in this sense carries on and transforms a tradition in which it remains dialectically embedded. Not just for its acute analysis of the economic origins of the family and for its genesis of contemporary socialist-feminism, but most of all because Marxism is a way of understanding the modern world that no one seriously concerned with politics can simply ignore, will our side-stepping it entirely seem to some readers a missed aspect of the problem. But that would have been another book. As a gesture of recognizing its importance—and an olive leaf, if not a branch, to our male colleagues—we end with an extract from a poem by one of this century's best-known Marxists, Bertold Brecht:

> The young Alexander conquered India.
> Was he alone?
> Caesar beat the Gauls.
> Did he not have even a cook with him?
> Philip of Spain wept when his armada
> Went down. Was he the only one to weep? . . .
>
> Every page a victory.
> Who cooked the feast for the victors?
> Every ten years a great man.
> Who paid the bill?[7]

We know that more often than not it is a woman who cooks the feast and pays the bill, but life is such that there will always be *someone* who must cook the feast and *someone* who must pay the bill. This is unavoidable. What is avoidable is the belief that cooking feasts has no value or, worse, that it precludes having valuable opinions about anything other than cooking. It is this avoidable mistake which occurs over and over again in the history of Western philosophy. If we are not to repeat the mistake, this is the lesson its history must teach us.

NOTES

1. Otto Von Gierke, *Das deutsche Genossenschaftsrecht* (Weidmannische Buchhandlung, 1881), Bd. 3, pp. 627-8.
2. George Sabine, *A History of Political Thought,* (Holt, 1961) 3rd edn. p. 333.
3. Mary Wollstonecraft, *A Vindication of the Rights of Woman* (Norton, 1975), p. 5.

4. Thucydides, *The Peloponnesian War,* trans. R. Warner (Penguin, 1954).
5. Anthony Crosland as quoted in A. Arblaster, *The Rise and Decline of Western Liberalism* (Blackwell, 1984) pp. 44.
6. S. Hampshire, 'Public and private morality', in S. Hampshire (ed.) *Public and Private Morality* (Cambridge University Press, 1978) p. 51.
7. B. Brecht, 'Questions from a Worker Who Reads', as quoted in A. Arblaster, p. 49.

1 Kant: 'An Honest but Narrow-Minded Bourgeois'?[1]

Susan Mendus

In their recent book, *Women's Choices,* Mary Midgley and Judith Hughes remark that:

When women read philosophy they tend to fall into an embarrassed habit of thinking that they ought not to criticize the ludicrous views which result, that it is unfair and anachronistic to think that people of this calibre ought to be able to avoid going into print with this sort of stuff.[2]

Nowhere is the embarrassment more keenly felt than in reading Kant's views on the nature of women and the role of women as citizens. The problem is not simply that Kant is dismissive about woman's status as a citizen (though this is in fact so), but rather that the explicit claims made in the political philosophy conflict markedly with what we might expect on the basis of reading the *Groundwork for a Metaphysic of Morals.* In *Groundwork* Kant emphasizes that the moral principles he proposes must be applicable not simply to men, nor even to human beings, but to rational beings as such. This generates the expectation that in the political philosophy women will be accorded equal status with men. Such expectations are, however, quickly disappointed, for when we reach the political philosophy, we find Kant insisting that women may be passive citizens only—never active citizens. Moreover, his reasons for insisting on this are far from clear: sometimes he gestures at reasons, sometimes he merely states baldly that this is so, but nowhere does he spell out explicitly and consistently exactly why women cannot be active citizens. The arguments of *Metaphysic of Morals, Theory and Practice* and *Anthropology* vacillate uneasily between the philosophic and the home-spun, and frequently Kant simply appears to indulge in an unthinking endorsement of the prejudices of his day and an uncritical acceptance of the dogma of others—notably Rousseau. However, it would be wrong to suggest or imply that it is only in the treatment of women as citizens that the expectations of the moral philosophy are disappointed: many commentators have remarked upon Kant's Janus-faced attitude in his political writings generally. Thus Rheinhold Aris notes that, 'he [Kant] attacked serfdom and defended the exclusion of the unpropertied members of society from all essential political rights almost in the same breath, in both cases in the name of reason'.[3]

Similarly, Kant's general disapproval of revolution is hard to square with his fulsome praise of the French Revolution as 'a moral cause', and this vacillation between adherence to the status quo and enthusiasm for change is amongst the most perplexing features of his political philosophy and the most difficult to analyse. Commentators have described these tensions variously as tensions between conservatism and radicalism; idealism and pragmatism; rationalism and empiricism; and as an aspect of the phenomena–noumena distinction of the *First Critique.* That the tensions exist, then, is not in doubt; what must be questioned is *why* they exist and how deep they run. We have seen already that Aris believed Kant to be simply incapable of spotting the inconsistencies of his own arguments. By contrast, Howard Williams, in his book *Kant's Political Philosophy,* interprets the tensions simply as a recognition by Kant of the limits of political endeavour; thus, 'at times, he appears to be advocating the most radical of political changes (when donning his philosophical hat), and, at others, he appears to be advocating the most cautious of conservatism (when donning his everyday, realist hat)'.[4]

For Williams, however, the tensions are simply a recognition of the limits of what is practically possible. Kant's radicalism expresses what he believes to be ideal; his conservatism expresses what he believes to be prudent and practical. A further diagnosis is provided by Cohen in his article 'A critique of Kant's philosophy of law'. Cohen suggests that the conflict in Kant's writings may be resolved only by ascribing to reason factors which are merely contingent and variable. 'Kant assumes', he says, 'that reason dictates that men can transmit their titles of nobility to their wives, but not conversely... This approach to the problem reduces Kant's position to such an absurdity that one may wonder how such a powerful mind could have been led to it even in old age'.[5] This criticism of Kant—that he confuses the dictates of reason with the merely contingent and socially determined—provides a third diagnosis of the difficulty involved in giving a coherent picture of his political philosophy. It must be repeated, however, that these are quite general difficulties involved in interpreting the political philosophy and in determining its relation to the moral philosophy, particularly the moral philosophy of the *Groundwork.* What is needed, therefore, is a general diagnosis of the cause of the tensions together with an inquiry into whether they explain Kant's view on the position of women; for it may be that there are specific problems involved in his account of women, over and above the general tensions mentioned here. In what follows I shall firstly try to elucidate Kant's stated views on the nature of women and their status as citizens, I shall then go on to say something about what accounts for these views, bearing in mind the three interpretations mentioned above. Finally, I shall attempt a reconstruction of Kant's doctrines to see whether there is anything in his moral and political thought which could give cause for optimism amongst feminists. I begin with Kant's theses about citizenship and the criteria for being a citizen.

CITIZENSHIP

The main texts in which Kant expounds his theory of citizenship are *Theory and Practice* and the *Metaphysic of Morals.* John Ladd, in his Introduction to Part I of *Metaphysic of Morals,* 'The Metaphysical Elements of Justice', points to an important difficulty in Kant's text. He notes that Kant has been criticized both for being a 'radical revolutionary' and for being an 'unregenerate reactionary'.

However, he defends Kant by urging that:

far from ignoring this seeming paradox, Kant makes it the central theme
of his inquiry. The whole book may be regarded as an extended
philosophical commentary on the relation between what is and what
ought to be, both in politics and law. In order to follow the various
discussions in the book, it is essential to realize that at times he is
discussing actual states and actual obligations, whereas at other times he
is discussing the ideal. [6]

Sadly for us, Kant rarely states explicitly when he is
indulging in idealism and when he is being pragmatic: it is
therefore left to the reader to disentangle these strands, and
this task is an extremely difficult one. At the moment, I can
do no more than mention this problem, and make no
attempt to resolve it. However, it is a point to which I shall
return later.

In *Metaphysic of Morals* Kant identifies three
characteristics or attributes which, he says, are 'inseparable
from the nature of a citizen as such'.[7] In *Theory and
Practice* these are referred to as 'three principles by which a
state can alone be established in accordance with pure
rational principles of external human right'.[8] They are:

1. The *freedom* of every member of society as a human
being.
2. The *equality* of each with all the others as a subject.
3. The *independence* of each member of a
commonwealth as a citizen.[9]

However, having stated these three principles, and having
insisted, in *Theory and Practice*, that they are not laws
given by an already established state but rather the laws by
which alone a state may be established, Kant immediately
goes on to insist that not everyone within the state will in
fact have the independence requisite for being a citizen.
Although all will be free as human beings, and all will be
equal as subjects, nevertheless not all will be independent as
citizens. Not all will have a hand in framing the law, even
though all will be equal as subjects under the law. Kant is
emphatic on this, urging that:

all are not equally qualified within this constitution to possess the right to
vote, i.e. to be citizens and not just subjects among other subjects. For

from the fact that as passive members of the state, they can demand to be treated by all others in accordance with laws of natural freedom and equality, *it does not follow* that they also have a right to influence or organise the state itself as *active* members, or to co-operate in introducing particular laws.[10]

The distinction between active and passive citizenship is therefore crucial for Kant and problematic for him, since it serves to justify the disenfranchisement of whole groups within society. We must therefore consider the criteria which Kant offers for distinguishing between active and passive citizens and try to establish whether the distinction can be made good and what it tells us about the assumptions of Kant's political philosophy.

In *Metaphysic of Morals,* Kant himself expresses a certain unease about proposing two classes of citizen, since this, he confesses, 'seems to contradict the definition of the concept of a citizen altogether'.[11] However, he then proceeds to provide examples of both active and passive citizens which, he says, 'may serve to overcome the difficulty'. His conclusion is that passive citizens are 'mere auxiliaries of the commonwealth, for they have to receive orders or protection from other individuals, so that they do not possess civil independence'. What is crucial for active citizenship, therefore, is being one's own master or being independent of the will of others, and such independence cannot be attributed to any servant (other than a servant of the state) or to anyone who sells merely his labour rather than the product of his labour. Those who must take orders from, or receive protection from, others cannot count as independent in this sense, and therefore cannot be granted the status of active citizen. To clarify yet further, Kant goes on to list passive citizens as:

apprentices to merchants or tradesmen, servants who are not employed by the state, minors *(naturaliter vel civiliter),* women in general, and all those who are obliged to depend for their living (i.e. for food and protection) on the offices of others (excluding the state)—all of these people have no civil personality, and their existence is, so to speak, purely inherent. The woodcutter, whom I employ on my premises; the blacksmith in India who goes from house to house with his hammer, anvil and bellows to do work with iron, as opposed to the European carpenter or smith who can put the products of his work up for public sale; the domestic tutor as opposed to the academic, the tithe-holder as opposed to the farmer; and so on—they are all mere auxiliaries to the commonwealth.[12]

Several points emerge here to which I would like to draw attention: firstly, that Kant construes independence very literally, arguing that no one can serve two masters and that anyone who is any sort of servant (other than a servant of the state) must, *for that reason,* be denied active citizenship. Presumably, his thought here is that if servants are allowed the vote, they may become the mere mouthpiece of their masters: economic servitude may become political servitude and economic mastery may lead to political coercion. I shall say more about this later.

The second point is that in this formulation of the independence criterion it might be thought purely contingent that women count as passive citizens only. For here Kant is anxious to emphasize the differences which might be relative to a given society. Thus the blacksmith in India is merely a passive citizen, whereas the European smith is an active citizen. This because the latter, unlike the former, is not merely a servant, does not sell merely his labour but sells the products of his labour to the public. Such distinctions between societies make a difference to whether any one individual within the society may be accorded the status of active citizen. Reading this, one might think that Kant would be prepared to allow that in some societies, even if not in eighteenth-century Germany, women might indeed be active citizens. Superficially, it appears to be simply a function of eighteenth-century German society that women were not independent in the requisite sense. Here then, in *Metaphysic of Morals,* the status of women as passive citizens appears to be merely contingent: it just so happens that women in that time in that country lacked civil independence, just as Indian smiths lacked independence, but circumstances might alter and there need be no objection in principle to women aspiring to the status of active citizenship. A final point emerges in the immediately following paragraph, when Kant argues that:

Whatever might be the kind of laws to which the citizens agree, these laws must not be incompatible with the natural laws of freedom and with the equality that accords with this freedom, namely, that everyone be able to work up from this passive status to an active status.[13]

The implication of this passage is that even the Indian smith, the apprentice and the domestic servant, might be allowed the opportunity to advance to active citizenship—to obtain the economic and social independence which bring with them civil independence. So the political status of the smith may vary from one society to another, but even the servant, who presumably counts as a passive citizen in *every* society, must be allowed the opportunity to 'better himself' by becoming something other than a servant. Even he must not be prevented from aspiring to an occupation which carries civil independence and active citizenship with it. Kant insists that '*everyone* be able to work up from this passive status to an active status', and we would hope that 'everyone' includes women.

It would seem, therefore, that although the situation of women is one of subordination and inferiority, there is nevertheless no principled objection to women being active citizens. At any rate, nothing which has been said so far precludes this possibility. However, if we turn from *Metaphysic of Morals* to *Theory and Practice*, we find that Kant offers different reasons for denying women the status of active citizens. Here he says that 'the only qualification required by a citizen (apart, of course, from being an adult male) is that he must be his own master *(sui-juris)* and must have some property (which can include any skill, trade, fine art or science) to support himself'.[14] In this stipulation it appears to be not merely contingent that women lack active citizenship; rather, women are ruled out from the start. By contrast with the formulation in *Metaphysic of Morals*, we are invited *first* to enquire into the sex of the individual and *then*, if the individual is male, to ask whether he satisfies the independence criterion. Of course, in this way, women, so to speak, never get past the starting post. They become, not persons occupying particular social positions but occupants of the position 'woman' which, by definition, fits them only for passive citizenship—and, unlike servants, they cannot hope to occupy a different position in the future. Thus they are eternally denied that possibility of advancement, which is open even to the lowliest of men. So, in *Theory and Practice* the exclusion of women is not contingent, but principled, and to understand why Kant might favour the exclusion of women as a matter of principle we shall need to look at his discussion of marriage in the *Metaphysical Elements of Justice* (Part I of *Metaphysic of Morals*). Before embarking on that, however, I shall digress briefly and say a little more about the independence criterion generally. This is necessary in order, ultimately, to assess the causes of the tensions in Kant's political philosophy.

We have seen already that Kant takes the term 'independent' very literally: he requires that citizens should serve no master other than the state, and that, for him, involves having something other than one's own labour to sell—the citizen must sell 'that which is his', and not 'allow others to make use of him'.[15] Now this insistence that the citizen sell only what is his (where 'what is his' must be something other than his labour) needs explanation, which Kant proceeds to provide in an extended footnote:

guaranteeing one's labour is not the same as selling a commodity . . . although the man to whom I give my firewood to chop and the tailor to whom I give material to make into clothes both appear to have a similar relationship toward me, the former differs from the latter in the same way as the barber from the wig-maker (to whom I may in fact have given the requisite hair) or the labourer from the artist or tradesman, who does a piece of work which belongs to him until he is paid for it. For the latter, in pursuing his trade, exchanges his property with someone else, while the former allows someone else to make use of him. But I do admit that it is somewhat difficult to define the qualifications which entitle anyone to claim the status of being his own master[16].

In this passage Kant employs two apparently separable criteria: first, he argues that to be an active citizen a man must sell that which is his—he must sell his alienable property, where merely guaranteeing one's labour is not something alienable. (In this context Kant assumes a sharp distinction between one's labour and the product of one's labour. Thus, the barber merely sells his labour; the wig-maker sells the product of his labour). Second, however, he insists that it is in this way alone that a man may be his own master: where he guarantees only his labour, he effectively allows himself to be used by others as a means to the fulfilment of their plans and purposes. These, however, are surely distinct features of the case, for from the fact that the barber takes instruction from, or serves his customers, it does not follow that the customer is his master in any sense which need affect the ability to attain the status of active citizen. Moreover, if the barber takes instructions from, and serves, his customer, it is surely also true that the wig-maker similarly serves and takes instructions from his client. Kant's desire to distinguish between active and passive citizens rests upon the belief that only those who are independent should have a hand in framing the law. Now it is indeed important that those who frame the law should not be coerced by others. They need to be their own masters and not the political tools of others. However, Kant construes as independent all and only those who have some skill or property to sell—and this is surely wrong, for the wig-maker is no more immune from coercion than the barber, and the tailor to whom I give material is just as much my servant as the wood-chopper. Of course, the social status of the wig-maker is higher than that of the barber, and the social status of the tailor is higher than that of the wood-chopper. But we need not believe, as Kant appears to, that fitness to vote is a function of social status.

By emphasizing these difficulties in the independence criterion we may see the source of the complaint that Kant is simply an honest but narrow-minded bourgeois, anxious to justify and strengthen the social status of his own class and fumbling ineffectively for reasons which will ground the justification. The discussion of the independence criterion, together with the earlier discussions, now give us three kinds of objection to Kant's treatment of women as citizens:

1. Women are relegated to the status of passive citizens and in the *Metaphysic of Morals* this move appears to be justified by appeal to the independence criterion. However, on inspection, the independence criterion

appears to make social status the test of fitness to vote, and it is far from clear why this should be accepted. So it seems the independence criterion fails in general and, *a fortiori,* fails to justify the exclusion of women from active citizenship.

2. Even if the independence criterion were coherent and plausible, still it is not invariably Kant's stated reason for the exclusion of women. In *Theory and Practice* women appear to be, by definition, incapable of independence.

3. This definitional exclusion of women makes them worse off than any male passive citizen, since it denies them any opportunity of advancing to active citizenship. This is a sinister and far-reaching implication of Kant's political thought; for, as we have seen, the opportunity to advance to active citizenship is a requirement of equality. Again, 'Whatever might be the kind of laws to which the citizens agree, these laws must not be incompatible with the natural laws of freedom and with the equality that accords with this freedom, namely, that everyone be able to work up from this passive status to an active status'.[17]

But if women are to be denied the possibility of advancement to the status of active citizens, then it is at least *prima facie* the case that they are also denied the equality which belongs to all men, whether active or passive citizens. And if this is so, then Kant appears not merely to be denying women a hand in framing the law, but worse, he is denying them the equality which he has already said belongs to all as subjects.

Why then are women denied the possibility of advancement, and what are the implications for Kant's view of women generally? To understand this we must turn to his treatment of the topic of marriage, to his doctrine of equality, and to his account of the nature of the sexes.

MARRIAGE

Kant's views about the nature of the marriage relationship are advanced in Part I of the *Metaphysic of Morals,* 'The Metaphysical Elements of Justice'. His treatment of the topic is notorious, an embarrassment to moral philosophers and philosophers of law alike. Few have found a good word to say about it, and at least one commentator has described Kant's views as 'shallow and repulsive'.[18] The salient features are these: Kant's view of sex is that it is basically animal, ultimately incompatible with the dignity of man and man's worth as a moral being. Even when contained within the confines of monogamous marriage, sex is still fundamentally animal and sexual love is not properly called love at all: 'it is a unique kind of pleasure *(sui generis)*, and the passion really has nothing in common with moral love, though it can enter into close union with it under the limiting conditions of practical reason'.[19] Indeed, Kant insists that yielding to the desire for sexual gratification is worse even than suicide:

the man who defiantly casts off the burden of life is at least not making a feeble surrender to animal impulse in throwing himself away; self-murder requires courage . . . But unnatural vice, which is complete abandonment of oneself to animal inclination, makes man not only an object of enjoyment, but still further an unnatural thing, i.e. a loathsome object, and so deprives him of all reverence for himself.[20]

This denial of one's own humanity is, however, permissable within the context of a monogamous marriage, where the relationship between the partners is reciprocal.

This conception of sex—as a form of mutual exploitation for which one must pay the price of marriage—has the ironic consequence that it turns one feminist objection on its head. In Kant's eyes, sex represents just as much an exploitation of the man by the woman as of the woman by the man:

The feminist complains that the man treats the woman as a sexual object. Kant suggests that the complaint is more deep-lying than this. According to him, both the man and the woman treat each other as things. This suggests that the feminist argument that sex takes on an exploitative form in modern society might best be reformulated not as an instance of the inhumanity of man towards woman, but as an instance of the general inhumanity of man (i.e. human beings in general) towards man.[21]

The exploitative and dehumanizing nature of sex is thus legitimized to some extent by the reciprocity involved in monogamous marriage. Yet Kant's appeal to reciprocity is both puzzling and misleading—puzzling because it is a central tenet of *Groundwork* that all employment of persons as things is immoral, and it is hard to see how that immorality can be modified or translated merely by the addition of reciprocity. 'Man is not a thing—not something used *merely* as a means.'[22] What separates man from mere things is precisely that persons, unlike things, are not to be used as mere means. Talk of reciprocity may also be misleading because it suggests that the marriage relationship is one of equality. However, as we shall see, reciprocity does not imply equality, and Kant never departs from his belief that man is naturally superior to woman, nor does he question the concomitant right of the husband to command the wife. I shall look at these points separately: first, the claim that the reciprocal nature of the monogamous marriage legitimizes that exploitation of one by the other which is involved in sex. It is important to note that Kant does not believe that sex within marriage is any less animal than fornication or adultery. The reciprocity is simply a guarantee for the wife that she will not be treated as a chattel or slave. In polygamous or adulterous relationships the woman's rights over the man are unequal and thus her position is reduced to one of servitude. The demand for reciprocity cannot therefore transform sex into something human, it can only ensure that the bargain struck is an equal one; that the exploitation of the woman by the man is matched by the exploitation of the man by the woman. Opportunities are equalized, but they are, nevertheless, opportunities to do what is fundamentally denaturing.

But doesn't reciprocity—so understood—imply equality? It does not. Kant's willingness to invest the wife with rights greater than those of a servant or chattel does not amount to a willingness to grant her equality, and he is quite clear that the natural superiority of the husband brings with it the right to command on his part, and the duty to obey on her part. Moreover, the marriage contract is one which ensures that the woman's position is one of subordination, for Kant tells us that by entering into marriage the woman, unlike the man, renounces her civil independence. Why should she do this? Why should a free and equal human being enter a contract that *always* places her in subjection and subordination to a male individual? To understand this we need to look more closely at Kant's account of equality.

EQUALITY

Kant is quite clear that the actual position of woman in marriage is not one of equality with her husband. However, he is ambivalent as to whether this *de facto* inequality is grounded in natural inequality. Sometimes he argues that wife and husband are naturally equal, but that the wife forgoes her equality for the sake of the common household good:

juridical law cannot be considered as contradicting the equality of the couple. Consequently, that domination has the sole objective of asserting, in the realisation of the common interest of the family, the natural superiority of the husband over the wife.[23]

Here the argument appears to be that superiority does not necessarily imply natural inequality: although the husband is superior to the wife, nevertheless she is his equal. However, recognizing his superiority over her, and mindful of what is in the interest of the family as a whole, she renounces her natural equality and submits to her husband. At other times, however, Kant claims that husband and wife (man and woman) are naturally *unequal,* but argues that this inequality is justified because reciprocal: in return for her lack of political power, the wife secures domestic domination; 'he loves domestic peace and readily submits to her regime'.[24] In this argument it is the chivalry of the man, not the self-denial of the woman, which explains the *de facto* inequality between them.

Either way, there is no reason for the married woman to be dissatisfied with her lot in life: if she has *voluntarily* renounced her equality, then she has no cause for complaint; equally, if she has exchanged subordination in one sphere for domination in another, she still has no cause for complaint. The two arguments, although divided on the question of woman's natural equality, both point to the same conception of woman's nature. The former argument, premised on the existence of natural equality which is voluntarily renounced, makes reference to a greater good than the equality of each with all others. In particular it implies that women are not ends in themselves, but are fully realized as women only when they submit to becoming means to some further social end—the unity and coherence of the family. The latter argument, premised on the assumption of natural inequality, makes explicit reference to woman's distinct and singular nature, and this appeal to the different nature of woman is fleshed out in Kant's claim that marriage is the means whereby woman obtains her genuine freedom and man loses his. The crucial point then is that, whether or not woman is formally equal with man, her nature is different from man's nature. This difference justifies her different status (as passive rather than active citizen) and explains why she becomes free by marrying, whereas the man loses freedom.

Summarizing, we may present Kant's views about woman's status as follows. Woman may be accorded the status of passive citizen only. Unlike a male passive citizen, she may not, by self-improvement or advancement, aspire to the status of active citizen. This is because of her intrinsic nature as exemplified in the marriage contract. By the marriage contract woman relinquishes her equality and allows the man to dominate in political life in exchange for her own domination in domestic life. It is fitting that a woman should do this, since she, unlike a man, gains her true freedom by entering into marriage. It is in woman's nature that her freedom should best be obtained by marrying. What, then, is woman's nature? And why is it so different from man's nature that the three characteristics of freedom, equality and independence are either denied women altogether or reinterpreted in their application to her?

WOMAN'S NATURE

The discussion 'Of the Nature of the Sexes' is to be found in the

Anthropology. Here Kant's mind, almost wholly uncluttered by any actual experience, is laid bare and the prejudice and bigotry are revealed. A great deal of what he has to say about the inherent nature of woman is merely ludicrous. For example:

'By extending favours towards men, the feminine character lays claim to freedom and simultaneously to the conquest of the entire male species. Although this inclination is in ill-repute, under the name of coquetry, it is not without a real justifiable basis. A young wife is always in danger of becoming a widow, and this leads her to distribute her charms to all men whose fortunes make them marriageable; so that, if this should occur, she would not be lacking in suitors.²⁵

And again:

In marriage the husband woos only his own wife, but the wife has an inclination for all men. Out of jealousy she dresses up only for the eyes of her own sex, in order to outdo other women in charm or pretended distinguished appearance. The man, on the other hand, dresses up only so far as not to shame his wife by his clothes. The man judges feminine mistakes leniently, whereas the woman judges very severely (in public); and young ladies, if they had the choice to have their trespasses judged by a male or female jury, would certainly choose a male jury for their judge.²⁶

And so it grinds on. One implausible remark following upon another. Most important here, however, is not this parade of blind prejudices or pretence to have discovered the intrinsic nature of woman as such. What is important, I believe, is the assertion in this same chapter that woman is to be identified with inclination and man with reason. Thus:

the woman should reign and the man should rule; because inclination reigns and reason rules.²⁷

It might be argued that it is wrong to place too much emphasis on this somewhat throw-away line, buried in a late and minor work. However, remarks made elsewhere do nothing to gainsay this observation in the *Anthropology:* we have already seen the desperate attempts to justify woman's status as passive citizen only; to explain the subordination of woman within the marriage relationship and her effective exclusion from all political life. Against this background, the identification of woman with inclination and of man with reason, even if not required, is hardly a bolt from the blue. Moreover, other aspects of Kant's philosophy of law mesh in with this final dismissal of woman. As Cohen notes, Kant seems to believe that the obedience of wife to husband is a requirement of natural law.[28] The honest but narrow-minded bourgeois in Kant fails to distinguish between what is merely conventional and accepted in his society and what is a command of reason. (This failure, it should be noted, is not confined to Kant's treatment of women: his view that life tenure for competent officials was a dictate of reason provides further evidence of his inability to distinguish the contingent and circumstantial from the *a priori*.)

From the beginning of the paper with the disappointing but not wholly surprising revelation that Kant will not enfranchize women, we have come a long way. The lack of independence of women is certainly not merely contingent in the way an apprentice's lack of independence may be thought to be contingent. Thus woman is denied not only the vote but also all hope of aspiring to it. Independence is eternally withheld from her. Then her freedom and equality are also threatened: the former by the radical dichotomy between woman's freedom and man's; the latter by a reinterpretation of the notion of equality as it applies to women (or, alternatively, by insistence that woman's equality is not denied, but merely voluntarily given up for practical purposes). Finally, it is denied—fleetingly and indirectly, but nevertheless denied—that woman's nature has a connection with reason. Woman's nature is identified with inclination, and it is for this reason that she must submit herself to man. It would appear that in the kingdom of rational beings there are only adult males. Kant even goes so far as to deny that there can be 'scholarly women': 'As for the scholarly woman, she uses her books in the same way as her watch, for example, which she carries so that people will see that she has one, though it is usually not running or not set by the sun'.[29]

In general, then, women are loquacious, quarrelsome, jealous and possessed of an overpowering inclination to dominate. It would be foolish and imprudent to allow them any power or authority in political matters since, Kant comes close to saying, they are not strictly rational. The downward spiral has brought us close to a situation in which it is hard to see what exactly distinguishes women from serfs or even animals, despite the lip-service Kant pays to the equality of women in marriage and the reciprocity of the marriage relationship.

What accounts for this massive underestimation of the value of women and suspicion of woman's nature? For even if the situation is not quite as bad as I have suggested, and as the texts quietly imply, nevertheless there can be little doubt that Kant took an extremely dim view of woman's nature and abilities. I have mentioned several times the excuse that Kant is merely a child of his time. Penned up in the narrow confines of Königsberg, starved of the company of women, it is surely, the argument goes, absurd to expect any more than this of him. It is not. At the beginning of this paper I quoted a remark from Mary Midgley and Judith Hughes's book *Women's Choices,* in which they comment upon the embarrassment which overcomes us when we read the views of the great dead philosophers on the subject of women. They comment too on the feeling that it is unfair and anachronistic to criticize the philosophers involved, but go on to conclude that even if excuses may be made for Aquinas, say, or Aristotle, nevertheless, 'When we get to the eighteenth century all such excuses fail, and it is important to say plainly that things went very badly wrong. Unthinking conformism was replaced by positive reactionary efforts to resist and reverse change'.[30]

Can we now say plainly that Kant's response to the question of women's status as citizens is rather more than mere unthinking prejudice, rather more than the reflections of an 'honest but narrow-minded bourgeois'? I think we can, and must. In this way, we may, I hope, find more far-reaching and useful lessons than the simple and by now unsurprising one that Kant 'got it wrong', for there is little point in establishing that he got it wrong without, at the same time, seeing how we might do better and without questioning whether the wrong done to women does not spring from a source which also involves doing wrong to others. In other words, is the wrong done to women simply the manifestation of a more deep-rooted and systematically misguided way of thinking? I now turn to these questions. My responses to them will be very partial and speculative. I recognize this and wish it were not so, but even a partial response may be better than nothing and I hope that what I say will suggest some lines of further inquiry.

At the beginning of the paper I noted the tensions in Kant's political philosophy and three accounts of the source of these tensions. Howard Williams' claim is that the tensions are merely part of Kant's general conservatism; his recognition that there are limits to what is practically possible in political life. Similarly, John Ladd's Introduction to the *Metaphysical Elements of Justice* suggests that the tensions represent a shrewd awareness of the gap between what is and what ought to be. That there is an element of this is undeniable; the most striking example of Kant's conservatism is perhaps his instruction always to obey the sovereign and his abhorrence of revolution. Thus he prefers to risk despotism rather than advocate the disobedience which would, he fears, result in chaos and strife. Other examples of conservatism are not hard to find in Kant's political philosophy and indeed in his own life (note, for example, his undertaking to Frederick William II not to mention religious matters either in his writings or in his lectures). However, it is difficult to see any element of compromise of this sort in his attitude to women; nowhere does he apologize for the low status he accords women. Far from it. In *Anthropology* he goes so far as to suggest that in civilized society woman's status is improved far beyond what it is in primitive society and even warns against the dangers of allowing women too much education. The same attitude is manifested in a series of letters concerning Maria von Herbert. This young woman had written to Kant about a romantic problem which was causing her great worry and unhappiness. Kant replied to the letters in stern moralistic tones and also sent them to Elizabeth Motherby, the daughter of an English friend, as a warning of what happens to women when they think too much and fail to control their fantasies![31] So even if the conservatism and caution are present in Kant's political philosophy, they cannot, I think, account for his treatment of women. For the problem here is precisely that there are no tensions at all: there is no radicalism or idealism to set against the pragmatism and conservatism, and it is this which distinguishes the treatment of women from, say, the discussion of revolution generally and the French Revolution in particular.

A second interpretation of Kant attributes the tensions in his political philosophy to straightforward failure to spot inconsistencies and contradictions. Thus Aris holds that Kant 'attacked serfdom and defended the exclusion of the unpropertied members of society from all essential political rights almost in the same breath, in both cases in the name of reason'.[32] This is true, but again not the whole truth. What is wrong with Kant's political philosophy in so far as it concerns the status of women is not simply that it expresses a cautious conservatism and eagerness to defend the status quo. Rather, the elevation of contingent practices to the status of requirements of reason represents a categorical denial on Kant's part that anything other than the status quo might be either feasible or permissible, and that is justified by appeal to pure reason. Thus the whole-hearted defence of capitalism, requiring that everything, even the marriage relationship, be understood in socio-economic terms; the defence of individualism generating the "shallow and repulsive" concept of marital relations, are all construed as demands of reason, not merely variable and changeable customs. Here we find a resistance to change which goes far beyond mere conservatism and elevates the principles and practices of eighteenth-century Germany to the level of undeniable and indubitable truth.

Still, the distinction between contingent practices and dictates of reason may not be quite as sharp as I have so far implied: in defending the status quo, Kant is not simply doing that. He is also defending his own individualism in *Groundwork*, and the difficulties he encounters are not, I think, peculiar to him, but are general difficulties which infect all individualist theories. In discussing Kant's views on woman's equality, I noted that he appears to be torn between, on the one hand, the belief that men and women are naturally equal, but that woman must renounce her natural equality for the common household good, and, on the other, the belief that men and women are *not* naturally equal: woman's singular nature renders inappropriate an equal division of authority and power. However, the problem here is a deep one—not only for Kant, but for

individualism generally and for feminist individualism in
particular. In all its forms, individualism runs the risk of failing
to do justice to the facts of our social lives. Caird makes this
point with particular reference to Kant's philosophy, pointing
out that in distinguishing between monogamous marriage and
concubinage Kant alludes to a social unity between two
persons which quite contradicts his original idea of right:

If we keep strictly to the category of reciprocity, and refuse to go on to the
higher category of organic community, each person would have to be
regarded as means to the other, and neither as end. This would answer to the
case of sensual indulgence in which each individual was a means to the
pleasure of the other, and no higher end was sought on either side. But Kant
really points to a higher social relation in which each individual loses himself
to find himself again in the common life to which he contributes.[33]

All individualist theories share this difficulty: in construing
persons as essentially independent, free and equal, they
support an atomistic model which cannot readily accommodate
those social units, such as the family, which transcend mere
atomism. The choice then is between abandoning individualism
and construing the family as itself a single unit, with the
husband as the head and decision-maker. The dilemma is
explained thus by Elizabeth Wolgast:

Husband and wife are different individuals with wills of their own. One would
think that, in the last determination, they form a small organisation which has
to make decisions in its own way, for which its members are jointly
responsible. But this would conflict with the atomistic model: from the point
of view of society, the parties would then neither be fully individuals, nor
together be one. It is simpler to say that the husband will represent them: that
saves the surface features of atomism. Like a single person, the head of the
family speaks for an atomic unit.[34]

And so it is with Kant: 'If a union is to be harmonious and
indissoluble, it is not enough for two people to associate as they
please; one party must be *subject* to the other'.[35] Against this
background Kant appeals to woman's nature to justify his claim
that it is she who should be subject; he who should dominate. At
this point, the honest but narrow-minded bourgeois appears, for
it is undeniable that here the contingent facts of eighteenth-
century German society are elevated to the status of eternal

truths. Nevertheless, the dilemma is thrown up by individualism itself, which dictates, as a central tenet, that *someone* must dominate, *someone* must give way. Even in Mill (champion of the emancipation of women), this problem arises, forcing him to appeal to woman's nature as a guarantee against the destruction of the patriarchal family. When individualism is feminist individualism, it still cannot escape its own internal demands. Thus the modern feminist may insist that at least sometimes the head of the family may be female, but it is never in doubt that *someone* must be the head and decision-maker. The language of domination and subordination is central to individualism and cannot be dispensed with except by abandoning individualism itself. Hence the charge that individualist feminism would turn women into psuedo-men.

In conclusion, then, it may well be that Kant is an honest but narrow-minded bourgeois, unable to see beyond the social conventions of his time. Nevertheless, we must beware of swapping one set of conventions for another: to abandon eighteenth-century German values for twentieth-century British values is not necessarily an improvement, particularly if the philosophical model underpinning both is faulty. The battle between individualist feminists and individualist misogynists will not be resolved satisfactorily until the implications of individualism are fully explained. As Kant himself says, in a different context:

As impartial umpires, we must leave aside the question whether it is for the good or the bad cause that the contestants are fighting. They must be left to decide the issue for themselves. After they have rather exhausted than injured one another, they will perhaps themselves perceive the futility of their quarrel, and part good friends.[36]

NOTES

I am very grateful to John Horton and Peter Nicholson for their extensive and helpful comments on an earlier draft of this paper.

1. The quotation is taken from Rheinhold Aris, *History of Political Thought in Germany, 1789–1815* (Frank Cass and Co., 1965) p. 87.

2.　Mary Midgley and Judith Hughes, *Women's Choices* (Weidenfeld and Nicolson, 1983) p. 45.

3.　Aris, p. 98. (Perhaps Aris exaggerates somewhat here: the denial of political rights to some members of society does not necessarily amount to applauding serfdom, as he suggests.)

4.　Howard Williams, *Kant's Political Philosophy* (Blackwell, 1983) p. 179.

5.　Morris R. Cohen, 'A critique of Kant's philosophy of law', in G.T. Whitney and D.F. Bowers (eds.) *The Heritage of Kant* (Russell and Russell, 1962) p. 296.

6.　*The Metaphysical Elements of Justice*, trans. John Ladd (Bobbs-Merrill, 1965) p. xxix.

7.　*Metaphysic of Morals*, sect. 46, in H. Reiss (ed.), trans. H. Nisbet, *Kant's Political Writings* (Cambridge University Press, 1970), p. 139. All page references to *Metaphysic of Morals* and *Theory and Practice* are to the Reiss edition, unless otherwise stated.

8.　*Theory and Practice* p. 74.

9.　*Ibid.*

10.　*Metaphysic of Morals*, sect. 46, p. 140.

11.　*Ibid.*, p. 139.

12.　*Ibid.*, pp. 139–40.

13.　*Ibid.*, p. 140.

14.　*Theory and Practice*, p. 78.

15.　*Ibid.*

16.　*Ibid.*

17.　*Metaphysic of Morals*, sect. 46, p. 140.

18.　Aris, p. 102.

19.　*The Doctrine of Virtue* (Part II of *The Metaphysic of Morals*), trans. M. Gregor (Harper and Row, 1964) p. 90.

20.　*The Doctrine of Virtue*, p. 89.

21.　Howard Williams, p. 118.

22.　*Groundwork for a Metaphysic of Morals*, Ak. 427–9.

23.　*Metaphysical Elements of Justice*, Ch. III., sect. 26, as quoted in B. Edelman, *The Ownership of the Image* (Routledge and Kegan Paul, 1979).

24.　*Anthropology from a Pragmatic Point of View*, trans. M. Gregor (Martinus Nijhoff, The Hague, 1974) p. 167.

25.　*Ibid.*, p. 168

26.　*Ibid.*, p. 170

27.　*Ibid.*, p. 172

28.　*Ibid.*, p. 285

29.　*Ibid.*, p. 171

30.　Midgley and Hughes, pp. 45–6.

31.　*Kant: Philosophical Correspondence, 1759–99*, ed. Arnulf Zweig (University of Chicago, 1967), p. 204 and Introduction, pp. 25–6.

32.　Aris, p. 98.

33.　E. Caird, *The Critical Philosophy of Kant* James Maclehose and Sons, 1889), vol II, 361, n.l.

34. Elizabeth H. Wolgast, *Equality and the Rights of Women* (Cornell University, 1980) pp. 145–6.
35. *Anthropology* p. 167.
36. *Critique of Pure Reason,* trans. N. Kemp Smith (Macmillan, 1929) A423/B451.

2 Virtue and Commerce: Women in the Making of Adam Smith's Political Economy

Jane Rendall

Adam Smith was by no means only a political economist. The *Wealth of Nations* (1776) was a part of a more wide-ranging project, 'an account of the general principles of law and government', incorporating all those subjects which formed part of the 'the science of a statesman or legislator'[1]. In this context, his ideas are frequently seen against the background of the development of liberal thought from John Locke to John Stuart Mill, united by the common themes of the pursuit of individual self-interest and the sanctity of contract, in a world of natural liberty restrained only by a minimal state. Yet Smith's analysis of his own commercial society—its gains and losses, its moral strengths and weaknesses—is a much more complex one, which does offer an opportunity to examine in depth some strands of eighteenth-century political thinking about the position of women. This subject may appear to be quite incidental to Smith's own aims, but the implications are fundamental to his view of the social and moral order. And his work formed an important theoretical stage in that redefinition of public and private spheres which is critical to our understanding of the relationship between the sexes in an industrial world. Throughout much of early modern Europe, definitions of the public sphere had looked to an older model of citizenship, that ultimately based on the pursuit of virtue within the classical republic. Though anachronistic, the classical rhetoric, based around the theme of the independent, virtuous, and by definition masculine, citizen, remained immensely powerful. Yet this was to be challenged as, increasingly, citizenship came to be seen as resting not on virtue, but on rights, the rights of the individual, both natural and contractual. The public world was no longer that in which the individual might find moral fulfilment. Inseparably associated with such a changing view of the public sphere, was the relocation of the pursuit of virtue within the private sphere, at its heart the life of the family and the moral inspiration of women. Adam Smith's writing on natural jurisprudence, on moral philosophy and on political economy was structured throughout by a sense of this critical transition, in which both public and private spheres received new definitions, dividing the commercial world of the market economy, from the domestic morality of the family.[2]

Recent studies of Smith have identified two major traditions of thought which shaped his ideas, and even at the risk of neglecting such fundamental contemporary influences as David Hume, and Montesquieu, these will be taken to exemplify the conflicting themes of 'virtue' and 'rights'. One such tradition is that described by J.G.A. Pocock as 'classical republicanism' or 'civic humanism'. The model for this was the small republic or city state in which the male citizen might find personal fulfilment, and attain a virtuous life, through full participation in public affairs of all kinds: for that citizen, private interests were to be subordinated to a public role of unceasing civic and military involvement sustained by patriotism. Classical authors—Aristotle, Cicero—clearly provided one source. Even more stimulating was that representation of republicanism found in Machiavelli's *Discourses* (1531), an immensely popular work in early modern Europe. Such classical republicanism underwent many shifts in meaning, identifiable only in precise historical contexts. By the beginning of the eighteenth century, in the work of 'old Whigs' like Walter Moyle, Viscount Molesworth, and the Scot Andrew Fletcher, the citizen had become a landed freeholder; the republic was interpreted as a commonwealth in which the constitutional elements were rightly balanced: and the sources of internal corruption and decay were to be found in the new machinery of commercial credit and finance, in the moral dangers of a new kind of luxury. Republicanism offered a language through which the concerns of those aware of the changing social and economic order might be expressed. Luxury, commerce, credit, all appeared to threaten the moral imperatives of the republic, the subordination of private to public good.[3]

The second tradition is that of natural jurisprudence. Such

jurisprudence had its roots in medieval and classical thought, but seventeenth- and eighteenth- century writers looked primarily to the great work of Hugo Grotius *De Jure Belli ac Pacis (Of the Law of War and Peace)* (1625). His most important later follower, Samuel von Pufendorf, who wrote the *De Jure Naturae et Gentium (Of the Law of Nature and Nations)* (1672), summarized as *De Officio Hominis et Civis (Of the Duty of Man and Citizen)* (1673) was to have a profound effect on Scottish political thinking in the first half of the eighteenth century. Both these writers grounded a theory of natural rights in a natural law which was distinguished from divine law, and from the positive laws of individual states. Natural law was divinely ordained, yet knowable not through revelation, but through 'right reason', as 'necessary for sociability between men'.[4] The only perfect duties towards one's fellows prescribed by the law of nature and valid even in the state of nature, were these: not to injure another person, and to make reparation for any injury or loss caused to another person. For the preservation of society it was necessary that, as a third duty, individuals should strive for the good of humanity: yet given the imperfections of human nature, such an aim could be secured only through a further obligation—that of keeping promises and contracts. Through the making of such promises arose the 'adventitious' or artificially created, voluntary obligations, whether in the relationships of property and commerce, in the personal relationships of husband and wife, parents and children, masters and servants, or in the formation of governments. Such obligations, once created, might be 'perfect' (absolutely binding on contracting parties), or 'imperfect' (morally binding only). Pufendorf stressed that individuals had rights only when they had claims, created by promises or contracts, on other individuals. Society then was bound together by a network of mutual obligations, rooted in the sociable nature of man, yet justified on utilitarian grounds as necessary to the welfare and preservation of that society. The implications of this were by no means necessarily liberal, since contractual relationships might justify an absolute government as easily as a liberal one.[5]

Pufendorf's work provided the basic framework for the teaching of moral philosophy and jurisprudence in the

University of Glasgow from the beginning of the eighteenth century until at least the 1760s. That framework was passed on by successive holders of the Chair in Moral Philosophy, Gershom Carmichael, who taught from 1695 to 1729, Francis Hutcheson, his direct successor, Professor from 1730 to 1746, and Adam Smith who after a brief interlude held the post from 1752 to 1764. Each of these teachers considered the derivation and meaning of the law of nature, and the obligations created by it: perfect natural rights, and perfect adventitious rights, as well as imperfect rights. Each included, under the heading of perfect adventitious personal rights, a chapter on the relationship of husband and wife. From Pufendorf to Smith, the content of that discussion was entirely transformed.

I

Pufendorf outlined his view of marriage briefly in his *Of the Duty of Man and Citizen,* though he treated the subject much more fully, with a wider range of references, in the *Law of Nature and Nations.* Natural law prescribed certain institutions for the good of human society. The first simple associations entered into in the state of nature were those of the household, and of those, the relationship of husband and wife was the first. Marriage, though an 'adventitious' or voluntary state was 'the first example . . .of the social life, and at the same time the nursery of the human race'.[6] The purpose of marriage was procreation, and other kinds of sexual pleasure were unnatural. Humanity had an obligation to marry and preserve their species, and individuals a personal duty to do so. Pufendorf listed the four irreducible articles of the marriage pact. First, the contract, to be initiated by the man 'in harmony with the nature of both sexes', had to contain the woman's promise of fidelity, in order to ensure legitimate offspring. Secondly, the woman must require the same promise of the man. Thirdly, there had to be a commitment to continuous cohabitation, and 'a mutual promise of such a life together as the nature of that alliance requires'. Fourthly, it was in agreement with 'the natural condition of both sexes' that the husband should be the head of the household, and 'in matters relating the marriage and the household the wife is subject to the husband's direction'.[7] To be valid, such articles had to be freely accepted by the two individuals, equal in rights before entering on such a contract, deriving their equality from the natural state of humanity:

For although, as a general thing, the male surpasses the female in strength of body and mind, yet that superiority is of itself far from being capable of giving the former authority over the latter. Therefore, whatever right a man has over a woman, inasmuch as she is his equal, will have to be secured by her consent, or by a just war.[8]

This view of marriage therefore rested on a contractual and utilitarian basis, in which the rights of husbands and wives sprang from the nature of the contract, though the positive laws of states, and divine law might impose further conditions. Uneasily, he argued that the superiority of the male sex did normally make the pact 'an unequal league', in which protection was exchanged for obedience. If the positive laws of states gave husbands absolute authority over their wives, that was not contrary to natural law. Nor were 'irregular and simple' marriages in barbarous societies, where women took the initiative, though these did not fit 'the condition of human nature' so well.[9] In a marriage normal according to natural and positive laws, parental authority over children similarly lay with the father.[10]. He had also to consider how far marriages which did not fit the western European model accorded with his argument: how far were polyandry and polygamy compatible with the purpose of marriage and its essential articles? Polyandry was dismissed as contrary to natural law, yet polygamy might be defended as fulfilling the ultimate purpose of marriage, the procreation of children. Women might consent to such marriages, which might be unequal but were not necessarily tyrannous. Monogamy, however, was 'the most decorous' and 'most conducive to domestic peace'.[11]

If the principal articles of the marriage pact were broken, then either husband or wife had a right to divorce. Yet Pufendorf, mocking John Milton's pamphlet on divorce, suggested that mere incompatibility could provide no justification. His argument is revealing:

It may, therefore, be better to keep our philosophy on lower levels, and taking into account the common genius of women, hold that a woman does her share for her husband when she devotes her energies to bringing forth and rearing children, and undertaking her share of the labour of the house, even though she may otherwise offer little aid in matters of philosophy.[12]

To fulfil the articles of the marriage pact, certain qualifications were required: the rationality and consent of both parties, the fulfilment of all the terms and conditions of the marriage, the absence of a previous marriage. Consanguinity was a fundamental barrier: the root of this prohibition was not easy to discover, since, Pufendorf maintained, it was not found among some more primitive peoples. Modesty and a sense of shame were, he argued, necessary to guard the chastity and good order of society, especially among the more civilized peoples. Such feelings were even more vital between those to whom reverence, or care, were owed, parents, children, and close relatives. That was the utilitarian reason for the preservation of such a barrier in the law of nature, at least between kin in close affinity.[13]

The contractual and utilitarian elements in Pufendorf's discussion have been stressed. But it is also true that on a broader front his account of the origins of private property and the eventual formation of governments was based not only on the formation of contracts, but on a gradual passage from the state of nature, which he rooted in its material context. Early families, hunters and shepherds, might separate as sons took their families to distant parts. But once families grouped together for protection, they gradually acquired the tastes of those who lived in towns and cities, for the products of manufactures and trade, for the arts and civilized life.[14] In his discussion of the marriage pact, however, Pufendorf never moved beyond rather indiscriminate use of historical and comparative material, though he often compared the customs of 'barbarian' peoples with those of more advanced nations. There is no suggestion in his work, unlike that of Smith, of any more structured approach to the history of the family.[8]

The responsibility for introducing Pufendorf's work into the teaching of moral philosphy in Scotland rests with an obscure figure, Gershom Carmichael, a committed supporter of the

Presbyterian regime after 1688 and of the Hanoverian succession. Pufendorf's *De Officio Hominis et Civis* was adopted by him as a textbook probably by the beginning of the eighteenth century, and in 1718 he published his own annotated edition of the work. It was sufficiently successful to be reprinted in 1724. In his preface, he pointed to his own differences with Pufendorf. He stressed the importance of rooting the obligations of the law of nature in natural theology. By that he meant not the revealed Christian message, but rather that understanding of the design of God for humanity which may be gained by closer study of human nature and human society. He stressed also the importance of the individual's quest for spiritual fulfilment, through the contemplation of the perfection of the Supreme Being. Carmichael's very full notes to Pufendorf's work stress this difference: he wanted to inject more positive moral concern, to *use* natural jurisprudence as a means of teaching ethics, of emphasising moral obligations. Among other commentators, he used extensively John Locke's *Two Treatises on Government* (1690) as a gloss on Pufendorf.[15]

In his notes to the chapter on marriage, Carmichael commented that the obligation to marriage did not arise primarily from the necessity of reproduction, or the desirability of a well-ordered society. Rather, the marriage pact, in its pure form adapted to the rational and social nature of humanity, entailing the right use of sexuality, would bring the right kind of upbringing for children, and with it a better informed and educated population.[16] And for that purpose, to secure the better education and care of children, the mutual promise of fidelity between spouses was essential. He does not appear to give the same primacy to a woman's obligation to fidelity, to secure legitimacy. Rather, he suggests that whether the contract originates from the woman or the man—a departure from Pufendorf—both seek to care for and to rear their own children.[17] He appears, then, to be marginally more sympathetic than Pufendorf to the notion of a degree of equality in marriage. In discussing the fourth article of the marriage pact, relating to the authority of the husband, he used parts of the more detailed discussion in the *Law of Nature and Nations* to argue that there was nothing in the law of nature to prescribe the subordination of a wife to her husband, beyond the need to vest authority in the family in the more prudent spouse: though it was true that custom normally gave that authority to the husband. Yet in a state of natural liberty, or among those ignorant of Divine revelation, such subjection might not be known.[18] His view of polygamy is much harsher than Pufendorf's, and he condemns it as 'a most iniquitious oppression'.[19] His comments on divorce are equivocal, his main stipulation that the primary purpose of marriage, the rearing of children, should never be infringed.[20]

The shifts of emphasis here are slight. But it is worth noting that Carmichael always stressed the way in which relationships were suited and adapted to human nature, rather than the pattern of authority and obligation rooted in contract. The relationship of marriage was rooted in its natural purpose, designed by God, not only that of reproduction, but of the moral improvement of humanity, 'especially in the shaping of the minds and habits of [children] to moral worth'.[21] The teaching of rights and duties could not, for him, be separated from the inculcation of virtue.[22]

Carmichael's direct successor was the moral philosopher Francis Hutcheson, who had attended his lectures as a student, and referred to him as 'by far the best commentator' on Pufendorf's work. Hutcheson was a much better known figure, both for his moral philosophy, grounded in human psychology, and for his liberal theology. Hutcheson too used Pufendorf's work in his teaching, though even before he had taken up his post he expressed some reservations about it, commenting that he seemed to have banished 'the natural affections and kind instincts' in favour of 'interest and some selfish view'.[23] In his inaugural lecture Hutcheson argued that Pufendorf's case had rested too greatly on the self-interest of individuals, omitting the sociable and benevolent side of human nature. That side was revealed first of all in that most 'mild, kind, and gentle' of societies, the human family, in the care of parents for their children, and in the mutual affection of brothers and sisters.[24]

In the early 1730s Hutcheson wrote his own series of lectures, published only after his death as the *System of Moral Philosophy* (1755). This fuller work amplified his *Short*

Introduction to Moral Philosophy (1742; English translation 1747). Hutcheson followed Pufendorf's framework of discussion, but there were two major differences in his outlook. First, his work was rooted in a clearly formulated and original study of moral psychology. He rejected the view that men could discover moral rules by the use of reason, and believed in the existence of a moral faculty, or sense, which perceived moral goodness, or experienced a feeling of moral pleasure. Providence had so ordered it for the good of mankind. His treatment of social and political issues was therefore based very much on the dual assumption that the individual's moral sense would indicate what was right, *and* that moral actions could be justified by the welfare and happiness of all. The language of the benevolent moralist and of utilitarianism could sometimes merge. Secondly, Hutcheson's arguments were overlaid by a clearly identifiable political standpoint. He acknowledged that he owed much to the 'republican' tradition of writing, and that tradition was to influence profoundly his treatment of political, social, and economic affairs.

As a republican and as a moral philosopher, Hutcheson was to view the terms of the marriage contract, and the relationship between public and private life, in a very different way from that of Pufendorf. He was infinitely more concerned with the moral qualities of the married state than with that network of obligations which Pufendorf had constructed. Like Carmichael, he also found the origin of that state in those reproductive instincts which humanity shared with the animal kingdom, distinguished from it by the length of time necessary to care for children. But he stressed the design of Providence in implanting those senses and affections in humanity which, repressing the brutal instinct of lust, brought to marriage 'delicate sentiments and finer passions of the heart of the sweetest kind', predisposing to a long and affectionate relationship.[25] This harmony within marriage made the caring and education of children a tolerable and fulfilling task. For Hutcheson it was 'this moral machinery of these instincts' which revealed the terms and obligations of the marriage contract, confirmed by 'the happy effects upon society' gained from following these instincts. The feelings had become a moral force, as 'all the concomitant generous passions' were distinguished from that original 'brutal impulse'. Indulged without such restraints, or channels for fulfilment, the sexual instinct would destroy family affections, reduce population, and bring 'general misery'.[26] Here as elsewhere Hutcheson contrasts 'calm' and 'turbulent' passions, as 'stable and conjugal love' is contrasted with 'the turbulent' passionate dispositions of tenderness'.[27] It was a profoundly optimistic view of the marital relationship, which stressed the bonds of affection, sentiment, and moral feeling.

In his examination of the four articles of the marriage contract, Hutcheson made several important alterations. The first article was the necessity of fidelity on the part of the woman. This meant that the loss of virginity before marriage could deprive a woman of her chance of conjugal life and affection, and the wrong done her by her seducer was the most grievous of injuries. The only remedy was a sense of the enormity of such a crime in a man, and the inculcation of habits of modesty in both sexes. Like Carmichael, in treating of the second article, Hutcheson denounced any suggestion that the obligation to fidelity and monogamy was not a reciprocal one: 'The natural passions of the woman as much require a friendly society, and unity of interest in the joint-education of the common offspring as those of the man'.[28]

On the third article, relating to 'continuous cohabitation', he stressed the mutal friendship of the partners, and, since true friendship was possible only for life, that the contract had to be a perpetual one, or marriage would become 'a mere servile bargain from procreation and joint labour'. Hutcheson's view was a much more exalted one than that of Pufendorf, of marriage as 'an equal friendship', 'a constant reciprocal friendship of two', 'a state of equal partnership or friendship'.[29]

Consistently, then, he also denied Pufendorf's fourth article, relating to the husband's right to head the household. And he rebutted John Locke's view that men's superior endowments, in body and mind, normally gave them that authority, arguing that such superiority was by no means universal, nor were those qualities in which women were usually superior taken into account. In a long and interesting paragraph, Hutcheson argued that there was no natural foundation for any right of authority in marriage. Such rights might well exist in positive law, but still

remained contrary to equity and humanity. In daily disagree-
ments, deference might in fact be shown to the partner of the
greatest abilities, and this might perhaps more often be the
husband. But where disagreement was fundamental, nature
suggested a reference to arbitration rather than a right to
command. Hutcheson does seem to have envisaged a broad
degree of equality in the relationship—but one which was
clearly based on a division of spheres: 'Domestic matters seem
indeed to be divided into two provinces, one fitted for the
management of each sex, in which the other should seldom
interfere, except by advising'.[30]

He denounced many civil laws, especially those depriving
women of property, suggesting that important affairs should be
entrusted to both partners equally. The parental power, for
example, rooted in natural affection, belonged equally to both
parents, though it was sometimes voluntarily surrendered by
the mother.[31] Contracts upon other terms, even validated by
positive laws, were contrary to nature. He followed Pufendorf
in continuing to discuss those impediments which might bar a
contract before marriage—the absence of proper consent, and
consanguinity—and the grounds on which divorce was possible.
Only the violation of the essential terms of the contract, through
adultery or wilful desertion, could justify it.[32]

In looking at the relationship between husband and wife,
Hutcheson appears to make a surprisingly egalitarian case. Yet
at the same time he also stresses a sharp division between the
worlds of men and women. Such a position was not necessarily
an inconsistent one, yet Hutcheson does find it hard to evaluate
the relative claims of public and private morality. As a
'republican' and as a moral philosopher he offers an ambivalent
interpretation, clearly caught between the two themes. For him
the highest morality was that 'calm, stable, universal, goodwill
to all', which remained the highest of aspirations. This meant
that 'the love of a society, a country, is more excellent than
domestic affections', for the more extensive, as well as calm, a
passion, the nearer it was to the ideal.[33] But at the same time, for
Hutcheson, the domestic affections offered a schooling in
moral sentiments, a means of improvement and development,
essential to the participation of the citizen in the public world.
The natural affections of the family were indeed 'the chiefest

springs of industry, and an incitement to zeal for our country's defence, and to all honourable services.'[34]

In his examination of the origins of property, Hutcheson had rooted the impulse to labour in the private desires of men to better themselves and their families, in 'the hopes of future wealth, ease, and pleasure to themselves, their offspring, and all who are dear to them'.[35] Yet such desires were not only private ones, but might be harnessed to the public good. Hutcheson recognized, and attempted to meet, Plato's objection to married life, that it was inward looking, introverted, leading individuals to neglect the public welfare in storing up wealth for their families. Communal property, and communal childrearing, were, Hutcheson argued, poorly adapted to human nature, and would deprive children of affection and care, and parents of 'life's sweetest enjoyments' in the conjugal and parental relationship. 'Higher knowledge and virtue must be introduced, and our natural affections suppressed, before industry, activity, labour, and dangers, can become agreeable from calm, extensive affection alone'.[36] Is it worth it? he seems to be saying. But in recognition of the difficulty of uniting public and private loyalties, he suggested that the state might introduce modest legislative changes, in matters such as education, elections to offices and honours, and inheritance law, which, in the public interest, would counteract any tendency to selfishness induced by family loyalty. These tentative suggestions seem to be analogous to his endorsement of an 'agrarian law' designed to curb excessive private wealth.[37]

The general good of society required the inspiration of the natural affections. Yet ultimately the world of citizenship remained entirely male. The task of the state was the promotion of virtue, seen in participation in public affairs, not merely the maintenance of justice and security. Virtue might be encouraged by the best forms of education and by freely electing the most virtuous men to public office. Besides the natural affections, the most necessary virtues were the cardinal ones of sobriety, industry, justice, and fortitude. In discussing the first two, Hutcheson revealed his idea of a state united by industry, not by luxury or excess consumption, in which the moderate comfort of many families, not the accumulation of wealth in a few, was the index of a virtuous republic. Such a state would be encouraged by a growing population, so that 'encouragement should be given to marriage, and to those who rear a numerous offspring to industry'.[38] Justice was to be embodied in simple laws, fortitude in the obligation of citizens to serve in the militia. This was the stuff of classical republicanism, in which women had no public role to play, excluded from the possibility of becoming virtuous citizens. Yet in Hutcheson that republicanism is linked, to a degree perhaps not found elsewhere, to a stress on the moral potential of domestic and family affairs, as the source and inspiration of the nobler affections of male citizens.

In his work republicanism was united with moral philosophy, and though he used the vocabulary of natural jurisprudence, the state of which he wrote had as its end the positive one of the pursuit of virtue. This uneasy combination meant that the balance between private and public spheres needed some redefinition. The pursuit of virtue was now to be founded on the fulfilment of the passions and instincts, 'calm' rather than 'turbulent', for which the original school was the family.[39] The sharpness of the division between the worlds of men and women, however, was never in doubt. Citizenship was still entirely male, but was defined by Hutcheson, both in the classical terms of participation in civic and military affairs, and with reference to the restrained and temperate pursuit of wealth. A healthy economy required a growing population, and the task of bearing and educating children for the republic was the sphere of women. In the work of Hutcheson's successor, Adam Smith, the republic was to be displayed by the market, as the arena of public life.

II

Adam Smith had attended Hutcheson's lectures as a student, and on his first arrival at Glasgow, initially as Professor of Logic, his first task was to lecture on Books 2 and 3 of Hutcheson's *Short Introduction,* dealing with 'Oeconomicks' and Politics. From 1752 to 1764 as Professor of Moral Philosophy, we know from a surviving account that his lectures were divided into four parts:

The first contained Natural Theology . . . The second comprehended Ethics, strictly so called, and consisted chiefly of the doctrines which he afterwards published in his Theory of Moral Sentiments. In the third part, he treated at more length of that branch of morality which relates to *justice* . . . .

In the last part of his lectures, he examined those political regulations which are founded, not upon the principle of *justice,* but that of *expediency,* and which are calculated to increase the riches, the power, and the prosperity of a State . . . . What he delivered on these subjects contained the substance of the work he afterwards published under the title of An Inquiry into the Nature and Causes of the Wealth of Nations.[40]

The Theory of Moral Sentiments was first published in 1759, though in later editions of 1761 and 1790 he made significant changes.[41] Like Hutcheson, Smith rested his understanding of moral rules not on the perceptions of 'right reason', but on his own view of human psychology, though he rejected the notion of an innate moral sense. Again, like Hutcheson, he wished to ground the principles of morality in the passions and instincts of humanity: yet his approach, as a practical moralist, was to deal with the ways in which individuals both acquire and internalize moral sentiments. Smith believed that through the exercise of sympathy, an individual, as a spectator, may attempt to sympathize with the motive of another person in a particular situation and estimate its appropriateness. That power of sympathy will also aid in the judgement of the merit of an action, in the degree to which the spectator enters into the gratitude or resentment of those affected by the action. That judgement constituted moral approval or disapproval, though where the individual's powers of sympathy were limited, recourse might be had to the accumulated experience of the 'impartial spectator', the conscience. Those moral rules, known through sympathy and judgement, would come to be recognized as the general principles of morality. Considerations of utility, though they might be relevant in reinforcing moral judgement, did not determine it.

Smith's survey of the different systems of moral philosophy, in Book VII, provides a useful introduction to his view of other contemporary systems.[42] He rejected a Stoicism founded on propriety of conduct in all circumstances, as one which prescribed 'perfect apathy', seeking to eradicate 'all our private, partial and selfish affections'. Nevertheless, especially in Book VI, added in 1790, he showed considerable admiration for the Stoic philosophy, and especially for the virtue of self-command. He reviewed those whose moral system depended on the principle of prudent self-interest. He pointed out that though the tendency of virtue to promote order and happiness in society might seem to offer a utilitarian critique of moral behaviour, yet such behaviour arose nevertheless from the operation of sympathy. Thirdly he wrote of those systems which, like Hutcheson's, rested on virtue as a calm benevolence. These, Smith suggests, ignored the 'inferior virtues' such as prudence, temperance, constancy, and others which sprang from self-interested, but perfectly praiseworthy motives: 'The habits of economy, industry, discretion, attention, and application of thought are generally supposed to be cultivated from self-interested motives, and at the same time are apprehended to be very praise-worthy qualities, which deserve the esteem and approbation of everybody'.[43]

All three systems contained some elements of what was to be his own. In rejecting Hutcheson's ideas, it has been suggested that here Smith is moderating not only the asceticism of the Stoic, but also the civic virtue of the republican: he is more concerned with the everyday virtues of those who live in a changing and commercial society.[44] Smith wrote of a range of different qualities, and of the man embodying the highest degree of virtue as one who 'to all the soft, the amiable and the gentle virtues, joins all the great, the awful, and the respectable'.[45]

The distinction is between those 'gentle virtues' arising from great sensibility, and those nobler qualities which stem from victory over one's own feelings, and which are found most of all 'under the boisterous and stormy sky of war and faction, of public tumult and confusion'.[46] There are many examples where this distinction appears to be used metaphorically as a sexual one: the point is stated unambiguously in an intriguing passage:

The propriety of generosity and public spirit is founded upon the same principles with that of justice. Generosity is different from humanity. These two qualities, which at first sight seem so nearly allied, do not always belong to the same person. Humanity is the virtue of a woman, generosity of a man.

The fair sex, who have commonly much more tenderness than ours, have seldom so much generosity... Humanity consists merely in the exquisite fellow-feeling which the spectator entertains with the sentiments of the persons principally concerned, so as to grieve for their sufferings, to resent their injuries, and to rejoice at their good fortune. The most human actions require no self-denial, no self-command, no great exertion of the sense of propriety. They consist only in doing what this exquisite sympathy would of its own accord prompt us to do. But it is otherwise with generosity. We never are generous except when in some respect we prefer some other person to ourselves, and sacrifice some great and important interest of our own to an equal interest of a friend or of a superior.[47]

That generosity might become the total devotion to duty, even at the cost of life, of a young officer in war, or the sacrifice by a Brutus of his own sons in the interest of Rome. Such perceptions of the propriety and beauty of public spirit could be attained only by the wisest.

This theme is echoed less directly, but surely with the same force, elsewhere. There is the continuous contrast between 'the soft, the gentle, the amiable' and 'the great, the awful and respectable'.[48] There is Smith's continuing reference to the necessity of balance. The 'delicate sensibility' of civilized nations may be in danger of destroying 'masculine firmness of character'.[49] A lack of passion may reveal weakness, as when 'the want of proper indignation is a most essential defect in the manly character'.[50] For men, Smith saw 'the contest between the two principles' as bringing, ideally, a proper balance of humanity and generosity.[51] It would seem that, for women, one side of that balance only was relevant. Women excelled in humanity, and the finest example of the principle of sympathy which Smith can offer is that of the mother's feeling for her sick child.[52] There was little suggestion that women might acquire the virtues of public life, lacking courage and the necessary capacity for self-command as they did.[53] They might, however, possess the ability to control their desires, to a lesser degree—on suffering the death of a relative, for example:

even a wise man may, for some time, indulge himself in some degree of moderate sorrow. An affectionate, but weak, woman, is often, upon such occasions, almost perfectly distracted. Time, however, in a longer or shorter period, never fails to compose the weakest woman to the same degree of tranquillity as the strongest man.[54]

In Book VI, added in 1790, Smith wrote of 'those gentler exertions of self-command', inculcating chastity, industry and frugality, less dazzling, but no less pleasing than the great qualities of the statesman or hero, leading to 'humble paths of private and peaceable life'.[55] Here surely there is a suggestion of virtues applicable to both sexes, in private life, and in economic matters.

One exception must be noted, and that is Smith's treatment of chastity. Like David Hume, he compared breaches of chastity in women to breaches of fidelity and the breaking of contracts by men. It was the one specifically female obligation, and it was to be judged by the unyielding standards, perhaps applied even more harshly, applied to all violations of faith: 'Breach of chastity dishonours irretrievably. No circumstances, no solicitation, can excuse it; no sorrow, no repentance atone for it. We are so nice in this respect, that even a rape dishonours, and the innocence of the mind cannot, in our imagination, wash out the pollution of the body'.[56] He returned to that subject in the lectures on jurisprudence. Here he treated the passion of love with some sympathy, in spite of what he saw as its dangers, its ridiculous features. Though the faculty of sympathy could not extend to love for a particular person, those high hopes of gratification, those 'expectations of romantic happiness', might indeed rouse the spectator's interest, as much in their vulnerability as in their possible fulfilment.[57]

Love, and the marital relationship, brought with it other important social virtues, of sensibility, kindness, friendship. A spectator might watch with pleasure a family ruled by love and esteem, companions for each other, with little difference between the members but that shown by 'respectful affection on the one side and kind indulgence on the other'.[58] These 'amiable passions' might be felt to an excessive degree, but they were never to be despised, as were the extremes of the unsocial passions. Extreme humanity and sensibility attracted pity, not contempt. The closest affections felt by anyone were those for the members of one's own family. Indeed those affections were but 'habitual sympathy' felt most closely within the family.[59] And it was the promotion of those family relationships which helped to create the operation of sympathy. For Smith 'domestic education is the institution of nature; public education, the contrivance of man. It is surely unnecessary to say which is likely to be the wisest'.[60] Rules of morality were first learnt through sympathizing with those nearest and dearest to us. On that family affection was built the willingness to accommodate to and identify with, neighbourhoods, associations, and one's country. He was describing a process of moral education which had the family, and those partial, humane values, at its centre. That education was dependent, not on the physical upbringing of the child, but on the moral responsibility asserted by the parents.[61]

Yet even within the *Theory of Moral Sentiments*, the role of the family may be seen in its historical context. He noted the contrast between family life in pastoral societies, where all branches of one family might reside together, and where tribal or clan links were fundamental, and those families of his own day, mobile, rapidly separated, soon losing all connection with all except their immediate family. It was not from any sense of kinship that any growth of 'natural affection' might be expected. But in this 'civilised' society:

the virtues which are founded upon humanity are more cultivated than those which are founded upon self-denial and the command of passions. Among rude and barbarous nations it is quite otherwise, the virtues of self-denial are more cultivated than those of humanity.

The material security of what were now humane and polished societies offered little scope for the military virtues. Only in such societies could the passion of love, and other emotions, be freely expressed, since savage and barbarian societies regarded such feelings as 'effeminacy'.[62] Yet civilization had its dangers too. Smith wrote of the desire to emulate the rich and great, from which women were by no means exempt '. . . place, that great object which divided the wives of aldermen, is the end of half the labours of human life'.[63]

Such emulation was 'the great and most universal cause of the corruption of our moral sentiments'—yet it might also be seen as the source of prosperity and economic growth. For Smith, the answer lay not in an easy equation of luxury and corruption, and Hutcheson's republican solution of legislation to curb private wealth and family accumulation.[64] For him, the answer lay in the sense of propriety, of fitness, of what was appropriate to one's station in life. And in the middling and lower ranks of life, the routes to virtue and to a reasonable wealth were not dissimilar, requiring a certain degree of ability, exercised with prudence and restraint. That sense of propriety splintered the unity of virtues required by the male citizen of the republican ideal.[65]

Smith's concept of virtue had balanced those qualities which he rooted in a martial society, barbarian or republican, against the humanity or natural affections, which played so much larger a part, he argued, in his own, more civilized world. The male citizen, ideally, would aspire to an appropriate balance. It is a balance which clearly had different implications for women. Their role in a civilized world was that of transmitting the humane virtues, and the natural affections, through the process of domestic education, though they could hope to achieve only occasionally those virtues which were primarily of a masculine character. They might however in private life exercise those qualities of self-restraint and self-command which Smith so much admired. Yet, finally, Smith says little of what propriety demanded of a woman, apart from that most fundamental obligation, to chastity.

In the lectures on jurisprudence, Smith followed his predecessors in outline. Two sets of lecture notes have survived. Those of 1762–3 (LJ(A)), recently fully edited, offer a much fuller guide to Smith's thinking than those of 1763–4 (LJ(B)), first published in 1896, not least in the section on marriage. In LJ(A), Smith declared that in discussing individual natural rights, following 'the distinction which Mr Hutchinson, after Baron Puffendorf' made between perfect and imperfect rights, he would describe only perfect rights in a state of 'commutative justice'.[66] Like his predecessors, he discussed the rights of the individual, and then those that belonged to a member of a family (husbands and wives, parents and children, masters and servants), and those of a member of a society. Though the ordering and intention remained the same, there were two major differences in Smith's treatment. First, rights were defined not as contractual obligations, nor in terms of the moral sense, but as arising from the way in which the 'impartial spectator' entered sympathetically into the resentment of the victim. It was a negative definition: that resentment, generalized by the working of sympathy, was to define natural rights and justice. Such natural rights, obvious and recognizable, could be distinguished from acquired or adventitious rights, which had to be related to their historical context. Smith might use the argument of utility, and frequently found it valuable, yet he was clear that the true origins of justice lay in the feelings of resentment of the individual who suffered injury. Secondly, Smith was writing an historical account, a history of rights, related to the four stages through which social institutions passed, each broadly characterized by a separate mode of subsistence: hunting, pastoral, agricultural, commercial. As well as writing about natural rights, then, he also offered a descriptive, historical account of the development of law, related to different patterns of subsistence. He was interested not in a voluntaristic theory of contract, or in a hypothetical state of nature, but in the customs and habits of different peoples, as their changing environment helped to mould their moral sentiments and their laws. Acquired rights were based on such changing customs and habits.[67]

Smith's discussion begins in a familiar way, in a passage on the origins of marriage in the sexual instinct, and in the necessity, among humans, for the lengthy care of the young. He promised then to sketch out the duties of both spouses and the rights and privileges of each. It must be said that this promise is not fulfilled, and that Smith departs significantly from the four articles of the marriage contract noted by Pufendorf and Hutcheson. The first duty of marriage, for Smith, is the wife's obligation to fidelity. Its foundation lay not only in the sense of injury felt by a husband, or the utility of securing legitimate offspring, but in the sympathy felt by a spectator with the jealousy of the husband:

The indignation of the public against the wife arises from their sympathy with the jealousy of the husband, and accordingly they are disposed to resent and punish it. The sentiment of jealousy is not chiefly founded, or rather not at all, upon the idea of a spurious offspring. It is not from the particular act that the jealousy arises, but he considers her infidelity as an entire alienation of that preference to all other persons which she owes him.[68]

The obligation here then rested not on the positive ends of marriage but negatively, on public sympathy with the injured husband. It would seem, unsurprisingly, that the public, or the 'impartial spectator', was in this instance evidently male. Smith is perfectly clear on this: 'The laws of most countries being made by men generally are very severe on the women, who can have no remedy for this oppression'.[69]

Elsewhere he contrasted the legislation of a celibate Catholic clergy, with no direct interest in the matter, and, presumably, no feelings of sympathy for the situation, with the oppressive inclinations of legislators who were also husbands. Smith acknowledged that a wife, in the case of her husband's adultery, might also feel a sense of injury: yet because the man was generally acknowledged to be the superior, the injury to his honour was the greater.[70] There was here no attempt to suggest that natural justice required any principle of equality, to be enforced through the articles of the marriage contract. Smith offered not an abstract, but a naturalistic account, using the two themes of a wife's obligation to fidelity and the perpetuity of marriage to trace the history of the marital relationship.

In the early stages of society, he suggested, the sentiment of love and the corresponding passion of jealousy were hardly felt. Where manners were 'rude and uncultivated' there was no strong desire that one's offspring should be legitimate: 'The foundation of jealousy is that delicacy which attends the sentiment of love, and it is more or less in different countries, in proportion to the rudeness of manners'.[71]

It is not altogether easy to relate Smith's history of the family to the four stages of society, never intended as a rigid guide, though references throughout the lectures can be pieced together. In the age of hunters, though he refers at one point to the mere coexistence of ten to twelve people of different sexes, he more frequently writes of people living together in a 'number of independent families', with no formal government, and the affairs of each family left to its own regulation. Contracts, settlements, and fixed obligations in marriage were unknown. The authority of the head of the household over its members was 'in the infancy of society' absolute.[72] There was no fixed property, and families maintained themselves by hunting, though sometimes, as among the American Indians, women practised primitive agriculture. Smith does, however, suggest that perhaps more regard was paid to women as 'rational

creatures' among those Indians, where women might fight and
be consulted on matters of government. Even in Anglo-Saxon
England, women such as powerful abbesses might have a share
in government deliberations.[73] In the age of shepherds, when
formal governments first commenced, they were little concerned
with intervening in private affairs, and simply attempted to
strengthen the authority of the head of the household. Though
marriage was intended to be perpetual, the husband alone had
an unlimited power of divorce. All members of the family were
expected nevertheless to contribute to the material support of
that family, and by doing so would earn a right to succeed to the
goods earned by their labour on the death of the master of the
family. The wife might be in a more favourable position than
slaves or servants, in that she had defenders in the male
relatives of her own family.[74]

Smith looked at the history of Europe from the classical
period onwards, to reconstruct the scale of the changes that had
taken place in marriage. In Greece and Rome, simple societies
based on a pastoral and agricultural life had given place to city
states whose inhabitants were increasingly involved in
manufacture and commerce, with correspondingly complex
governmental and legal arrangements. Changes in wealth
brought changes in the marriage pattern, settlements and
contracts. In the early stages of the Roman republic, for
example, a wife was entirely in her husband's power, and
subject to his right of divorce, for she brought with her so little
wealth that she had no bargaining power. Yet the poverty of the
Roman republic became the wealth of the Roman empire,
and:

the women, who are in all polite and wealthy countries more regarded than
they are by a poorer and more barbarous nation, came to have large fortunes
which they could confer on their husbands; they could not submit, nor would
the friends allow it, to the subjection that attended the old form of
marriage.[75]

In the new form of marriage devised for their needs, both
husband and wife had the right of divorce, and the wife's
property was protected by a trust. Smith suggested that the
consequence of this, and the great freedom enjoyed by such
women in the Roman empire, was their notorious lack of

chastity: 'it tended plainly to corrupt the morals of the woman'.[76]

That situation came to an end with the barbarian invasions, and reversions to the earlier, absolute form of marriage relationship. In the rural world of early medieval Europe, women could not inherit either allodial or feudal property, since they could not serve a monarch militarily or in the council, though at a lower level, since they could do 'the country work', they might hold land in socage tenure. Only as feudal tenure came to be seen as property, rather than as military service, could women again inherit land in their own right.[77] The introduction of Christianity equally transformed the pattern of marriage in medieval Europe, for the clergy, as 'impartial judges', put both partners on a much more equal footing, and introduced the indissolubility of marriage. It was this, according to Smith, which brought a new significance to the choice of a partner who would be lifelong, and a new attitude to the passion of love, once seen as trivial and ridiculous. Smith suggested that, both as a result of the introduction of Christianity, and as a product of the refinement of manners, the status of women within the family had steadily risen up until his own day.[78] Smith is always careful to relate the pattern of authority within the family both to its material context, and to those general moral sentiments about the nature of marriage which had come to be accepted in particular societies.

Where Pufendorf and Hutcheson had written of the four articles of the marriage contract, Smith's concern, in dealing with identical themes, is to describe the four family types which he has recognized as existing in different societies. One, not yet considered, was that of polygamy. Like Pufendorf Smith did not see polygamy as intrinsically unjust, since a woman entered into a voluntary contract in such a marriage. Nevertheless he did see it as contrary to 'a well regulated police', and as an inexpedient institition for a number of reasons. Such marriages were damaging to population growth, and adverse to the happiness and morality of men, women, and children within the family. Perhaps as important, he suggested that polygamy, found in the most 'despotic and arbitrary' governments of the world, was itself harmful to liberty, in eliminating the possibility of that small but powerful hereditary nobility, which had resisted absolute power and defended popular liberties in western Europe.[79]

Of monogamous marriages, Smith recognized three types: where the husband only had the power of divorce, as in early societies; where both husband and wife had that power, as in the Roman Empire; where divorce did not exist, or was determinable only by the civil magistrate. The two former, according to Smith, both had considerable disadvantages: the absolute power of the head of the household, the licentiousness of morals induced in the Roman Empire. His view was that, of these four types, the best was that prevailing in contemporary western Europe. His treatment of polygamy surely exemplified another facet of the European fascination with 'oriental despotism' which allowed eighteenth–century writers to define what was *not* European, but socially, culturally, and politically alien. The indissoluble, monogamous marriage saw the wife occupying a 'middle rank' between the independence of the Roman woman of the empire and the servitude of primitive societies.[80] Within this marriage, Smith did not necessarily rule out divorce altogether, for he thought that the infidelity of the wife, and other injuries exciting a similar degree of resentment, might justify divorce, though it was always better that 'the knot should be too straight than too loose'.[81]

A further theme is the way in which the property of the couple was affected by the different types of marriage. In a polygamous marriage, a wife, 'the slave of the husband', had no right of any kind to property. In a primitive marriage, equally, the whole estate of the wife became the husband's, and at his death she was treated similarly to a daughter. In a marriage in the Roman Empire, the husband had no right to a wife's property more than a power of administration, and property returned to the wife on the husband's death. The 'separate interests' of such a marriage made it, according to Smith, unstable and uncertain. In the contemporary monogamous marriage, on the other hand, husband and wife were said to have 'one common interest', and he detailed the vagaries of Scots and English property law on this subject.[82]

Smith concluded his discussion of the marriage relationship with a consideration of the degrees of consanguinity which barred marriage. As Knud Haakonssen has suggested, this discussion, though based on similar issues to those of Pufendorf and Hutcheson, did 'exemplify the full scale of Smithian principles of analysis in the law'.[83] The disapproval of the 'impartial spectator' was universal in the case of mother and son, for a son owed obedience to his mother and could not exercise authority as a husband. The marriage of a father and daughter was also shocking, though not to the same extent, since the principle of authority was not contravened. A few such marriages therefore were tolerated in primitive societies. The principle of utility, of the expediency of 'a well-regulated police', might however be invoked to cover a much wider degree of affinity, for instance that between a man and his sister-in-law.

Marriage, therefore, for Smith, as a formal legal institution, could not be described in terms of the rights and duties of the law of nature, or of the abstract end of marriage. Its obligations were rooted in that sense of injury felt by men at the infidelity of a wife. Sympathy with that sense of injury became the basis of social and legal rules: and acting impersonally, though in the masculine interest, it was to restrain and moderate individual practice. Custom and historical process were to shape the form of marriage, the pattern of legal codes, the prevalent moral sentiments. The direction of that change in Western Europe since the end of the classical period had been towards the moderation of the authority of the head of the household, partly because of the growing influence of Christianity, partly because of increasing material wealth. The family form of his own day seemed to represent to Smith the high point of social evolution in this respect, typical of contemporary commercial and civilized society, and parallel to the political improvements which also typified the states of Western Europe. In this prosperous society, as has already been seen, there was little scope for the older republican virtues. The qualities of humanity and prudence appeared more relevant, to private life and economic relationships respectively. In his historical account of marriage, Smith linked the material situation of a wife—in particular her material wealth—to her strength in the marital relationship. It remains relevant to consider how far propriety dictated, for women of different classes, a role as economic agents in the eighteenth century economy.

Poor women undoubtedly figure in the *Wealth of Nations* (1776) occasionally. Smith assumed that their paid labour was necessary to the bringing up of a family, though he does not discuss the relative contributions of husband and wife.[84] He refers elsewhere to coarse household manufactures, and to linen spinning, as the work of women and children all over Scotland.[85] As has been recently emphasized, he was, in the *Wealth of Nations,* concerned for the proper distribution of wealth, in a prospering economy.[86] This was put both in terms of justice and utility. It was mere equity that those who produced wealth should be 'tolerably well-fed, clothed and lodged', but it was also advantageous to society that a growing population be encouraged by these means. Poverty did in fact seem to encourage the birth of children, where luxury tended to produce barrenness, but the mortality of the children of the poor was high, significantly more so than among people of fashion. The poor 'cannot afford to tend them with the same care as those of better station', and such care was undoubtedly the responsibility of the mother, who carried the burden of 'necessary attendance on the children' as well as that of providing for herself.[87] Clearly Smith saw it as desirable that families should reap the 'liberal reward of labour', allowing them to bring up their children better. Women's participation in the economy was limited then, and, given a better distribution of wealth, would be limited even more, by the proper care of their families.

The best known reference to women in the *Wealth of Nations* is that contrasting the admirable education received by girls with that of boys:

There are no public institutions for the education of women, and there is accordingly nothing useless, absurd or fantastical in the common course of their education. They are taught what their parents or guardians judge it necessary or useful for them to learn; and they are taught nothing less. Every part of their education tends evidently to some useful purpose; either to improve the natural attractions of their person, or to form their mind to reserve, to modesty, to chastity and to economy; to render them both likely to become the mistress of a family, and to behave properly when they have become such. In every part of her life a woman feels some conveniency or advantage from every part of her education. It seldom happens that a man, in any part of his life, derives any conveniency or advantage from some of the most laborious and troublesome parts of his education.[88]

The classical education which so dominated the masculine curriculum in grammar schools and universities, offered a man of the middling classes no training for the public world. For Smith that public world was surely not the city-state or commonwealth, but commerce and the professions. But Smith did surely outline here what propriety dictated for the woman of the middling and perhaps the upper classes—the life of a mistress of a family.

Unlike some of his contemporaries, Smith did not write of the 'oeconomy' of the household, either in its own right, or as a model for the 'political oeconomy of the state'.[89] He did, however, recognize the importance of the household in creating a demand for commodities. This is one of the major factors in the shift from a demand for services to one for consumer goods, their character dictated by changing taste, and by fashion. This meant of course that the household was not exempt from the dilemma facing the male merchant or landlord: what constituted the proper pursuit of prudent self-interest? Smith argued that the demand for goods was favourable to public wealth, since it created, through emulation, a broader demand, it brought credit, for artistic merit, to the country, and it was indeed more favourable to the important virtue of frugality than riotous living. Such expenditure, as well, would employ more people. Yet at the same time, Smith noted that this expenditure might not spring from the same 'liberal or generous spirit' as that on good living. Was it more liberal to entertain one's friends in lavish hospitality, or to store up private goods, 'the little ornaments of dress and furniture, jewels, trinkets, gewgaws', the collecting of which might imply 'not only a trifling but a base and selfish disposition'?[90] Within the household, also, the commercial society had its moral pitfalls, from which, surely, the wives of aldermen mentioned in the *Theory of Moral Sentiments* were not immune. Yet these might be overcome by restraint, by frugality, by prudence, the key moral qualities of the market economy.

It is not perhaps surprising that there is so little discussion of the household and family in Smith's greatest work. The household did have an important consuming function, but, more important, it had a moral and social task. Through this survey of the development of natural jurisprudence, it should have been clear that the family, and the part of women in the family, had taken on a new significance. From that largely abstract network of obligations sketched out by Pufendorf, in which women's part of chastity, labour, and childbearing, went largely unquestioned, Francis Hutcheson created a far more optimistic view of the family, with women, as wives and mothers, playing a vital part in the schooling of republican virtue, a source of immense strength, yet in the last resort subordinated to the public good. But in Smith's civil and commercial society, firmly rooted in the present, the republican version of the civic and military virtues was becoming irrelevant. As J.G.A. Pocock has written, a citizen with such qualities was 'so much of a political, and so little of a social animal' as to be archaic.[91] He has suggested that a reluctance to abandon that model of behaviour altogether—a reluctance certainly present in Smith—brought a redefinition in terms of a concept of 'manners', which allowed the pursuit of virtue through a refined and polished sense of propriety. But this is to look only at one side of the question. The pursuit of virtue was first to be relocated in the conjugal family, as an instinctual haven of the natural affections and 'habitual sympathy', to be contrasted with the market economy, and the social world, inspired by emulation, expediency, and the restrained pursuit of self-interest. The emotional bonds of wider political units—tribes, clans, republics—had gone. The family was to be the source of emotional and moral strength, of the natural feelings. That early education was prior to the entry of the male citizen into the polite and refined culture of the cities of eighteenth-century Britain—the clubs, associations, and intellectual life of Edinburgh, for instance, which Smith knew so well, and which might exemplify the world of polite 'manners'. That early experience in the family was women's responsibility, as guardian, though by no means exclusively, of 'the soft, the gentle, the amiable virtues'. Smith portrayed a civilized society in which the influence of women, and those virtues, seen as primarily their own, was increasing, yet at the cost of an increasingly clearcut division of spheres between the economic world in which the male citizen acted, and the household, which, though consuming goods, might lie largely outside production and commerce. When Alasdair Macintyre, tracing the fate of the 'Enlightenment project' to relocate the pursuit of virtue in the modern secular world, wrote that: 'the restricted households of Highbury and Mansfield Park have to serve as surrogates for the Greek city-state and the medieval kingdom'[92] he might have written of more than Jane Austen.

Smith's work was not profoundly original, more a revealing and stimulating patchwork. It must be seen in the context of Glasgow in the 1750s and 60s, and his dual inheritance of natural jurisprudence and classical republicanism. Yet there were important elements in his treatment of the role of women, though largely unnoticed, which were fundamental themes in what has come to be thought of as the 'Victorian' concept of womanhood: his implication that women were the moral educators of the family; the limited social and economic role of women of the middling classes; his view of the monogamous European family as representing the highest form of family life. And the emergence of political economy as the most dynamic element of his all encompassing philosophical survey suggests that the changing boundaries of public and private life were in the future to be as dominated by the requirements of the market as those of the state.

NOTES

1.   Adam Smith, *An Inquiry into the Nature and Causes of the Wealth of Nations*, ed. R.H. Campbell, A.S. Skinner, and W.B. Todd, 2 vols., (Oxford, 1979), Vol. I, IV. Introduction; *The Theory of Moral Sentiments*, ed. D.D. Raphael, and A.L. Macfie, (Oxford, 1976), VII. iv. 37. References are to these editions throughout, and I have followed the editors of the Glasgow edition in giving references not to page numbers, but to paragraphs.

2.   Of many detailed studies of Smith's work, the most relevant here are: J. Cropsey, *Polity and Economy. An Interpretation of the principles of Adam Smith* (The Hague, 1957); A. Skinner, *A System of Social Science. Papers relating to Adam Smith* (Oxford, 1979); D.A. Reisman, *Adam Smith's Sociological Economics* (London, 1976); J. Ralph Lindgren, *The Social Philosophy of Adam Smith* (The Hague, 1973); K. Haakonssen, *The Science of a Legislator. The Natural Jurisprudence of David Hume and Adam Smith* (Cambridge, 1981); Donald Winch, *Adam Smith's Politics.*

An essay in historiographic revison (Cambridge, 1978). The most valuable recent work, essential to any discussion, is the collection of essays edited by I. Hont and M. Ignatieff (eds.) *Wealth and Virtue. The Shaping of Political Economy in the Scottish Enlightenment* (Cambridge, 1983).

However, very few writers have touched upon the role of women, or the family, in Smith's ideas. E. Fox-Genovese, 'Property and Patriarchy in Classical Bourgeois Political Economy', *Radical History Review,* 4, 1977, pp. 36–59, is a most stimulating article. For other discussions of the 'liberal' tradition, see Mary Lyndon Shanley, 'Marriage Contract and Social Contract in seventeenth-century English political thought', *Western Political Quarterly,* 32, 1979, pp. 79–91; M. Butler, 'Early Liberal Roots of Feminism: John Locke and the Attack on Patriarchy', *American Political Science Review,* 72, 1978, pp. 135–50; Jean Bethke Elshtain, *Public Man and Private Woman. Women in Social and Political Thought* (Princeton, N.J., 1981), Ch. 3; Z. Eisenstein, *The Radical Future of Liberal Feminism* (New York, 1981); S.M. Okin, *Women in Western Political Thought* (Princeton, 1979).

3.   This theme is most fully explored in J.G.A. Pocock's great volume, *The Machiavellian Moment. Florentine Political Thought and the Atlantic Republican Tradition* (Princeton, N.J., 1975), and in his 'Machiavelli, Harrington, and English political ideologies in the eighteenth century', in *Politics, Language, and Time* (London, 1972). For his most recent review of the issue, and Smith's relationship to that tradition, see his 'Cambridge paradigms and Scotch philosophers: a study of the relations between the civic humanist and the civil jurisprudential interpretations of eighteenth century social thought', in Hont and Ignatieff (eds.) *Wealth and Virtue.* Also useful is Caroline Robbins, *The Eighteenth Century Commonwealthsman* (Cambridge, Mass., 1959). For Smith and the republican tradition, see esp. the work of Donald Winch, *Adam Smith's Politics,* Ch. 2, and his 'Adam Smith's 'enduring particular result': a political and cosmopolitan perspective', in Hont and Ignatieff (eds.) *Wealth and Virtue.*

4.   Samuel Pufendorf, *De Officio Hominis et Civis juxta Legem Naturalem.* . . . 2 vols., (New York, 1927), translated by F.G. Moore, vol. II, 'Greeting to the Reader', p. x. References are to this edition, by section and paragraph, throughout.

5.   There are very few studies in English of natural jurisprudence. See R. Tuck *Natural Rights Theories. Their Origins and Development* (Cambridge, 1981), esp. pp. 156–62, 174–7; L. Krieger, *The Politics of Discretion* (Chicago, 1965): D. Forbes, *Hume's Philosophical Politics* (Cambridge, 1975), Chs. 1–2; P. Stein, *Legal Evolution* (Cambridge, 1980) Ch. 1.

6.   Pufendorf, *De Officio Hominis et Civis,* II.ii.i. There was of course a long previous tradition of writing about marriage in terms of natural law, going back to the late thirteenth century, when Western thinkers began to discuss the subject on the basis of the works of, or attributed to, Aristotle (the *Ethics, Politics,* and *Economics*). Aristotle's vocabulary, combined with that of contemporary legal and theological discussion, was to form a reservoir of concepts and terms, on which later writers continued to draw in a variety of

ways. I am here, however, not concerned with the nature of the debt to this earlier tradition, but with the direct transmission of the particular framework established by Pufendorf. I am greatly indebted to my colleague Dr P.P.A. Biller for discussion on this point, and for assistance with Latin translation.

7.   *Ibid.,* II. ii. 4.

8.   Pufendorf, *De Jure Naturae et Gentium . . .* 2 vols., (Oxford, 1934), translated by C.H. and W.A. Oldfather, vol. II, VI. i. 9. All references are to the translated text.

9.   *Ibid.,* VI. i. 9–13.

10.   *Ibid.,* VI. ii. 3.

11.   *Ibid.,* VI. i. 18.

12.   *Ibid.,* VI. i. 24.

13.   *Ibid.,* I. i. 29–35.

14.   *Ibid.,* IV. iv *passim;* VII. i. 5–7; and see Hont and Ignatieff, 'Needs and justice in the *Wealth of Nations',* in Hont and Ignatieff (eds.) *Wealth and Virtue,* pp. 32–5.

15.   On Gersholm Carmichael, see: Robert Wodrow, *Analecta: or materials for a history of remarkable providences; mostly relating to Scotch ministers and Christians,* 4 vols., (Glasgow, 1843), vol. I, pp. 95–6; James Moore and Michael Silverthorne, 'Gershom Carmichael and the natural jurisprudence tradition in eighteenth-century Scotland', in Hont and Ignatieff (eds.) *Wealth and Virtue:* W.L. Taylor, 'Gershom Carmichael: a neglected figure in British poltical economy', *South African Journal of Economics,* 13, 1955, pp. 252–5.

16.   S. Pufendorf, *De Officio hominis et civis juxta legem naturalem,* libri duo. Supplementis & observationibus in Academiciae juventutis usum auxit & illustravit Gerschomus Carmichael. Editio secunda priore auctior & emendatior, Edinburgh, 1724, II. ii. 2. note 1. All references to Carmichael's work are to this edition.

17.   *Ibid.,* II. ii. 4. notes 2 and 3.

18.   *Ibid.,* II. ii. 4. note 4.

19.   *Ibid.,* II. ii. 5. note 1.

20.   *Ibid.,* II. ii. 6. note 1.

21.   *Ibid.,* II. iii. 2. note 1.

22.   *Ibid.,* Preface, xvii–xviii.

23.   For Hutcheson's comments on Carmichael's work, see Francis Hutcheson *Short Introduction to Moral Philosophy . . . containing the elements of ethics and the law of nature . . .* translated from the Latin (Glasgow, 1747), p.i; Wodrow, *Analecta,* vol. IV, p. 185. For his comments on Pufendorf, see his *Reflections upon Laughter, and the Fable of the Bees* (Glasgow, 1750), pp. 6–7. The *Reflections upon Laughter* first appeared in the form of articles for the *Dublin Journal* in 1725.

On Hutcheson's career, see W.R. Scott, *Francis Hutcheson. His life, teaching, and position in the history of philosophy* (1900, reprinted New York, 1966).

24.   Francis Hutcheson, *De Naturali Hominum Socialitate* (Glasgow, 1756), pp. 17–18, 23.

25. Hutcheson, *A System of Moral Philosophy*... 2 vols., (London, 1755), vol. II, p. 152.

26. *Ibid.*, vol. II, pp. 153–5.

27. *Ibid.*, vol. I, p. 69.

28. *Ibid.*, vol. II, p. 159.

29. *Ibid.*, vol. II, pp. 159, 161–3. The *Short Introduction to Moral Philosophy*, pp. 260–1, gives articles three and four of the marriage contract as 'a perpetual union of interests and pursuits' for the prosperity and education of the family, and the perpetuity of the marriage bond. The *System of Moral Philosophy* suggests no fourth article to replace Pufendorf's.

30. *System of Moral Philosophy*, vol. II, pp. 164–5.

31. *Ibid.*, vol. II, p. 190.

32. *Ibid.*, vol. II, pp. 180–3.

33. *Ibid.*, vol. I, p. 69.

34. *Ibid.*, vol. II, p. 186.

35. *Ibid.*, vol. I, p. 321.

36. *Ibid.*, vol. II, p. 186.

37. *Ibid.*, vol. II, pp. 187, 248–9. Hutcheson acknowledged the influence of James Harrington's *Oceana* (1656) here.

38. *Ibid.*, vol. II, p. 319.

39. Compare Pufendorf's comment, 'nor is it altogether safe, in eliciting the law of nature, to consult the mere judgement of the senses and passions, since the opposite conclusion can be reached, that things to which the senses and passions are strongly attracted are enjoined by the law of nature, while most of them are in fact clearly opposed to that law', *De Jure Naturae et Gentium* VI. i. 28.

40. Dugald Stewart, 'Account of the Life and Writings of Adam Smith LL.D. from the Transactions of the Royal Society of Edinburgh...' reprinted in Adam Smith *Essays on Philosophical Subjects*, ed. W.P.D. Wightman (Oxford, 1980) pp. 274–5. The account, by John Millar, is quoted and discussed by the editors in, Smith, *Lectures on Jurisprudence*, Introduction, pp. 3–4.

41. Smith, *Theory of Moral Sentiments*, Introduction, pp. 46–52. References which are to material added in 1790 have been indicated. On Smith's moral philosophy generally, see T.D. Campbell, *Adam Smith's Science of Morals* (London, 1971).

42. Smith, *Theory of Moral Sentiments*, Introduction, p. 4.

43. *Ibid.*, VII.ii.3.16.

44. N. Phillipson, 'Adam Smith as civic moralist', in Hont and Ignatieff (eds.) *Wealth and Virtue.*

45. Smith, *Theory of Moral Sentiments*, III.iii.35 (1790).

46. *Ibid.*, III.iii.37 (1790).

47. *Ibid.*, IV.ii.10. Compare David Hume, on the sense of compassion: 'Add to this, that pity depends, in a great measure on the continuity and even sight of the object; which is a proof, that 'tis derived from the imagination. Not to mention that women and children are most subject to pity, as being most guided by that faculty, *Treatise on Human Nature*, ed. E.C. Mossner

(Harmondsworth, 1969), p. 418. Clearly Hume's influence upon Smith, especially with respect to the distinction between the natural and the artificial virtues, is a most important one here.

48.   Smith, *Theory of Moral Sentiments,* I.i.5.1.
49.   *Ibid.,* V.ii.12.
50.   *Ibid.,* VI.iii.16 (1790).
51.   *Ibid.,* VI.iii.19 (1790).
52.   *Ibid.,* I.i.1.12.
53.   *Ibid.,* I.ii.3.5.
54.   *Ibid.,* III.iii.32 (1790).
55.   *Ibid.,* VI.iii.13 (1790).
56.   *Ibid.,* II.iv.13. Hume treats chastity as an artificial virtue, justified on utilitarian grounds by the need to secure legitimacy of offspring. The restraints imposed upon women to secure this had become internalized into a sense of reputation, and shame at its loss. *Treatise of Human Nature,* p. 621.
57.   Smith, *Theory of Moral Sentiments,* I.ii.1–5.
58.   *Ibid.,* I.ii.4.2.
59.   *Ibid.,* VI.ii.1.7.
60.   *Ibid.,* III.iii.12–13 (1790); VI.ii.1.10 (1790).
61.   *Ibid.,* VI.ii.1.14 (1790).
62.   *Ibid.,* V.ii.8.
63.   *Ibid.,* I.iii.2.8.
64.   See, for example: *Ibid.,* I.iii.2.1–9; I.iii.3.7; VII.ii.4.12
65.   *Ibid.,* I.iii.2.5; I.iii.3.5 for two paragraphs which clearly describe 'the chief characteristics of the behaviour of a private man', and V.ii *passim.*
66.   Smith, *Lectures on Jurisprudence,* LJ(A) i.12–16.
67.   The most useful general study of Smith's jurisprudence is Haakonssen, *Science of a Legislator,* esp. Chs. 4–5; see also R. Meek, *Social Science and the Ignoble Savage* (Cambridge, 1976), Ch. 4.
68.   Smith, *Lectures on Jurisprudence,* LJ(B), 102–3 (pp. 438–9). It is unfortunate that the relevant section of LJ(A) is missing here.
69.   *Ibid.,* LJ(A) iii.13.
70.   *Ibid.,* LJ(A) iii.16.
71.   *Ibid.,* LJ(B) 104 (p. 439).
72.   *Ibid.,* LJ(A) i.27; iv.10; LJ(B) 105 (p. 439).
73.   *Ibid.,* LJ(A) iv.121; LJ(B) 105 (p. 439).
74.   *Ibid.,* LJ(A) i.94; iii.7; iii.89.
75.   *Ibid.,* LJ(A) i.156; iii.54.
76.   *Ibid.,* LJ(A) iii.10.
77.   *Ibid.,* i.141-5. Allodial land is land held on absolute ownership, whereas feudal land is held of a superior. Socage tenure was land held on condition of labour service not military service.
78.   *Ibid.,* LJ(A) i.111; iii.13–22.
79.   *Ibid.,* LJ(A) iii.23–49.
80.   *Ibid.,* LJ(A) iii.54.
81.   *Ibid.,* LJ(A) iii.51.
82.   *Ibid.,* LJ(A) iii.52–8.

83.   *Ibid.,* LJ(A) iii.59–75; Haakonssen, *Science of a Legislator,* p. 125.

84.   Smith, *Wealth of Nations,* vol. I, I.viii.15.

85.   *Ibid.,* vol. I, I.viii.51; I.x.b.50–1; vol. II, IV.viii.4.

86.   Hont and Ignatieff, 'Needs and justice in the *Wealth of Nations,* in Hont and Ignatieff (eds.) *Wealth and Virtue.*

87.   Smith, *Wealth of Nations,* vol. I, I.viii.36–40, 42.

88.   *Ibid.,* vol. II, V.i.f.47.

89.   See, for example, the views of Sir James Steuart's *Inquiry into the Principles of Political Oeconomy* (1767): 'Oeconomy, in general, is the art of providing for all the wants of a family, with prudence and frugality . . . What oeconomy is in a family, political oeconomy is in a state . . .', quoted in Keith Tribe, *Land, Labour and Economic Discourse* (London, 1978), pp. 83–4. In Chs 4–5 Tribe explores the shift from that definition of 'oeconomy' which was dependent on the household as a productive unit. He sees Smith's work as transitional, with an important emphasis on the concept of productive labour, but an older view still of 'political oeconomy' as a branch of a legislator's science.

90.   Smith, *Wealth of Nations,* vol. I, II.iii.38–42; on this theme see N. Rosenberg, 'Adam Smith's Consumer Tastes, and Economic Growth', *Journal of Political Economy,* 76, 1968, pp. 361–74.

91.   J.G.A. Pocock, 'Virtue, Rights, and Manners. A Model for Historians of Political Thought', *Political Theory,* 9, 1981, p. 365.

92.   Alasdair Macintyre, *After Virtue. A study in moral theory* (London, 1981), p. 224.

3 Rousseau's Two Concepts of Citizenship

Margaret Canovan

In any feminist Chamber of Horrors Jean-Jacques Rousseau would occupy a prominent place. While most great political thinkers have taken for granted the subjection of women, Rousseau's patriarchalism is particularly blatant because it contrasts so violently with his views on the proper condition of men. His denunciation of personal dependence and demand for moral and political autonomy for men throw into stark relief his recommendations for women, while his glorification of the public sphere of citizenship makes still harsher woman's exclusion from it. Rousseau's writings might, therefore, seem an unpromising place to search for inspiration on the subject of women as citizens. This is one of the many areas, however, in which his ideas have implications extending far beyond his own intentions.

The range of Rousseau's influence is not the least paradoxical thing about this most paradoxical of political thinkers. When we consider that he explicitly limited the scope of his political ideas not only to men but to small communities of simple, pre-industrial peasants, we must wonder at the ease with which his backward-looking rural utopia has turned into an inspiration for modern industrial societies. Clearly, Rousseau holds the place he does within the canon of political thought because he is read selectively. His stipulations about small size and rural simplicity are tacitly set aside, and in the same way comment-ators often ignore his restriction of citizenship to males, assuming without further argument that it is permissible to read 'men' as 'persons'. To do this, however, is to make much more than a marginal adjustment to his theory. Rousseau did not simply ignore women: he deliberately excluded them from his vision of public life, and we cannot take for granted that the latter can be extended to women while remaining otherwise intact. Can his conception of citizenship in fact be given a feminist form? That is the question I shall attempt to answer in this essay.

TWO CONCEPTS OF CITIZENSHIP

Interpreting Rousseau is a hazardous undertaking, and those who embark upon it do well to bear in mind that, in the words of one of their number, 'more nonsense has been written about Rousseau than about any other major political theorist'.[2] The variety of interpretations that have been plausibly offered suggests in itself that his theory cannot be quite as clear and consistent as some of his interpreters maintain.[3] One of the reasons for his enormous influence is, in fact, the multiplicity of different strands to be found within his writings, providing disciples and commentators with seemingly endless opportunities to choose different leading ideas and to argue about the relations amongst them. This is not the place to enter into the continuing debate whether or not his apparently contradictory ideas can be reconciled,[4] and I shall take it as given that there are at the very least tensions within his work. Perhaps the most politically relevant is that between his longing for autonomy (to the point of solitude), on the one hand, and for integration (to the point of self-annihilation), on the other[5]—between, as he put it, the life of the 'man' and of the 'citizen'.[6] Judith Shklar has argued that he expressed his overriding impulse to judge and reject contemporary society in terms of two different utopias which were consciously offered as alternatives: on the one hand, citizenship in a Spartan republic; on the other, domesticity in an idyllic household as described in the latter part of *La Nouvelle Hélöise*.[7] While taking Shklar's point, one can, I think, go beyond it to recognize a further refinement of complexity that bears directly on the question of whether or not Rousseau's conception of citizenship could be extended to women. I shall suggest that Rousseau offers not *one* concept of citizenship but two different ones, which I propose to label *juristic* and *Spartan*, respectively.[8]

Juristic Citizenship

The 'juristic' side of Rousseau's ideas on citizenship is the better known of the two. It is this side of his thought that has influenced political philosophers from Kant down to our own time and that dominates the most frequently read parts of *The Social Contract*, namely Books I and II. A brief description will, therefore, suffice. This line of thought, which is deeply indebted to the juristic tradition of seventeenth- and eighteenth-century political thought,[9] is based on the familiar model of a social contract among individuals in a hypothetical state of nature. The individuals concerned are abstract specimens of humanity, free and equal and (Rousseau argues) under no obligation to render obedience without consent. They are morally autonomous: as Rousseau says, their freedom consists in obeying laws which each lays down for himself. Incorporating them into a legitimate republic therefore involves a problem which Rousseau states with great precision: 'How to find a form of association which will defend the person and goods of each member with the collective force of all, and under which each individual, while uniting himself with the others, obeys no one but himself, and remains as free as before'.[10]

As every schoolgirl knows, Rousseau solves the problem in a brilliantly original way, arguing that these free individuals can join together in a social contract to form a sovereign body that will rule itself by its own general will. The climax of his juristic theory is the noble vision of autonomous, responsible citizens discovering the general will in themselves and setting it above their own private wills to achieve public harmony and justice.

This conception of citizenship, like those of the jurists before Rousseau and Kant after him, is rational, general and abstract. In particular, Rousseau's conception of freedom through self-government is premised upon an abstract legalistic distinction between the roles of sovereign and subject. He distinguishes between the individual *qua* citizen, bearing a public personality, and the same individual as a private person. When the citizen attends the public assembly, he leaves his private life behind him, and moves into a public realm concerned only with general issues; similarly, the citizen's general will is distinct from his private will, and is not concerned with his particular interests; it can express itself only in laws framed in general terms and applicable to citizens as such. A further refinement of abstraction is that although the citizens are different and unequal as private persons, the public realm confers upon them an artificial equality as citizens which supersedes their private characteristics.[11]

Although Rousseau wrote explicitly with small city-state republics in mind, this abstract, juristic side of his views on citizenship is framed in legalistic terms that are readily universalizable, and it has of course been interpreted more and more widely by subsequent political thinkers. However, while it is an authentically Rousseauian conception,[12] it stands in an uneasy relation to another very different vision of citizenship.

Spartan Citizenship

As Rousseau's early draft of *The Social Contract* makes plain, the abstract, universalistic way of thinking about politics that he inherited from the jurists was severely qualified by his own sense that citizenship is in fact possible only in special circumstances and within limited areas. In sharp contrast to the traditional picture of natural man hearkening to the universal dictates of natural law, he argued that only the intense loyalties of small communities originally made possible a sense of justice, and that universal conceptions were generalizations and dilutions of the moral and political principles developed by this small-scale socialization: 'We conceive of universal society only as a result of our particular societies, the establishment of little republics makes us dream of a great one, and we only start to become men, properly speaking, after having been citizens'.[13]

The problem of establishing political justice, therefore, is not simply an intellectual problem of showing that autonomous individuals can concur in a rational general will. It has another, more demanding side to it: that of creating the kind of community within which citizens would in fact be capable of willing such a general will in preference to their own private interests. As a result, as soon as Rousseau moves on in *The Social Contract* from defining the general will to spelling out the circumstances in which it might exist, his picture of citizenship changes. The abstract, rational, juristic image fades into the background, and the stern model of Sparta takes it place.

The first casualty of this change is the juristic citizen's rational autonomy. The free individual laying down his own laws for himself is replaced by a mass-produced product of intensive socialization. The prerequisite for a good state is a good people, and to form such a people, a law-giver is necessary, modelled on Lycurgus, who made the Spartans what they were. Rousseau is quite explicit about the assault on individual autonomy involved in this exercise.

> Whoever ventures on the enterprise of setting up a people must be ready, shall we say, to change human nature, to transform each individual, who by himself is entirely complete and solitary, into a part of a much greater whole, from which that same individual will then receive, in a sense, his life and his being. The founder of nations must weaken the structure of man in order to fortify it, to replace the physical and independent existence we have all received from nature with a moral and communal existence.[14]

Since the people will not be able to appreciate the wisdom of the laws until they have been moulded by them, the law-giver must be a charismatic figure, pretending supernatural powers and hoodwinking the people for their own good.[15] Using the authority he has gained by these dubious means, he must tell them what their general will really is, and embody it in sacred laws. Thereafter, the virtue of the citizen will consist rather in remaining true to this foundation than in thinking for himself. As long as the citizens remain virtuous they will be at one, and their solemn assemblies will be reaffirmations of their ancient customs and rededications to patriotism rather than occasions for rational debates.[16]

In the more 'Spartan' sections of Rousseau's political writings, the role of citizen ceases to be a juristic abstraction and becomes an all-absorbing way of life. Within *The Social Contract* itself, Rousseau proposed a 'civil religion' to foster patriotism and to counter the privatism and factionalism encouraged by Christianity in its various forms.[17] Elsewhere in his writings he gave more detailed and vivid accounts of the formation and duties of the 'Spartan' citizen. He maintained in the essay on 'Political Economy', for example, that 'to form citizens is not the work of a day; and in order to have men, it is necessary to educate them when they are children'. Such patriotic education ought to ensure that its products are totally absorbed in their role as citizens: 'If, for example, they were early accustomed to regard their individuality only in its relation to the body of the state, and to be aware, so to speak, of their own existence merely as a part of the state',[18] then they would achieve the public spirit appropriate to citizens.

Rousseau's clearest picture of this kind of intensive citizenship occurs in his 'Considerations on the government of Poland', in which he stresses over and over again that a citizen should be obsessed by his country:

When first he opens his eyes, an infant ought to see the fatherland, and up to the day of his death he ought never to see anything else. Every true republican has drunk in love of country, that is to say love of law and liberty, along with his mother's milk. This love is his whole existence; he sees nothing but the fatherland, he lives for it alone.[19]

These prescriptions add up to a vision that has been described as 'totalitarian'[20]: a closed, militaristic, unanimous society in which the (male) citizens are totally absorbed in their public life. In the present context, there are two particularly notable features of Rousseau's 'Spartan' citizenship. The first is its total, unmediated quality. As Rousseau says explicitly at the beginning of *Emile*, one can be either a citizen or a 'natural man' but not both, and the virtue of losing one's individuality to be a citizen in this unmediated way is that it makes for wholeness, and does not divide a man against himself.[21] The Spartan citizen loses his own identity so completely in the republic that he is not torn by inner conflict, for patriotic virtue comes naturally to him. This is an important point, to which we shall return later. Let us note for the moment, however, that the integrated Spartan citizen forms a sharp contrast to the 'juristic' citizen, who is aware of both his general will and his private will, and has to use his reason and self-control to keep the two in their appropriate places.

The other feature we need to note about Rousseau's 'Spartan' citizenship is that although all-embracing in its intensity, it is severely limited in its scope. Rousseau never supposed that it could apply to men as such (and still less to women), but only to a small select group of men holding the privileged status of citizens within a few tiny city-states. He makes it clear that exclusiveness and intensity are directly related: 'it is necessary in some degree to confine and limit our interest and compassion in order to make it active';[22] 'every patriot is harsh towards foreigners: they are only men, they are nothing to him'.[23] He was even willing to acknowledge that, in Sparta itself and in the other ancient city-states that he admired, freedom for the citizens had been made possible only by slavery. He commented defiantly, 'What? Is freedom to be maintained only with the support of slavery? Perhaps. The two extremes met. Everything outside nature has its disadvantages, civil society more than all the rest'.[24]

The modern reader who is attracted by the early 'juristic' sections of *The Social Contract* is likely to be puzzled and repelled by the later parts of the book and by the even more 'Spartan' tone of Rousseau's other political writings. What, she may wonder, has happened to those autonomous, rational individuals who made the original social contract? Surely they are no longer recognizable in the socialized automatons of Rousseau's 'Spartan' vision? There may be an inconsistency here,[25] but it is important to realize that Rousseau did have a good reason for moving on from the 'juristic' general will to the quasi-totalitarianism of Sparta. In effect, his reason is that men will not behave like rational, juristic citizens and find their freedom in willing the general will unless they have first been subjected to patriotic socialization. The intensity of Sparta is a necessary though apparently unlikely precondition of juristic citizenship (in much the same way that, according to Max Weber, an obsessional Protestant ethic was a necessary precondition for the rational, calculating behaviour of the early capitalist).

This is a point to which we shall have to return when we come to consider whether Rousseau's conception of citizenship can be extended to include women. We shall have to ask whether either version, 'juristic' or 'Spartan', can take a feminist gloss and, if only one of them can, whether it is detachable from the other. First, however, since Rousseau himself excluded women from citizenship and consigned them emphatically to private life, we must consider why he did so.

WOMEN SHOULD BE NEITHER SEEN NOR HEARD

In *The Social Contract* Rousseau did not mention female citizenship even to refute it. Elsewhere, however, he made it quite clear that woman's place was in the home, not in the public sphere. Why did he take this view? No doubt part of the explanation is to be found simply in convention: up to a point he may have resembled other men of his own and previous times in simply overlooking women's claims to participate in politics. It was hard for any eighteenth-century man to take seriously the idea that men and women might be political equals, just as it was hard for the American revolutionaries to take seriously the idea that the human rights they claimed might also belong to their black slaves.[26]

This explanation will not take us very far, however, for Rousseau was not a conventional writer. If he reaffirmed a strongly traditionalist view of women's role, it was certainly not for lack of the imagination and mental energy to consider alternatives. He could be startlingly radical about other well-established customs: why not about this? Furthermore, he did not lack examples of emancipated women. Apart from the dutiful Thérèse, most of the women in his life were active, energetic, dominant personalities who were perfectly capable of taking any opportunities to participate in public life—one thinks of Mme de Warens, Mme Dupin, Mme d'Houdetot. During the period when he worked for the Dupin family, he even collaborated with Mme Dupin in the writing of feminist essays, though whether she ever agreed with what he wrote may be doubted.[27]

Add to these experiences his admiration for Plato, who had proposed to include women among his philosopher-kings, and it is clear that he must have had stronger reasons than mere convention for his determination to keep women strictly out of public life. Some of these reasons were no doubt disreputable biographical ones. It seems likely that Rousseau was profoundly afraid of women, partly because he was ashamed of his own submissive impulses toward them, and that he saw unmitigated domesticity not just as the proper role for their weakness but also as an appropriate remedy for their strength.[28] To be fair, his desire to keep women in the home was also a reaction against the kind of public life that actually existed in France rather than against female *citizenship*. The emancipated women he encountered were not moving in a public world of free politics, since no such world existed. Instead, when they left their homes to appear in public, their stage was high society, the society of the salons.[29] It is entirely comprehensible that Rousseau should have reacted against a public life so riddled with hypocrisy and intrigue, so obsessed with fashion, personal display and love affairs, and have exalted domesticity by comparison. Similarly, when he saw d'Alembert's proposal for a theatre at Geneva as a threat to the city's republican virtue, his fear was partly that if the theatre drew women out of their homes into a society on the Parisian model, this public world of society would absorb and eclipse the authentically political (and exclusively male) life of the city.[30]

Be that as it may, Rousseau held steadfastly to beliefs about women that put female citizenship out of the question. They were, he believed, fitted by nature 'to please and to be subjected' to man:[31] to take the subordinate role within a patriarchal family. It was in *Émile* that he made his views most explicit, when, having described the education of the truly natural man, he went on to consider that appropriate for the truly natural woman, Émile's predestined bride, Sophie.

His first assumption was that men and women are naturally different and complementary to one another in mind and character as well as in body. Each sex has, he maintained, a separate path marked out for it by nature so that 'a perfect man and a perfect woman should no more be alike in mind than in face'.[32] Woman's sexual role is to be 'weak and passive' in face of the man's strength, and this basic sexual difference corresponds to a subordinate role in life, together with abilities and attitudes appropriate to it. Women are naturally modest, for example, because it is their job to guard their virginity and their husband's honour; they are naturally interested in dress and self-adornment because it is their role to please men; naturally cunning because they must rely on wiles rather than strength to get their own way; naturally docile to fit them to obey their husbands: 'Woman is made to give way to man and to put up even with injustice from him. You will never reduce young boys to the same condition, their inner feelings rise in revolt against injustice; nature has not fitted them to put up with it'.[33] As for their mental powers, women, according to *Émile*, are less intellectual than men, and their reason is not strong. They have ready tongues and good heads for practical detail, but are less capable of grasping general principles: 'Woman has more wit, and man more genius; woman observes and man reasons'.[34]

In short, women are conveniently fitted by nature to be wives and mothers. Rousseau argued elsewhere[35] that the family should be patriarchal, partly because it needs a single authority, which could not be the wife because of her reproductive activities, but also because a man must control his wife to make sure that her children are really his. He repeatedly argued that a good woman should stay within the family circle, avoiding social distractions, let alone political ones. When Ancient Greek women married, they disappeared from public life; within the four walls of their home they devoted themselves to the care of their household and family, and, said Rousseau, 'This is the mode of life that nature and reason prescribe for the sex'.[36] Unlike the Greeks, however, Rousseau did place a high value on the domestic life to which he wanted to relegate women. Among his other claims on the attention of posterity, it was he more than anyone else who generated the modern ideal of the family, based on relations of intense intimacy between the adults plus a sustained attention to the development of the children. The domestic idyll which he described in the latter part of *Julie* and of which his heroine is the patron saint[37] forms an alternative utopia to his ideal city, a world in which, in a sense, women come into their own.[38]

Unappealing as Rousseau's views on women may be now, they do at first sight seem clear and consistent. As Susan Okin has pointed out, however, they contain some odd contradictions.[39] What connection can there be, for example, between Rousseau's repeated references to the 'naturalness' of the patriarchal family and his account of the natural state of human beings in the *Discourse on the Origin of Inequality?* In that *Discourse* he described the original condition of mankind as a non-domestic and non-patriarchal one in which individuals of both sexes wandered by themselves in the forests, meeting only occasionally and accidentally. Children conceived in their casual encounters were tended by the mother until they could fend for themselves: their fathers did not even know they existed, still less have authority over them or their mother.[40] The family, with its accompanying inequality between the sexes, arose during the second stage of human evolution, as part of the development of the first rude societies; but although Rousseau's essay is purportedly concerned with the origins of inequality, he does not provide any explanation at all of the transformation of independent women into domestic inferiors.

Apart from the blatant contradiction entailed by saying in one place that the family is not natural, and in another place that it is, Rousseau's account of the nature of women also involves an inconsistency of a more fundamental kind. Where the nature of man was concerned, he emphasized the difficulty of distinguishing between 'what is original and what is artificial',[41] and castigated those who merely looked at men as they appeared in contemporary society. To identify genuine human nature, he said, we need to lay aside all the accretions and corruptions of centuries of social life.[42] But when he wrote about women he continually committed the very error that he had himself identified, pointing to the characteristics of women as he knew them, such as their trivial chatter or their fondness for finery, and using these as evidence of their fundamental nature.[43] Clearly, he had made up his mind what women ought to be like, and was much more interested in that than in discovering what they actually were.

In any case, even if his account of woman's nature had been more plausible, it could not by his own criteria have provided a conclusive argument against admitting women to citizenship. For one of his most reiterated claims was that citizenship was unnatural to *men*, too—it was a thoroughly artificial condition, superimposed upon nature and in tension with it.[44] If it is necessary to 'change human nature'[45] in order to create citizens, why should female nature pose any more of an obstacle? After all, Rousseau's revered Plato had not let women's biological limitations stand in the way of his scheme for an ideal republic.

If Rousseau's observations about nature and man undermine his view of the position of women, so does his discussion of power and legitimacy. His most fundamental argument for the subordination of women is that men are naturally the stronger sex, particularly during the sexual act itself. As he himself argued in *The Social Contract*, however, strength does not in itself establish a right to power; legitimate authority comes only from the consent of those commanded.[46] More pragmatically, he also argued that power tends to corrupt—a view which has an obvious application to the patriarchal family, however optimistically he may have relied on the 'natural inclinations' of fathers to ensure their benevolence.[47] There is, besides, a profound dissonance between the ideal of individual autonomy that (in his less Spartan moments) he recommended for men,[48] and the dependence on father, husband and public opinion that he preached for women. The contrast is made all the more dramatic by his portrayal in *La Nouvelle Hélöise* of a heroine who is not trivial and mindless, but whose intelligence and capacity for moral autonomy far surpass those of her lover.

If the 'juristic' side of Rousseau's concept of citizenship is at odds with his view of women because of its stress on autonomy, the 'Spartan' side is no easier to reconcile with his account of the feminine role. The heroic examples of ancient citizenship that he was so fond of quoting depended on the sacrifice of 'natural' domestic affections to public virtue. Brutus ordered the execution of his own sons so that impartial public justice might be done, and he is nothing to Rousseau's prize exhibit, the Spartan mother: 'A Spartan mother had five sons in the army, and awaited news of the battle. A Helot arrives; trembling, she questions him. "Your five sons have been killed." "Vile slave is that what I asked you about?" "We have gained the victory." The mother runs to the temple and gives thanks to the gods. That is a citizen'.[49]

This story graphically makes the point that citizenship is artificial and at war with natural feelings. In conjunction with Rousseau's view of women, however, it raises difficulties more intractable than the obvious point that Spartan women at any rate were evidently as capable of citizenship as men. For if women were to be kept rigidly out of public life and all their energies directed to their families, then every wife and mother must represent a subversive influence, drawing the male citizen's will away from the general will and his heart away from the republic.[50] This is a problem that we shall return to later.

CAN ROUSSEAU BE GIVEN A FEMINIST GLOSS?

Rousseau's arguments for confining women to private life are a farrago of contradictions, rendering this aspect of his theory far from impressive. But what follows from this? Can we consign his patriarchalism to the dustbin of history and proceed to read 'persons' wherever he writes 'men'? Could women be Rousseauian citizens? Let us consider this question in relation to each of his two models of citizenship, taking the Spartan version first.

As Jean Bethke Elshtain remarks, 'Rousseau's public world takes up a great deal of space'.[51] This is certainly true of his 'Spartan' citizenship, the essential feature of which is its total, unmediated quality. Public life is all-embracing; private life is virtually non-existent. One must choose between being a citizen *or* a man [52] (or person), and if one is a citizen, one is so every minute of the day, perpetually mobilized for political and military duties. For a woman to be a citizen in this sense poses physical difficulties analogous to those faced by women trying to combine motherhood with a career as an athlete or ballet dancer—female biology really does get in the way. Even Rousseau's Spartan mother had to take time off to bear and nurse the infants she then so willingly relinquished, so that in spite of her patriotic attitude of mind, she could not have exercised equal citizenship with men.

If citizenship is conceived as such a full-time job, and if the bearing and probably most of the rearing of children is to continue to be done by women, then it is not unreasonable to argue that women cannot be full citizens, and that if they cannot be more than second-class citizens, they would be better out of the public arena altogether, lest they dilute public values. On the other hand, the advent of reliable birth-control and test-tube babies opens up the prospect of releasing women from biological constraints and allowing them to be full-time citizens as well. If we were prepared to relinquish the entire private sphere of personal and family affections, we could in principle revive something like Plato's utopian scheme for the incorporation of women into an all-inclusive public sphere on the same terms as men, and out-Sparta Rousseau himself. But in spite of the willingness of some radical feminists to contemplate artificial reproduction,[53] a universalization of Spartan citizenship would be unlikely to appeal even to them. Feminism, as has often been pointed out,[54] is an offshoot of liberalism, and in common with other liberal standpoints it places a value on individual freedom that is quite at variance with the more totalitarian aspects of Rousseau's vision. If we are to adapt Rousseau to feminism, it is therefore the liberal, 'juristic' strand in his political thought that we must follow up. It is this side of his thought, of course, that continues to interest male political philosophers: the ideals of personal autonomy, of laying down laws for oneself, of coming to agreement with others on a general will, and of being simultaneously sovereign and subject within a participatory democracy.

Within this aspect of Rousseau's thought (as in liberal thought generally) public and private spheres are distinguished from one another in such a way that the (male) citizen can participate in both, wearing different hats. Unlike the Spartan, the juristic citizen is not a unified person totally dedicated to the state, but a dual personality able to move in two worlds and make an abstract distinction between them. Citizenship is for him a role that he knows how to play: a legal *persona* that he can adopt or discard. He can distinguish between his general will and his particular will; he understands the difference between acting *qua* member of the sovereign and *qua* subject of the state; he is so adept at abstract thinking that he can cope with sophisticated legal niceties like the process by which a governing body is established, in which, according to Rousseau, the people in their capacity as sovereign first decree that a particular type of regime should be set up, and then resolve themselves into an executive democracy for the purpose of appointing its officials.[55]

For Rousseau himself, of course, as for Locke and other liberal thinkers, this duality of roles applied only to one sex. Men were expected to cope with the distinction between public and private spheres, but women were confined exclusively to the latter. Nevertheless, the very abstractness of the distinction appears to open up the possibility of extending Rousseau's conception of the free, participating citizen to women. If private and public life are distinct, and the citizen participates in the latter by abstracting from his role in the former, where is the difficulty about including women? Why should not men and women be equal as citizens in public regardless of their differences in private? Once Rousseau's beliefs about the different natures of men and women are discarded, then his arguments about the natural autonomy of man and the need to base legitimate authority on consent and participation seem to apply equally well to women, carrying with them his juristic concept of citizenship.

Most modern non-feminist commentators on Rousseau have in fact read him in this way. Ignoring or dismissing both his Spartan side and his view of women, they have universalized his juristic concept of citizenship without asking whether it is compatible with women's other role within the family, and without paying heed to Rousseau's own warnings against splitting human beings between different loyalties. More recently, however, feminists have argued that this strategy is superficial, and that to extend Rousseau's theory to women is much more difficult than might at first appear. I propose to look at these objections, though I shall argue that they are not in fact conclusive.

There are two different kinds of feminist objections to the familiar strategy of reinterpreting Rousseau's ideas so that 'citizens' can include women, and part of the persuasiveness of these objections is that both of them are very much in the spirit of Rousseau's own thought. I shall indicate briefly what these objections are before going on to discuss them at greater length. The first line of objection is practical: just as Rousseau argued that citizenship, however abstractly it may be conceived, needs the support of a whole world of social practices to be effective, so some feminists have argued that formal political equality between men and women cannot be given real substance without thoroughgoing social change, particularly in the family. The second line of objection, which is, again, a very Rousseauian one, is that the splitting of persons between different roles and conflicting loyalties is in principle undesirable.

The first, practical objection is that women's admission to public citizenship on the same formal terms as men cannot be other than a sham because of women's private position as wives and mothers. In spite of universal suffrage, women are not really equal citizens even in the non-participatory democracies with which we are familiar. How, then, could they cope with the more demanding role of Rousseauian citizen? Carole Pateman has summed up the current political situation of Western women as follows: 'An important long-term consequence of women's enfranchisement, and the other reforms that have led to women's present position of (almost) formal political and legal equality with men, is that the contradiction between civil equality and social, especially familial subjection...is now starkly revealed'.[56]

The objection that women's citizenship must be nullified by their domestic role is clearly a serious one, and it is easy to envisage historical and contemporary cases in which there is no doubt that it is so. Suppose, for instance, that women had been enfranchised along with men during the French Revolution. Given the unashamedly patriarchal structure of the eighteenth-century French family, and the continual pregnancies to which wives were subject, women could hardly have combined subordination in private with equality in public. In many of the countries where women have been given the vote as part of the standard modern package of 'national liberation', the same situation exists today. So much is relatively uncontroversial; but many feminists wish to go beyond this and to argue that even in societies like contemporary Britain and the USA, where contraception is almost universal and families less patriarchal than ever before, women still cannot be equal citizens because they are still held responsible for childrearing. To quote Carole Pateman again, 'If women are to participate fully, as equals, in social life, men will have to share equally in childrearing and other domestic tasks. While women are identified with this "private" work, their public status is always undermined.'[57]

At first sight, this position looks very persuasive. Nevertheless, we need to make a distinction within 'social life', and to recognize that the necessary conditions for equal *employment* and equal *citizenship* are not the same. Where employment is concerned, particularly in a profession with a competitive career structure, there can be no doubt that motherhood almost invariably poses great problems. Apart from the few women rich enough to employ first-class nannies, and the even fewer fortunate enough to find husbands willing to take on the role of 'mothering', women tend to be caught between the demands of career and domestic life, and to spend a great deal of their time and energy feeling guilty both at home and at work. The same considerations of course apply to a career as a professional politician, and explain why so few young women become MPs or Congresspersons. But while the disadvantages of this low proportion of women in legislatures should not be under-estimated, we must not make the mistake of identifying citizenship, especially Rousseauian participatory citizenship, with making a career out of politics—after all, the over-whelming majority of *male* citizens are not professional politicians, either. Participatory citizenship is essentially an amateur, unpaid activity without a career structure, and it is less clear that this activity is in fact systematically incompatible with the family as we know it. Certainly women with small children may find it hard to participate in politics (though a surprising number manage to do so); certainly women who are struggling to keep home and job going simultaneously may feel that to expect public spirit of them as well is too much. But the reverse of the coin is that older women, housewives or part-time workers, may have *more* time and energy to spare for politics and other voluntary work than most men, and do indeed form the backbone of many groups in which something like a Rousseauian ideal is realized.[58]

It is important to recognize also that the problem of making equal citizenship a reality in the face of social differences is not a straightforwardly sexist problem. If many women find it hard to exercise their citizenship, so do many men. It is not only babies and the washing-up that can keep one out of the public arena; so can long working hours, physically exhausting jobs, the demoralization of being unemployed, lack of education or belonging to the wrong social group (not to mention lack of inclination). Where the role of citizen is formally open to all, some women do find the resources to make use of it, and most men do not. The fact that Britain's first woman prime minister is a mother of twins ought to be enough to check hasty generalizations about the contemporary subordination of women. At present, effective citizenship is considerably easier for women in some social classes than for men in others, and while equal sharing of the burdens of domesticity would no doubt release some women into public life, there is no reason to suppose that it would produce genuinely equal citizenship for all.

Some feminists would answer that the political and the economic cannot be separated, and that to admit that motherhood tends to put women at an economic disadvantage is also to say that equal citizenship for them is impossible. Most women, after all, are economically dependent on their husbands while their children are small, and although the majority do now return to paid employment later, 'women's jobs' are in general less well-paid than those traditionally done by men, so that many working women belong to an underclass. This is an objection that has a great deal of force, since it is obvious that economic dependence or disadvantage must be a poor basis for political equality. All the same, it is important to recognize that the gap between formal citizenship and the economic conditions for full political equality is not a specifically sexual problem, but a general social one. Not all women are economically dependent, and, conversely, not all men are economically powerful; compare a married woman teacher with an unemployed man. No one could reasonably assert that all men in advanced industrial countries have equal employment opportunities, or deny that some women have much better opportunities than many men. Insofar as citizenship is closely tied to economic status, therefore, it cannot be specifically linked to sex. Economically dependent women are simply one of several underclasses (the unemployed, the handicapped, ethnic minorities) who suffer social and economic barriers to full citizenship.[59] Rousseau's general point that citizenship requires social preconditions still stands, but it is simplistic to suppose that the abolition of the current family structure is either a necessary or a sufficient element in those social conditions.

A more subtle barrier to genuine female citizenship may be that domestic life limits not only women's economic opportunities but also their outlook. Certainly women have in the past tended to be less interested in politics than men,[60] and it has also been suggested that they may be less fitted for it because their position in the family focuses their moral energies on private affections directly opposed to public standards of universal justice. In an interesting article, Carole Pateman has argued that one of Rousseau's reasons for regarding women as a 'permanently subversive force within the political order'[61] was that 'love and justice are antagonistic virtues: the demands of love and of family bonds are particularistic and so in direct conflict with justice, which demands that private interest is subordinate to the public (universal) good'.[62] Rousseau insists on keeping women segregated in the home and apart from men as much as possible because they are 'a corrupting influence on men. Their disorder leads them always to pull men away from civic virtue and to mock at justice'.[63]

Pateman suggests that Rousseau's worries about women (and similar observations by Freud) represent profound insights into a genuine problem which the formal enfranchisement of woman has not solved. As long as most women continue to be mainly concerned with childrearing inside the family, their moral understanding will be directed by particularist love, not universal justice. This is an argument very much in the spirit of Rousseau, recalling not only his insistence on the need for proper socialization of citizens but also his fondness for stark, mutually hostile alternatives, such as that between 'man' and 'citizen'. However, although it does highlight a potentially important conflict of political loyalties, it is not entirely persuasive. For one thing, even if it is true that contemporary women are socialized to respond to the moral demands of 'love' rather than those of 'justice', this is not necessarily politically subversive. Pateman seems to be arguing that 'love' necessarily leads one to take a particularistic view of politics, concerned only with the interests of one's own family. While it is undoubtedly true, however, that mothers (and fathers) are inclined to put the interests of their own children above those of others, there is another, less particularistic side to this 'love'. A common phenomenon on which much of the promotional material of international relief agencies is based is the sense of solidarity that many mothers (and fathers) feel with *all* mothers—their concern with *all* children, simply because they can imagine so vividly what other parents feel when their children are suffering. This impulse is also at work in the women's peace movement, and while it is all too easy to sentimentalize the virtues of bringing 'maternal thinking'[64] into politics, it is certainly an oversimplification to assume that such maternal thinking necessarily produces a 'Sanjay'-style particularism and corruption.

It is in any case rash to suppose that particularism/love can be attributed to women in general and universalism/justice to men in general. Considering how much women in the past have suffered from overgeneralized accounts of the characteristics of the two sexes, it surely behoves feminists to be particularly careful to avoid such errors themselves. The very fact that female political thinkers can raise the issue of universalism[65] shows that even within the existing social structure women are not impervious to the demands of justice; conversely, it would be the height of naïveté to suppose that men are necessarily more responsive to these demands. Most men are in fact no better qualified to be Rousseauian citizens than most women are. The social world they inhabit is not the universalist sphere of the citizen but the particularistic world of civil society, and they are not in general conspicuous for public spirit.

The practical objections to extending a universalized, juristic, non-Spartan version of Rousseauistic citizenship to women on the same terms as men do not, therefore, seem to me to be very strong. I suspect, however, that many of those who find these objections persuasive may do so because they are in sympathy with Rousseau at a deeper level—in sympathy with his objection to abstractions and divisions within a single human life, and with the profound desire for wholeness which was one of the most persistent themes of his own fragmented life and work. Himself a thoroughly unintegrated personality torn between opposed impulses and contradictory self-images, Rousseau desperately longed for unity, immediacy, integration. Time and again he returned to this point: 'Make man one, and you make him as happy as he can be'[66].

While Rousseau's willingness to sacrifice almost anything to the cause of inner peace may be explicable in biographical terms, what makes it important is that he gave unparalleled expression to longings that pervade the modern world [67] and highlighted a paradox of modern life that stands in the way of the feminist appropriation of his theory proposed here. The paradox is this. Looked at from one point of view, an abstract concept of citizenship, distinguishing public from private life and detached from Spartan concomitants, is much more plausible now than in Rousseau's own time because we are all used to making abstract distinctions between social roles. The process of bureaucratic rationalization chronicled by Weber has accustomed us to this: we are used to dealing with strangers rather than with kinsmen and clients, and we distinguish without any great effort between our official job and our private interests, between the public funds and the private purse. It seems that we no longer need the heroic, unnatural virtue of a Brutus to do justice in court or to be an honest tax-collector: the replacement of particularism by universalism in society has imperceptibly solved political problems that had been intractable for centuries. Ernest Gellner has made this point, remarking that premodern states, finding it hard to recruit public servants who would not as a matter of course sacrifice public interest to their private loyalties, adopted a variety of devices to overcome the problem, such as the employment of eunuchs, celibate priests or slave warriors like the Mamluks. As Gellner remarks, we are all Mamluks now:[68] abstract distinctions between roles, including the distinction between public and private, are part of the social atmosphere we breathe.

What is paradoxical, however, is that this bureaucratic development, which should on the face of it make equal citizenship for both sexes much easier to practise, has generated its own reaction, of which Rousseau was himself the prophet. The splitting of the modern person into a set of abstract roles, including the division between public and private, is attacked in the name of a Rousseauian craving for immediacy, a romantic aversion from bureaucratic abstraction, an aversion to be found in all modern radical movements, including feminism. Feminists therefore find themselves torn between two opposite impulses: the desire, on the one hand, to affirm an abstract concept of citizenship and to claim admission to public life on the same terms as men, leaving aside as irrelevant their private identity as women; and, on the other hand, the impulse to challenge the public–private distinction itself not only as a patriarchalist ploy but as an alienating destruction of authenticity.

R.P. Wolff has analysed both contradictory impulses in a fascinating article, 'There's Nobody Here But Us Persons'[69]. From one point of view, Wolff affirms, liberal industrial society is to be congratulated for establishing an abstract concept of the person. As rational individuals in the public sphere, equal before the law, possessors of rights as citizens, we are not tied down to ascriptive statuses based on race, religion, occupation or sex. Nevertheless, he simultaneously finds himself deploring the depersonalization involved in this abstract citizenship which ignores the great realities of human life, birth, personal relations and death: 'the steady draining away from the public realm of the human dimensions of the human condition',[70] as everything real about people is held to be irrelevant to their public position.

Wolff admits that he finds himself in a quandary. He recognizes the value of a concept of public personality that no longer discriminates against someone because they are a woman or a Jew, but he also deplores the dehumanization entailed by the split between public and private. And this quandary is surely not peculiar to Wolff but finds constant expression in the feminist movement, whose members are often unsure whether liberation consists in making their private identity as women genuinely irrelevant in public, or whether, on the contrary, what they want is to overcome so alienating a division altogether and appear in politics precisely *as* women.

The dilemma is a genuine one, to which there may be no entirely satisfactory solution. I suspect, however, that it might not look quite so intractable if we were to be more critical than is customary of the Rousseauian quest for immediacy. The romantic critique of fragmentation is so widely accepted that we often forget to ask ourselves whether integration is really so overwhelmingly desirable. There is a lot to be said for moving between different life-worlds, being familiar with a variety of different experiences and responding to a plurality of different values, even though there may be difficult adjustments to be made between them. While bearing in mind Wolff's sardonic remark that to escape from genuine dilemmas it is not enough simply to 'use the word "dialectical" a lot',[71] we should also recognize that contradictions of this kind can present an opportunity and a challenge as well as a problem.

Looking at Rousseau's legacy from the point of view of a modern woman, we may seem to be faced with an all-or-nothing choice. On the one hand, we have the public life of the citizen, which must be lived with Spartan intensity if it is to be lived at all; on the other hand, we have the private life of personal intimacy and child-centred domesticity. If we are true to Rousseau's ideal of authenticity, we must choose: we cannot have citizenship without Sparta, and Spartan citizenship is irreconcilable with family life for women. If we are not willing, therefore, either to retreat into domestic life or to sacrifice the family to an exclusively public life, we seem to be left with the conclusion that Rousseau—and perhaps the whole tradition of male-dominated political thought—has nothing to say to us, and that we must start again from scratch.

Although this kind of uncompromising conclusion would be very much in Rousseau's own spirit, however, it is not the conclusion I wish to recommend. I suggest that we should pay less attention to Rousseau's spirit than to his practice, for in spite of his rhetoric of authenticity and his fondness for radical dichotomies, he himself did *not* choose, and did not bequeath a single consistent message to posterity. On the contrary, his continuing fascination lies precisely in the range of options he offers his readers, one of which is an abstract but nevertheless inspiring conception of self-government through participatory citizenship.

CONCLUSION

I set out in this essay to consider whether it is possible to give

Rousseau's understanding of citizenship a feminist form, and my answer is a severely qualified Yes. It is clear that in order to do so one must select ruthlessly from among Rousseau's ideas, rejecting many of the views that he himself most strongly held. One must jettison not only his specific views on the nature of women, but also the 'Spartan' side of his political writings, together with his emphasis on authenticity and on the need to make radical choices between total ways of life. Feminist political theorists have therefore been quite right to point out that to press Rousseau into the service of women's liberation requires not merely a minor adjustment but a real breach with the spirit of his thought. However, it does not follow that Rousseau has nothing to say to modern women about citizenship and political freedom, for his works are not all of a piece, and the abstract, juristic side of his theory that is regularly meditated upon by contemporary male political thinkers is just as relevant to women.

In his writings on the relation between 'medium' and 'message', Marshall McLuhan used to distinguish between 'hot' and 'cool' media, the 'hot' being those with high definition, like print, which leaves little to be filled in by the person on the receiving end, whereas the 'cool' ones, like speech, have low definition and demand a high degree of participation by the hearer to reconstruct a meaningful whole from the information received by the senses.[72] If we were to extend this distinction to political theory, Hobbes would be comparatively 'hot', but Rousseau would be the 'coolest' of them all. There are many different messages to be found in his work, and we should allow neither revulsion from his chauvinism nor sympathy with his romanticism to blind us to the importance of his abstract conception of the free self-governing person, neither male nor female.

NOTES

1.   Julie, *La Nouvelle Hélöise* in *Oeuvres Complètes de Jean-Jacques Rousseau* (Paris, Bibliothèque de la Pléiade, 1959–69), II, p. 305. I am grateful to Professor Martin Harrison for advising me on this translation.

Subsequent translations from Rousseau are mine except where otherwise indicated.

2. S. Ellenburg, *Rousseau's Political Philosophy: An Interpretation from Within* (Ithaca and London, Cornell University Press, 1976), p. 28.

3. *Ibid.*, p. 14; R.D. Masters, *The Political Philosophy of Rousseau* (Princeton N.J., Princeton University Press, 1968),p. vi.

4. Cf. M. Canovan, 'The limits of seriousness: Rousseau and the interpretation of political theory', *European Studies Review* 2 (1972), pp. 1–24.

5. For a sensitive exploration of these tensions, see M. Berman, *The Politics of Authenticity* (London, Allen and Unwin, 1971), sections II to IV. Joel Schwartz argues that the key to Rousseau's ambivalence about politics is his even more fundamental ambivalence about sex (J. Schwartz, *The Sexual Politics of Jean-Jacques Rousseau,* Chicago, University of Chicago Press, 1984, Ch. 1).

6. *Émile,* in *Oeuvres Complètes de Jean-Jacques Rousseau,* IV, p. 248.

7. J.N. Shklar, *Men and Citizens: A Study of Rousseau's Social Theory* (Cambridge, Cambridge University Press, 1969) p. 3.

8. Cf. B. Groethuysen, *J.J. Rousseau* (Paris, Gallimard, 1949), pp. 91–9.

9. Rousseau's debts are documented in R. Derathé, *Jean-Jacques Rousseau et la Science Politique de son Temps* (Paris, Presses Universitaires de France, 1950).

10. J.J. Rousseau, *The Social Contract,* trans. M. Cranston (Harmondsworth, Penguin, 1968), p. 60.

11. *Ibid.,* pp. 62–83, 136–54.

12. Though one which is much less prominent in Rousseau's own writings than in those of his interpreters.

13. First version of *The Social Contract,* in *Oeuvres Complètes de Jean-Jacques Rousseau,* III, p. 287. Cf. Masters, *Political Philosophy of Rousseau,* Ch. VI.

14. *The Social Contract,* p. 84.

15. *Ibid.,* p. 87.

16. Cf. R. Fralin, *Rousseau and Representation* (New York, Columbia University Press, 1978), pp. 3, 96, 106; Shklar, *Men and Citizens,* p. 181.

17. *The Social Contract,* pp. 176–87.

18. 'Discourse on Political Economy', J.J. Rousseau, *The Social Contract and Discourses,* trans. G.D.H. Cole (London, Dent, 1913), p. 251.

19. 'Considerations on the government of Poland', in *Rousseau's Political Writings,* trans. F. Watkins (Edinburgh, Nelson, 1953), p. 176.

20. J.L. Talmon, *The Origins of Totalitarian Democracy* (London, Secker and Warburg, 1952), pp. 38–49.

21. *Émile,* pp. 248–9.

22. 'Discourse on Political Economy', p. 246.

23. *Émile,* p. 248.

24. *The Social Contract,* p. 142.

25.   Though cf. Masters, *Political Philosophy of Rousseau*, pp. 351, 362, 421.

26.   On the successive reinterpretations of Jefferson's 'self-evident truth', see J.R. Pole, *The Pursuit of Equality in American History* (Berkeley, University of California Press, 1978).

27.   M. Cranston, *Jean Jacques* (London, Allen Lane, 1983), p. 206.

28.   Cf. V. Wexler, ' "Made for Man's Delight": Rousseau as antifeminist', *American Historical Review* 81 (1976). See also Schwartz, *Sexual Politics of Rousseau*, passim.

29.   Cf. H. Arendt, *The Human Condition* (Garden City, Doubleday, 1959), p. 36.

30.   *Politics and the Arts: Letter to M. D'Alembert on the Theatre*, trans. A. Bloom (Glencoe, Free Press, 1960), *passim*, but see, for example, p. 111.

31.   *Émile*, p. 693.

32.   *Ibid.*, p. 693.

33.   *Ibid.*, p. 750.

34.   *Ibid.*, p. 737.

35.   'Discourse on Political Economy', p. 234.

36.   *Émile*, p. 705.

37.   Shklar, *Men and Citizens*, p. 3.

38.   But see Susan Okin's acute observations on 'the fate of Rousseau's heroines', S.M. Okin, *Women in Western Political Thought* (Princeton, N.J., Princeton University Press, 1979), pp. 167–94.

39.   *Ibid.*, pp. 106–66.

40.   Rousseau devoted a long footnote to refuting Locke's argument that the family is natural ('Discours sur l'origins et les fondements de l'inégalité', in *Oeuvres Complètes de Jean-Jacques Rousseau,* III, pp. 147, 214–8').

41.   *Ibid.*, p. 123.

42.   *Ibid.*, p. 122.

43.   *Émile*, pp. 707, 718.

44.   *Ibid.*, p. 249.

45.   *The Social Contract*, p. 84.

46.   *Ibid.*, pp. 52–3.

47.   'Discourse on Political Economy', p. 235.

48.   According to Stephen Ellenburg, the 'insistent demand for absolute liberty permeates and animates Rousseau's philosophy', and 'Rousseau judged every conceivable instance of social dependence in terms of the difference between liberty and slavery'. Like most other students of Rousseau, Ellenburg does not appear to notice the contradiction between Rousseau's claims for men and his views on women. (Ellenburg, *Rousseau's Political Philosophy*, pp. 118, 132).

49.   *Émile*, p. 249.

50.   Okin, *Women in Western Political Thought,* pp. 192–3; C. Pateman, ' "The Disorder of Women": women, love, and the sense of justice', *Ethics* 91 (1980), pp. 20–34.

51.   J.B. Elshtain, *Public Man, Private Woman* (Princeton N.J., Princeton University Press, 1981) p. 165.

52. *Émile*, p. 248.
53. S. Firestone, *The Dialectic of Sex: The Case for Feminist Revolution* (London, Cope, 1971), pp. 233, 63, 70, 73.
54. For example, Z.R. Eisenstein, *The Radical Future of Liberal Feminism* (New York, Longman, 1981), p. 4.
55. *The Social Contract*, p. 145.
56. C. Pateman, 'Feminist critiques of the public/private dichotomy', in S.J. Benn and G.F. Gaus (eds.), *Public and Private in Social Life* (London, Croom Helm; New York, St Martins Press, 1983), p. 292.
57. *Ibid.*, p. 299.
58. As far as contemporary liberal democracies are concerned, the conventional wisdom in political science is that women are not only rare as political leaders, but also participate less in all political activities than men. (See, for example, S. Verba, N.H. Nie and J.O. Kim, *Participation and Political Equality: A Seven-Nation Comparison*, Cambridge, Cambridge University Press, 1978, p. 234). The gap is small, however, and seems to be declining. Furthermore, employment outside the home does not seem to diminish rates of political participation but to increase them—an indication that what is at issue is motivation rather than leisure time. (V. Randall, *Women and Politics*, London, Macmillan, 1982, pp. 37, 62). There is conflicting evidence concerning the effect of children. One would expect that having small children to look after would hamper political participation, and there is some evidence to support this (e.g. G. Pomper, *Voters' Choice*, New York, Dodd Mead, 1975, p. 72). But other researchers have suggested that motherhood does not necessarily have this effect (S. Welch, 'Women as political animals? A test of some Explanations for male–female political participation differences', *American Journal of Political Science*, 21 (1977), 711–30, esp. 724; C.B. Flora and N.B. Lynn, 'Women and political socialization: considerations of the impact of motherhood', in J. Jaquette (ed.), *Women in Politics*, New York, Wiley, 1974). On the activity of middle-aged housewives in community action groups, see Randall, *Women and Politics*, p. 41. It could perhaps be argued that the direct action of the women at the Greenham Common Peace Camp is particularly close to the participatory ideal.
59. It has been suggested that much, if not all of the comparative political apathy of women is due to their overrepresentation in those social and economic groups (the old, the poor and the less educated), whose male members tend not to participate in politics either (Randall, *Women and Politics*, p. 65).
60. On the continuing gap between men and women in 'ideological sophistication', see M.K. Jennings and B.C. Parah, 'Ideology, gender and political action: a cross-national survey', *British Journal of Political Science* 10 (1980), 219–40.
61. Pateman, 'Disorder of Women', p. 20.
62. *Ibid.*, p. 24.
63. *Ibid.*, p. 28.
64. Elshtain, *Public Man, Private Woman*, p. 336.

65. The most celebrated female political thinker, Hannah Arendt, was especially notable for thinking in terms of public principles rather than private loyalties. See, for example, H. Arendt, *Eichmann in Jerusalem*, (London, Faber, 1963), pp. 245–52.

66. 'Du bonheur public', in *Oeuvres Complètes de Jean-Jacques Rousseau*, III, p. 510. Cf. *Émile*, p. 251; Shklar, *Men and Citizens*, p. 55.

67. Cf. Berman, *Politics of Authenticity*, passim.

68. E. Gellner, *Nations and Nationalism* (Oxford, Blackwell, 1983), pp. 15, 18, 36.

69. R.P. Wolff, 'There's Nobody Here But Us Persons', in C.C. Gould and M.W. Wartofsky, (eds.), *Women and Philosophy: Toward a Theory of Liberation* (New York, Capricorn, 1976).

70. *Ibid.*, p. 135.

71. *Ibid.*, p. 143.

72. M. McLuhan, *Understanding Media* (London, Routledge and Kegan Paul, 1964), p. 22.

4 Humboldt and the Romantics: Neither *Hausfrau* nor *Citoyenne*—The Idea of 'Self-Reliant Femininity' in German Romanticism

Ursula Vogel

What could be uglier than over-emphasised femininity, what more repulsive than exaggerated masculinity as they prevail in our morals and opinions today? ... Only *self-reliant femininity* and *gentle masculinity* can be called good and beautiful.

Friedrich Schlegel[1]

INTRODUCTION: THE ROMANTIC GROUP— THE IDEAL OF SOCIABILITY

Jena, some day in December 1799: A visitor calling at the house of the literary critic August Wilhelm Schegel would have been witness to an astonishing scene. A group of young men and women—who would later enter the history books as the pioneers of German Romanticism[2]—were gathered around a hospitable dinner table to follow a daily routine of reading poetry, talking philosophy (probably Kant and Fichte) and trading every piece of irreverent gossip that might scandalize the literary establishment. On this day they were in a particularly jolly mood. Laughter 'nearly swept them under the table'.[3] They had been reciting a standard piece of German classical literature—Friedrich Schiller's 'Song of the Bell'. Generation after generation of German children have been made to memorize its rhymes and to imbibe its lofty ideal of human striving and fulfilment. Many have been tempted, but few will have dared, to giggle at the following passages:

> The Husband must enter
> The hostile life,
> With struggle and strife
> To plant or to watch,
> To snare or to snatch,

To pray and importune,
Must wager and venture
And hunt down his fortune...

Within sits Another,
The chaste Housewife;
The mild one, the mother—
Her home is her life.
In its circle she rules,
And the daughters she schools,
And she tames the boys...

Locks the chest and the wardrobe, with lavender smelling,
And the hum of the spindle goes quick through the dwelling;
She hoards in the presses, well polished and full,
The snow of the linen, the shine of the wool;
Adds shine to the good, and from care and endeavour
Rests never![4]

According to Friedrich Schlegel's sarcastic comment on this and other similar poems by Schiller, the poet had indeed idealized the nature of man and woman, albeit in the wrong direction—downwards and below the level of truth. Both stereotypes—conqueror and *hausfrau*—lack the features of a fully human person.[5]

We commonly associate the term 'romantic' with notions of sentimental love, with unbounded feeling (at the expense of reason), with yearning for harmony and nostalgia for the past. It is difficult to recover from this usage the characteristic mood of early Romantic thinking: enthusiasm for building a new world of beauty and love, coupled with a radical spirit of criticism. 'Sublime impertinence' was the motto under which the first Romantic journal waged war against the prevailing literary fashions.[6] And the same irreverence towards cherished orthodoxies was manifest in the love and friendship relations inside the Romantic group.

In its earliest and most revolutionary phase, German Romanticism was essentially a collective enterprise. The critique of the prevailing view of women's nature and place in society grew directly out of experiments in 'communal living'. It reflected the determination of a small circle of friends to create in their personal life and work new forms of sociability that would transcend the conventional divide between male and female roles. The ideal of sociability (*Geselligkeit*) does not fit into the confined space of the nuclear family. Nor does it resemble any kind of political association constituted by rules, hierarchies and power. It rests, indeed, upon intimate personal bonds like friendship and love (usually at odds with the legal forms of marriage), but these expand into intellectual companionship and a sense of common mission (expressed in terms like *sympoetry, symphilosophy, symrevolution*).[7]

The most important feature of the Romantic group, for our purpose, is the participation of women in its literary and philosophical projects.[8] Caroline Schlegel contributed to the translation of Shakespeare; Dorothea Veit wrote novels; both collaborated on the journal. Although in terms of published output their achievements cannot compare with those of the men, they seem to have given decisive intellectual impulses to the discussions in which the Romantic doctrine originated. Evidence of their co-operation can be found not only in the innumerable volumes of private correspondence but also in the typical literary genres of early Romantic theorizing—the dialogue and the epistolary letter.

In both women were represented as equal partners and authors of ideas.

SCHLEGEL: 'DO NOT WASTE FAITH AND LOVE IN THE POLITICAL WORLD!'[9]

Why was Schiller's idyllic portrait of woman's dignity and special mission in the world so unacceptable to the Romantics? On what grounds did they challenge the dominant ideology of their time in which time-honoured conservatism had been powerfully reinforced by Rousseau's endorsement of female submissiveness? Surprisingly perhaps, after what has been said about the rebellious mood in the face of sacred traditions, the Romantics did not join radical reformers in the quest for women's equal rights. They were contemporaries and, for a brief spell, even enthusiastic supporters of the ideals of the French Revolution. Yet they were remarkably unconcerned about women's inferior legal and political status.

Equality of right and citizenship were not the issue here. The Romantic writers rebelled against the equation of femininity, Nature and domesticity because it was incompatible with the ideal of *Bildung*—with the full development in each individual of her particular potential. *Bildung* entails the commitment to a life-long, *open-ended* process of self-education in which all our human faculties are activated and extended. It is obvious that the fixation of human beings in natural roles and rigid sexual polarizations does not admit of genuine individuality. In particular, it denies scope to those of our faculties which the Romantics valued above all others: imagination and creativity. They are, of course, central to the artist's vision and to his experimenting with ever new forms of creative self-expression. But they occupy an equally important place in the lives of 'ordinary' human beings, enabling them to play with, and thereby free themselves from, the confines of seemingly natural roles (like, for example, those of sexual behaviour).

The political realm, as commonly understood in our discipline, is left out of the Romantic argument about women. So are the constraints of economic necessity; neither household chores nor the need to earn a living seem to exist in the aesthetic domain of *Bildung*. Yet, in compensation for the vacuum, the latter has nonetheless something important to offer. For it is not from the outset defined by male characteristics; its ideals are equally accessible to men and women. Could it not therefore offer space for an unbiased reflection on the differences between the sexes—unburdened, that is, by the entrenched divisions of labour and power which must be the *starting-point* of any development of women's political emancipation?

To put the case more provocatively: with its emphasis on the important place of sensuality in the individual's development, together with the value which it assigns to diversity and differentiation as necessary incentives for self-realization, Romantic aesthetics could encourage us to take a fresh look at the loaded question of significant sexual differences. Precisely because it stays aloof from the struggle for equal political rights, it need not insist, for the sake of effective propaganda, on uniformity in the constitution of female and male character. It can afford to explore the possibility of contrasts that may be appreciated and enjoyed without providing yet another excuse for justifying inequality.

We have to look at such a possibility as an open question. The Romantic experiment is a precarious one. It has to dissociate the idea of a woman person from fixed conceptions of gender—without, however, losing the distinct attributes of femininity in the abstract notion of a sexless humanity.

HUMBOLDT: 'WOMAN IS CLOSER TO THE IDEAL OF HUMANITY THAN MAN—BUT LESS OFTEN REACHES IT.'[10]

A brief excursion into Wilhelm von Humboldt's early writings will indicate the direction in which a solution to this dilemma could be sought. Like Schiller, with whom in the 1790s he entertained close friendship, Humboldt wanted to overcome the Kantian antagonism between rational and sensual faculties by calling upon the sense of beauty as a mediator. The demands made upon 'man' as a rational agent were mitigated by, and eventually took second place to, the quest for 'the highest and most harmonious development of his powers to a complete and consistent whole'.[11] As a vital source of our creative energies, sensuality was rehabilitated, and with it those non-rational inclinations which had often been taken as evidence of woman's lower nature and incapacity for freedom. Moreover, since the study of the individual as an aesthetic being put premium not upon any particular excellence but upon the feeling of beauty that 'binds all human capacities together in a single whole',[12] and since, as we shall see, this disposition towards harmony was considered an attribute of female rather than male character, women could make considerable advance on the ladder of the philosopher's esteem. Two implications inherent in Humboldt's ideal of *Bildung*, as individual *self*-realization, have particular importance in the context of our argument. First, the emphasis on liberty—as the necessary condition for making one's own choices (and mistakes!)—led him to deny to marriage any public function to be guarded by the state.[13] Human associations, he argued, will always tend to frustrate the individual's creative energies and self-determining course of action unless they are formed and maintained spontaneously. Marriage must, therefore, be understood as a voluntary union between two human beings sustained entirely by their mutual affection. Since enforced permanence would have a disastrous effect upon each person's development, divorce must be possible 'at any time and without excuse'[14] (a conclusion which was too radical even for J.S. Mill). Second, Humboldt's ideal of the fully and harmoniously developed character does not abstract from the sexual differences between individuals. On the contrary, the dissimilarity and polarity between male and female nature import vital energies to the process of self-development. Genuine individuality thrives on contrast and confrontation while equality of life-situations has always a dull and enfeebling effect.[15]

On these assumptions, it should be possible to define the distinct, constitutive elements in both femininity and masculinity so as to allow for genuine diversity without falling back upon any hierarchical scheme of evaluation. Humboldt approaches the task from seemingly value-free territory—classical Greek sculpture in the different presentations of female and male beauty; comparative anthropology; observation of polarity and attraction as the creative principle in all nature. At first sight, the comparisons seem to work much in favour of feminine qualities. Women, Humboldt believes, are closer to the ideal of perfect humanity because their natural disposition tends towards harmony and wholeness.[16] Whereas man, given to restless striving in the external world, invests and dissipates his energy in a multitude of fragmented pursuits, woman experiences and understands everything in relation to an *inner* centre; her mind is infinitely receptive, open to everything that is good and beautiful, yet she remains at one with herself.

However, the emphasis on harmony and receptivity in the idea of genuine femininity has problematic implications. It leads Humboldt to disapprove of active self-assertion and of all manifestations of outstanding talent—such as wit, brilliance of mind, vivacity—in which a person's character will strike us as interesting and original. Whereas in a man such accomplishments are admired as features of excellence, in a woman they betray an unfeminine disposition because they disturb the equilibrium of a harmonious character which derives from an unassuming, 'unambitious striving' for goodness and beauty.[17] One-sidedness of disposition and achievement is a male predicament. Yet, on Humboldt's own premises, it is also a privilege—the mark of freedom, proof of the capacity to leave the confines of nature behind: 'Man strives for freedom, woman for moral harmony' (Humboldt, quoting Goethe).[18]

Moreover, women's superior qualities remain essentially and causally connected to the domestic sphere. Not only are they said to be inseparable from the experience of motherhood; they depend upon a daily routine which is free from the taxing demands of the outside world, in which all tasks are more like play, leaving the inner person undisturbed.[19] In the last instance, genuine femininity is tied to the natural destination of the wife and mother—confined to an inner circle surrounded by, and separate from, the world in which men act and develop themselves.

There is no doubt that Humboldt himself did not consider women inferior, and that his essays betray a new appreciation and evaluation of female character. But the dynamic element in the notions of masculinity and femininity is encumbered by a *natural basis* of gender which remains static and entrenched in absolutes. There is no crossing of borders, at least not in both directions. Humboldt does suggest that men would gain if they 'attuned their inner life to gentleness'.[20] He does not, however, hold out a similar promise for women that they might attain 'masculine' independence of mind. This combination was to be explored in Friedrich Schlegel's theory of femininity.

SCHLEGEL: 'EXAGGERATED FEMININITY'— A CRITIQUE OF MODERN PREJUDICE

In his earliest critical works (written at about the same time as Humboldt's essays)[21] Friedrich Schlegel chooses a similar historical route to the study of woman's character. He too, searches in the great art works of classical Greece for a model conception of femininity. But his account is more critical and brings to light the defects in both modern and ancient attitudes. Unlike Humboldt, who does not relate the artistic represent- ation of female character to a wider social and political environment, he is keenly aware that, especially in 'free' Athens, the majority of women were excluded from the very activities—public education, gymnastics, citizenship—which had enabled the Greeks to reach the ideal of perfect humanity. And for him, second to none in his enthusiasm for everything Greek, that exclusion casts a shadow upon the ideal:

The female sex lacked all those opportunities for self-development; kept out of the realm of sociability it was confined to the narrowest circle of domestic life. Repression and general contempt brought about its degeneration.[22]

But there were also exceptions. By careful combination of fragmented textual evidence, Schlegel sets out to reconstruct the character and life-situation of those women who were exempt from the repressive conditions of Greek society. And here he detects possibilities in feminine nature which reveal the corruption in modern attitudes towards the female sex:[23] that women—like Diotima in Plato's *Symposium* and the female pupils of the Pythagorean school[24]—were deemed capable of a philosophical education; that in Sparta they took part in masculine exercises and were, as mothers, willing to sacrifice the most 'natural' feelings to the demands of patriotism. Facts like these contradict and offend modern notions of propriety. To the guardians of contemporary morality the 'masculine' pursuits of Greek women must appear as the destruction of femininity itself, just as Sappho's poetic genius will not be honoured among those censors of taste who, like Rousseau, believe that women are by nature incapable of genuine enthusiasm and artistic creativity.[25]

Why are we moderns, Schlegel asks, so loath to see in those examples from the past a higher, more developed form of womanhood? Because we have exaggerated the natural differences between the sexes into a rigid scheme of mutually exclusive qualities. We find it difficult even to imagine that there was a time when in Sparta 'women possessed masculine strength and independence while young men displayed female modesty, shame and gentleness'.[26] What to us seems but a perversion of nature's imperatives is, in fact, proof of the human capacity for freedom—freedom to move beyond the separate prescriptions of male and female virtue towards a common ideal of *Menschlichkeit*.[27]

This is the salient point in Schlegel's account of Greek femininity: it challenges any belief in an immutable sexual nature. Such a tribute to the determining power of nature would, he claims, be incompatible with the demands of morality and beauty. For to accept that Nature has locked up the potential for human development behind the prison walls of a sexual role makes nonsense of the idea of freedom. The selfless, unbounded devotion of a wife—extolled by many writers as the most admirable among female virtues—is, in fact, a shameful renunciation of independence, a symptom of a woman's 'absolute lack of character' (since she passively receives the maxims of her actions from another person, i.e. her husband).

Both the impatient will to dominate in man and a self-denying submissiveness in woman are exaggerated and ugly. Only self-reliant womanhood and gentle manhood deserve to be called good and beautiful.[28]

That these stereotypes, each made up of an extensive catalogue of exclusively male and female characteristics, have assumed the status of self-evident truths is due to self-interest as well as delusion.[29] Schlegel recognizes that the ideal of pure femininity, with its emphasis on innocence and helplessness, serves as an instrument of male dominance—a convenient belief to rationalize the desire that women should exist *for* men. Self-interest is reinforced by confusion: people fail to distinguish the essential, constitutive attributes of an idea from its contingent associations. Thus they crowd into the notion of femininity numerous attributes which are derived from experience and thus attributable to particular circumstances of time and place.

That does not mean that Schlegel adopts the stance of a rationalist who relegates sexual identity and difference to insignificant, merely contingent attributes.[30] The notions of femininity and masculinity have not become redundant. It is his ambition—and that of Romantic thinking in general—to harness the diversity of male and female dispositions to the energies which encourage a rich and many-faceted personality. But those differences must not be allowed to constitute closed roles, since these would prevent intimate communication and mutual enrichment in relations of friendship and love—and, through them, the striving for a common goal of *Menschlichkeit*.

Whether Schlegel can bring about such a precarious synthesis—whether it can be achieved at all—is the question which we shall now approach through his later writings.

LOVE AS VOCATION

Schlegel's novel *Lucinde*, written in the heyday of Romantic sociability, portrays the history of a perfect love in which all the desires of an undetermined, unconstrained sexual nature will find gratification. From the time of its first appearance (in 1799), *Lucinde* was surrounded by scandal which continuously refuelled itself until well into the twentieth century.[31] It is now difficult to understand why Schlegel's contemporaries condemned the book as immoral. One looks in vain for spicy, pornographic rarities. There was more sensational literature around, especially for those who read French. What shocked the reading public was the idea that a woman should, like a man, be able and be permitted to feel sexual passion. This clearly offended the common notions of chastity and saintliness which propriety demanded of the wife and mother. It was not surprising that the respectable bourgeois was scandalized by passages like the much quoted 'Dithyrambic Phantasy about the most Delightful Situation', which praises the pleasure lovers will derive from swapping masculine and feminine roles in sexual intercourse:

One among all situations I consider the funniest and most beautiful: when we exchange roles and compete in childish delight who of us is better at imitating the other—whether you are more successful in pretending to the cautious impetuosity of a man, or I in feigning the attractive passivity of a woman.[32]

That this was not a scandalous account of perverse practices but, in its unashamed tribute to sensual passion, at the same time an allegory intimating the perfection of both female and male nature towards full humanity, escaped most readers.

Love as portrayed in *Lucinde* expresses the Romantic dissatisfaction with any one-sided and therefore divisive account of human nature. It is a protest against the separation of sensual from spiritual elements in our involvement with a beloved person. Its prime target is that false modesty ('Englanderism', as the Romantics called it), in which society has successfully curbed women's natural desires and extinguished what are original and truly human feelings.[33] It would, however, be equally wrong to see in Schlegel's novel merely a plea for the 'emancipation of the flesh'. Its intention is more ambitious. It claims that a genuine love relationship, unconstrained by artificial rules of propriety, will gratify and develop all human desires and faculties, 'from the most exuberant sensuality to the most spiritual spirituality'.[34] Thus Lucinde and Julius are, each for the other, passionate lover, best companion, perfect friend, all in one person.

Romantic love does not ignore nor discard the different sexual identities of women and men—but it continuously shifts their boundaries. It allows for the possibility that both will find and cultivate in themselves attributes commonly ascribed to the other sex. What is possible on the basis of female and male sexuality is not predetermined by nature; it is something with which individuals have the freedom to play and experiment. This is an attractive idea but one beset with considerable conceptual problems (though these are not Schlegel's alone). If gender is not a determining power of pervasive range, we must be careful not to grant too much to unalterable facts of sexual nature. If, on the other hand, it is not a merely contingent attribute of a person's life, we must assume some core element in human nature which lies outside the individual's freedom and open development. What, then, are the possibilities that an individual can realize because she is a woman and not a man? And what, conversely, are the constraints imposed by this fact? Where is the line beyond which we cannot ascribe observable differences between the sexes to convention alone?

In his earliest reflections on the matter, Friedrich Schlegel had, for polemical purposes, adopted an agnostic position, similar to the one later espoused by J.S. Mill: we do not yet know what woman's nature is, because what appears to us natural is all too often but entrenched custom, prejudice in the guise of self-evident truth. To the extent, however, that love between woman and man became the focus of his interest, this strategy proved more difficult to maintain. Although narrow conceptions of sexual role could be challenged, the polarity of male and female character could not be denied or minimized without depriving the Romantic idea of love of its specific meaning.

WOMAN IS A DOMESTIC BEING

The case that I have presented so far in Friedrich Schlegel is that of a radical thinker who rejects the whole ideology of separate spheres. Unfortunately, the departure from the old conception of sexual roles is not as complete as we might have expected. Women's special ties with the domestic world and her peculiar mental and emotional constitution have not disappeared, although they no longer bear the stigma of inferiority.

Since gender polarities are admitted and, indeed, welcomed as stimulating contrasts, it is not implausible to suggest that love affects woman and man in a different manner. 'It would be absurd', in Schleiermacher's words, 'not to acknowledge sexual characteristics of the soul'.[35] But, as has already been observed in Humboldt's case, the problem is whether these dissimilarities can be so described that the notions of male and female nature do not slide back into the old clichés.

The only sense, Schlegel contends, in which we may legitimately refer to femininity as an *essential* attribute of a woman's character is that, for her, living and loving mean the same.[36] Love is, so to speak, a woman's calling; she is unable to experience it as only a partial interest or feeling. Because her love is 'total' and self-contained, it can transform a man's life by imparting to it a sense of unity, a direction towards an inner centre. She, on the other side, gains from his love an extension of herself—self-consciousness, knowledge, contact with the outside world. As one of the female correspondents in Schleiermacher's fictional *Letters on Schlegel's Lucinde* puts it, 'You develop us, but we give you roots'.[37]

If we abstract from the tone of enthusiasm and elation in which man and women converse with each other in these dialogues (and which makes very tortuous reading indeed), do such statements not in the end reaffirm the very orthodoxies that the Romantics set out to challenge? Man's business is freedom and striving towards the infinite, while woman is there to provide harmony and roots! We must, again, concede to the Romantic position that these differing attitudes towards love, although original, are not absolutes. They can be mutually transferred and acquired. It would be unacceptable, Schleiermacher maintains, to explain a man's less comprehensive capacity for love as an unalterable fact of nature. To expand this capacity must, and can, be made the object of his endeavour.[38]

Yet, however much we emphasize the flexibility of the concepts used to convey a contrast of original disposition, woman's sexual nature remains associated with the inner life *(Innerlichkeit).* Moreover, it is in an indirect way realigned with domesticity: 'Whether it be a device of nature or an artificial design of man, the truth of the matter is—woman is a *domestic* being.'[39] Schlegel, it is true, insists that we make a distinction between the *typical situation* of a woman's life and its *ultimate purpose (Bestimmung).* The latter has nothing to do with domesticity; indeed, is diametrically opposed to it. Like man, woman must strive for the ideal of *Bildung.* He regrets that, even under optimal circumstances, marriage, motherhood and family tend to pull women downwards, to entangle them in the restrictive circle of mere needs and petty responsibilities. He is aware, too, that all too often such circumstances are powerful enough to obliterate even the consciousness of an alienated existence. But he does not seem to conceive of the possibility that a woman's external environment could be any other than domestic. Given his keen sense of the historicity of society's institutions, he might have argued that the typical situation in which women find themselves is mainly a consequence of social convention. Instead, he links domesticity to Nature and thus brings back a whole set of implications which run counter to the ideal of liberated femininity: a woman's biological organization is directed towards the one beautiful purpose of motherliness *(Mütterlichkeit)*; this is an original and essential quality of physical nature. To it corresponds, on the plane of emotional and mental disposition, the capacity for sympathy—a capacity to harmonize all experience and knowledge from an inner centre of intuitive understanding and reflective feeling.

For a woman, therefore, *Bilding* will always tend towards inner independence rather than towards self-assertion in the world outside. This does not mean—and here Schlegel must not be misunderstood—that she should resign herself to typically female pastimes, like needlework or tinkling on the piano, or that she should pursue art and philosophy with less sincerity than a man. The narrow focus of a mind trapped in domestic duties should be widened through the study of Plato, Kant and Fichte. On the other hand, it is *not* a woman's vocation to get involved in the affairs of civil society—a world that a man, however reluctantly in the case of the Romantic poet, will always have to confront.[40]

Is it at all reasonable to expect that even a generous dose of *The Critique of Pure Reason* will eventually weaken the stranglehold of domestic and political oppression? Julius, the hero in Schlegel's novel, praises in Lucinde the independence of mind and strength of character that have enabled her to defy the restrictive moral conventions of her environment. But nothing is said about the fact of her economic dependence, nothing about the nature of a society whose laws still treated women as the property of their husbands or fathers, and which made no provisions whatsoever for their education.[41]

These are, it seems, good reasons for charging the Romantic theory of self-reliant femininity with a fundamental inconsistency: while it postulates the transcendence of women's inferior position in the realm of love, sociability and *Bildung*, it takes for granted the material and legal conditions which sanction and perpetuate this inferiority. In bed, sexual roles are reversed and moral conventions toppled, but the conventions of economic and political life are left unquestioned. The fact that 'women did virtually not exist for the state' is but of little concern.[42]

Yet, if Romantic love is capable of transcending the constraints of inequality and subjugation imposed by the conventional form of marriage, why should its transformative power not reach further, into the legal and political sphere? The main protagonist in Schleiermacher's *Letters* seizes on this very point. To her, the perfect love relationship in *Lucinde* seems curiously and unacceptably impotent as regards the world outside: 'In a world where civil institutions crush women, the person who loves a woman has the duty to... enter public life and be active there'.[43] Her interlocutor admits that the novel does, indeed, abstract from civil society and its concerns: 'but because that world is so corrupt, its omission is absolutely necessary in a work of art wholly dedicated to love'.[44]

This opposition is a recurrent theme in Romantic thinking: civil society appears as the arena of petty and vulgar concerns when contrasted with a world of the individual's own *creation*. It is no accident, of course, that Lucinde and Julius are artists (painters). As it develops, the history of their love becomes more and more indistinguishable from a process of artistic creation:

At the same time as his art became more accomplished and as he succeeded in what previously (i.e. before his love to Lucinde) he had been unable to attain even with great effort and devotion—his life, too, turned into a work of art... He now saw all the different parts of his life in the right proportion and recognised the structure of the whole, because he had found the centre.[45]

In *this* world, a woman's particular capacities are not inferior. From the Romantic viewpoint, and in deviation from accepted meanings, it might even be said that her feminine qualities and talents constitute a genuinely 'political' sphere—in so far as she translates love into the 'art of sociability': 'Lucinde united and sustained this group of individuals; and gradually there evolved a free society or rather, a large family whose members remained interesting to each through their *Bildung*'.[46]

THE UTOPIA OF A FREE SOCIETY

In conclusion, we have to return to the question raised at the beginning of the paper: how central is the political sphere to the cause of women's liberation? Some interpreters of Romanticism—and this applies not only to older works written in the 'prehistory' of the women's movement—have contended that the Romantic ideal of independent womanhood goes far beyond, and is superior to, the Enlightenment's concern with equality of right and citizenship.[47] Political emancipation, it is argued, allows women only the freedom to become like men; Romantic sociability, on the other hand, envisages a situation where they can express and develop their specifically feminine qualities which will liberate men, too, from the fetters of conventional roles.

Although it underestimates the importance of *political* changes, this criticism sheds light on the specific (i.e. limited) goals that can be attained through politics. As far as the Romantic critics of dependent womanhood are concerned, they would, themselves, not have accepted the charge that their vision of the individual's liberation in love and friendship was 'unpolitical' simply because it did not aim at the state and its institutions. They took seriously, as matters of common human concern, only those political events which had a direct impact upon the personal relationships among individuals. This is why they applauded the French Revolution as long as it held out the promise of a regeneration not just of the French state but of mankind's moral condition, and why they turned away from it when they realized that it did not go beyond legal and governmental changes. They envisaged a process of change which would work in the opposite direction: the reform of society would originate in the centres of private life and would radiate outwards from relations in which individuals had attained a new self-understanding. In this sense, they saw themselves as citizens of a new world built upon the intimacy of liberated personal relations, on the one hand, and a sense of universal 'brotherhood', on the other: 'instead of an artificial society, there should only be marriage between the two estates of women and men, and a universal brotherhood of all individuals'.[48] The space normally occupied by the functions of the state did, indeed, not exist in this utopia.

The Romantic position thus differs from the commitment of reformers like Mary Wollstonecraft and Condorcet, who saw the strategic centre for women's liberation in the struggle for equal political rights. Mary Wollstonecraft believed that in order to make a convincing case for women's equal abilities and civic competence, one had to de-emphasize the importance of love (a 'tumultuous passion')—precisely because it was commonly associated with attitudes that rendered women humble and dependent on men.[49]

The Romantic strategy for liberation has, on the other hand, some resemblance with premises on which some groups in the women's movement today have entered politics. They too, want to transform the routines of the established political system—and, in a sense, the meaning of politics—by bringing the personal experience of the 'private' sphere to bear upon political activity. For instance, Petra Kelly's most recent book, *Fighting for Hope*, ends with the plea 'for an erotic society'.[50] It sees in the human capacity for love and erotic experience the most powerful 'weapon' with which to combat the life-destroying forces of the modern world.

The utopia of an 'erotic, non-violent, loving society'[51] has much in common with the Romantic ideal of love. In both cases the vision of a free society is closely linked to—indeed, made dependent upon—the liberation of women, of those persons whose particular, (and as the Romantic sees it, superior) capacity for love has been most severely curtailed under the existing system of conformity and enforced subordination. There is, furthermore, the same insistence that a revolutionary transformation of this kind cannot be enacted by political means. That is, it cannot be expected from, nor wait for, legal changes—it must begin in everyday life. Yet where the 'Romantics' of today most differ from their predecessors is in their willingness to make some concessions to the need for political participation. They are prepared, albeit with numerous reservations, to use the established political institutions for the realization of a more-than-political goal.

The Romantic thinkers discussed in this paper placed the ideal of self-reliant femininity in a political vacuum. To say that they should have adopted a more positive, activist attitude towards politics is to miss the point. Citizenship, in the Rousseauian sense, could never rank prominently amongst Romantic values, and this applies to men as well as women. But the Romantics failed to see—and this is, I think, the lynchpin in Mary Wollstonecraft's strategy—that women will not be able to realize their capacities in intimate personal relationships as long as they are not recognized as equal persons in the public sphere.

NOTES

1. Friedrich Schlegel, *Theorie der Weiblichkeit,* ed. W. Menninghaus (Frankfurt, Insel Verlag, 1983), p. 60 (my emphasis).

2. Romanticism—even if we confine ourselves to the German case alone—is a highly complex and heterogeneous movement which includes different groups and geographical centres as well as several distinct phases of development. I shall concentrate here on what one might call the core group of German Romanticism in so far as here the terms 'romantic' were placed at the centre of a new aesthetic and cultural programme. This *Jena Circle* (largely recruited from an earlier Berlin group) consisted of the following members: the brothers August Wilhelm Schlegel and Friedrich Schlegel—with their women companions/wives, Caroline Bohmer-Schlegel-Schelling and Dorothea Veit-Schlegel; Novalis; Schleiermacher, Schelling. For a group portrait constructed from biographical material (mainly correspondence), cf. G. Dischner, *Caroline und der Jenaer Kreis: Ein Leben zwischen bürgerlicher Vereinzelung und romantischer Geselligkeit* (Berlin, Wagenbach, 1799); E. Klessmann, *Caroline: Das Leben der Caroline Michaelis-Bohmer-Schlegel-Schelling, 1763–1809* (Munchen, Deutscher Taschenbuch Verlag, 1979). For the philosophical and aesthetic doctrine of early German Romanticism, cf. A. Lovejoy, 'The meaning of "romantic" in early German Romanticism', in A. Lovejoy, *Essays in the History of Ideas* (Baltimore and London, Johns Hopkins Press, 1948) pp. 183–206; 'Schiller and the genesis of German Romanticism', *Ibid.,* pp. 207–27; R. Wellek, *A History of Modern Criticism, 1750–1950.*

2. *The Romantic Age* (Cambridge, Cambridge University Press, 1981), Chapters. 1–3.

3. Caroline Schlegel, Letter of 27 December 1799, quoted in G. Dischner, *Friedrich Schlegel's Lucinde und Materialien zu einer Theorie des Müssiggangs* (Hildesheim, Gerstenberg Verlag, 1980) p. 24.

4. *The Poems and Ballads of Schiller,* trans. Sir Edward Bulwer Lytton (London and New York, Frederick Warne and Co., 1887), p. 248 f. In two instances I have changed the translation slightly.

5. Friedrich Schlegel, *Theorie der Weiblichkeit,* p. 197. His older brother, August Wilhelm, tried his hand at a parody of Schiller's 'The Dignity of Women' (the poem was never published in Schlegel's lifetime):

Friedrich Schiller	*August Wilhelm Schlegel*
Honour to Women! to them it is given	Honour to Women! They knit all those socks
To embroider life with the roses of heaven,	For men to conquer puddles and rocks.
To weave love's enchanting bonds.	They never rest mending their heroes pants.
Secure in their faithful hearts	They cook wholesome soups be it morning or night,

Rests what men waste without
            care—
Mankind's most sacred arts

From the bounds of truth
            careering
Man's strong spirit wildly
            sweeps,
With each hasty impulse
            veering
Down to passion's troubled
            deeps.
And his heart, contented
            never,
Greeds to grapple with
            the far,
Chasing his own dream
            for ever,
On through many a distant
            star.

They dress pretty dolls for the
            children's delight
And thriftily handle the kitchen
            money
But man, the clumsy fellow,
Has no taste for such delicate
            virtues.
He smokes a big pipe
While his beer-mug he nurtures.
Grumbling like a bear tied to
            a chain
He nags at his offspring but
            for ever in vain.
At night, then, in bed
He at once turns his back
On his sweet little wife.

Cf. *The Poems and Ballads of Schiller,* p. 230 f. (I have changed the translation of the first stanza); August Wilhelm Schlegel's parody is quoted in Friedrich Schlegel, *Theorie der Weiblichkeit,* p. 197 f.

6.   Friedrich Schlegel, letter to August Wilhelm Schlegel, 31 October 1797, quoted in G. Dischner, *Caroline und der Jenaer Kreis,* p. 95. The journal in question is the *Athenaum,* the first issue of which appeared in May 1798.

7.   Cf. G. Dischner, *Caroline und der Jenaer Kreis,* p. 96.

8.   Cf. *Ibid.,* pp. 81–152; E. Klessmann, *Caroline,* pp. 176–212; *Frauenbriefe der Romantik,* ed. K. Behrens (Frankfurt, Insel Verlag, 1981), pp. 247–370. Good examples for the conversational and 'sociable' construction of Romantic theorizing are Friedrich Schlegel, 'Gesprach uber die Poesie' (1799), *Kritische Schriften,* ed. W. Rasch, (Munchen, Carl Hanser Verlag, 1956), pp. 183–339, and F. Schleiermacher, *Vertraute Briefe über Schlegel's Lucinde* (Frankfurt, Insel Verlag, 1964), pp. 91–164.

It should be noted that the women members of the Romantic group did not address themselves *publicly* to the question of women's emancipation as a general social problem. What they thought can only be gleaned from the writings of their male companions.

9.   Friedrich Schlegel, *Kritische Schriften,* p. 108.

10.   W. von Humboldt, *Werke, Vol. 1* (Stuttgart, Cotta, 1960), p. 80.

11.   *Ibid.,* p. 64. For the general context of Humboldt's aesthetic and political ideas, see P.R. Sweet, *Wilhelm von Humboldt: A Biography, Vol. 1* (1978); J.W. Burrow, 'Introduction to Wilhelm von Humboldt' in *The Limits of State Action* (Cambridge, Cambridge University Press, 1969), pp. i to xiiii; U. Vogel, 'Liberty is beautiful: von Humboldt's gift to

liberalism', in *History of Political Thought, Vol. 3 no. 1* (Jan. 1982), pp. 77–101.

12.   Quoted in Sweet, *Wilhelm von Humboldt*, p. 162.

13.   Cf. Humboldt, *Werke, Vol. 1*, pp. 80 ff., 162 f. (English text in *Limits of State Action*, pp. 30 f., 95).

14.   Humboldt, *Limits of State Action*, p. 95. For Mill's comment see J.S. Mill, *On Liberty* (London, Dent, 1972), pp. 158–9.

15.   Humboldt, *Werke, Vol. 1*, pp. 64 f., 268, 349.

16.   *Ibid.*, pp. 79 f., 334 f., 375; also Kluckhohn, *Auffassung der Liebe*, pp. 263–66.

17.   *Ibid.*, p. 331 f.

18.   *Ibid.*, p. 80.

19.   *Ibid.*, pp. 79 f., 368.

20.   Humboldt, *Werke, Vol. 1*, p. 335. Kluckhohn, *Auffassung der Liebe*, p. 266, comments that, in the last instance, Humboldt judged the female character by those qualities which are particularly valuable *for* men.

21.   'Über die weiblichen Charaktere in den griechischen Dichtern' (1794); 'Über die Diotima' (1795), in Friedrich Schlegel, *Theorie der Weiblichkeit*, pp. 11–38, 39–84.

22.   *Ibid.*, p. 14.

23.   *Ibid.*, p. 55.

24.   *Ibid.*, p. 39 ff., 51.

25.   *Ibid.*, pp. 59–65. Schlegel holds Rousseau responsible for having 'strung together an infinite number of common platitudes into a coherent doctrine of femininity in which nonsense was so well presented that it could not fail to meet with general applause', *Ibid.*, p. 129.

26.   *Ibid.*, p. 59.

27.   *Ibid.*, pp. 60, 91 f.

28.   *Ibid.*, p. 61.

29.   *Ibid.*, pp. 67 f., 60 f.

30.   A good example is T.G. von Hippel, *Über die bürgerliche Verbesserung der Weiber* (1793) (Frankfurt, Syndicat, 1977). This was perhaps the most radical defence of women's equal rights advanced in Germany at that time.

31.   G. Dischner, *Friedrich Schlegel's Lucinde*. In his doctoral dissertation of 1922, Ludwig Marcuse took this scandal as prime evidence in reconstructing the 'history of indignation': L. Marcuse, *Obszön, Geschichte einer Entrüstung* (München, 1962), pp. 63–115.

32.   Friedrich Schlegel, *Lucinde*, p. 12.

33.   F. Schleiermacher, *Vertraute Briefe über Schlegel's Lucinde, Ibid.*, p. 104 ff. Schleiermacher refers to an English governess and her typically English indignation—'Good heavens, how dare you talk about suspenders in the presence of women!'—as a source of constant amusement in the Romantic circle. See also Friedrich Schlegel, *Theorie der Weiblichkeit*, p. 72.

34.   Friedrich Schlegel, *Lucinde*, p. 10.

35.   Quoted in Kluckhohn, *Auffassung der Liebe*, p. 462.

36.   Friedrich Schlegel, *Lucinde*, p. 10. For Schleiermacher, see Kluckhohn,

Auffassung der Liebe, p. 347 f.

37.   Schleiermacher, *Vertraute Briefe,* p. 152.

38.   *Ibid.,* p. 158.

39.   Friedrich Schlegel, *Theorie der Weiblichkeit,* p. 88. These ideas are to be found in a later essay (written in the same year as *Lucinde),* 'On philosophy. For Dorothea' (1799), *Theorie der Weiblichkeit,* pp. 85–119.

40.   *Ibid.,* p. 96.

41.   On the legal condition and subjugation of women in Germany at that time, cf. R. Huebner, *A History of Germanic Private Law,* trans. F.S. Philbrick (London, John Murray, 1918), pp. 620–23; 632 f., 648 f. For the deplorable state of women's education, see F. Giese, *Der romantische Charakter,* p. 8 ff.

42.   *Ibid.,* p. 9.

43.   Schleiermacher, *Vertraute Briefe* in Friedrich Schlegel, *Lucinde,* p. 110.

44.   *Ibid.,* p. 161.

45.   *Ibid.,* p. 63.

46.   *Ibid.,* p. 64.

47.   G. Dischner, *Friedrich Schlegel's Lucinde,* pp. 21, 26. A similar defence of Humboldt's non-political views has been offered by Sweet, *Wilhelm von Humboldt, Vol. 1,* p. 169: the case for equal rights (?), he claims, 'is very much present in Humboldt's . . . essays, though they are far from being pamphleteering broadsides for women's liberation such as some of his contemporaries were writing'. The editor of von Hippel's 'On the Civil Improvement of Women', on the other hand, explains the oblivion which this radical and rationalist plea for women's emancipation has suffered for more than 150 years and the curious lack of interest on the part of feminists by the fact that Hippel's commitment to the theory of natural rights did not allow him to make any concessions to the fashionable belief in typically *feminine* qualities and virtues: cf. von Hippel, *Von der bürgerlichen Verbesserung der Weiber.* The tendency of the older literature, of which Kluckhohn's excellent study offers a good example, was to stress the superiority of the Romantic conception of woman's 'inner independence' over the demand for mere external (i.e. superficial) freedom of citizenship. See Kluckhohn, *Auffassung der Liebe,* pp. 116 ff.

48.   Friedrich Schlegel, *Lucinde,* p. 70.

49.   Mary Wollstonecraft, *A Vindication of the Rights of Woman,* ed. M. Kramnick (Harmondsworth, Penguin Books, 1975), p. 110 f. See also Condorcet, 'On the admission of women to the rights of citizenship' (1790), in *Selected Writings,* ed. K.M. Baker (Indianapolis, Bobbs Merrill Company, 1976), pp. 97–104.

50.   P. Kelly, *Fighting for Hope,* trans. M. Howarth (London, Chatto and Windus, 1984), pp. 111–118.

51.   *Ibid.,* p. 113.

5 Women and the Hegelian State

Joanna Hodge

Hegel explicitly excludes women from political life in his treatise on politics, *The Philosophy of Right* (1821). This appears to leave no room for questions about the rights of women in his political theory. Nevertheless attempts have been made to discuss the position of women in politics, using elements of Hegel's political analysis. These attempts can take two forms. Minimally, Hegel's analysis attributes to women a valuable and indispensible contribution to human society, quite distinct from the contribution of men. Thus Jean Bethke Elshtain (1981) has argued that Hegel's rigorous separation of spheres between women and men permits an affirmation of the values of selflessness and familial loyalty, traditionally embodied by women.[1] Carol B. Landes,[2] attempts to mobilize Hegel's authority in support of a liberal feminist analysis, claiming the centrality of rights in political theory, as opposed to a radical feminist analysis of patriarchy. She suggests that Hegel's threefold distinction between the ethical life of the family, the public sphere of economic production and legal regulation, and the political sphere, the state, puts in question 'the contemporary radical feminist assertion that the exercise of male power occurs in an identical fashion in family and society'.[3] Hegel's questioning of a historical theorizing makes the radical feminist assertion look still more dubious. However, this use of Hegel's work to defend liberal against radical feminist analysis can be complemented, as this paper will show, by detecting radical feminist themes in Hegel's work.

Long before radical feminists declared men to be the enemy, Hegel had declared women to be the enemy of the community.

He writes in *The Phenomenology of Spirit* (1807):

Since the community only gets its existence through its interference with the happiness of the family, and by dissolving individual self-consciousness into the universal, it creates for itself in what it suppresses and what is at the same time essential to it an internal enemy—womankind in general. [p. 288]

Hegel thus identifies the interests of women with the interests of the family, rejecting without discussion the possibility that women, like men, might have interests, both individual and collective, which are not identical with those of families. He construes women exclusively as a collective, making it impossible for him to conceive of women acting in any way other than in the defence of the family's collective interests. As the defenders of family interests, women become for Hegel the enemy of the public, political community. Thus, like Christine Delphy,[4] he identifies women as a class, with nothing but a collective claim over the spheres of public and political life, which he conceives as reserved for men.

Hegel's work is just one example out of many in the Western, European tradition of political theory, which has not concerned itself with the interests of women.[5] In this tradition, the interests of European men have been treated as the interests of the whole of humanity. This renders the tradition inimical to women and to non-Europeans, who refuse to accept honorary male, European status. It is possible, however, to radicalize Hegel's political theory and to bring this lack of concern into question. Hegel seeks to chart the realization of reason and freedom in the history of the world. He writes in the introduction to his *Lectures on the Philosophy of World History* (1830): 'World history is the progress of the consciousness of freedom, a progress which it is our business to comprehend' (p. 54). If that progress is seen to require the opening of the public and political spheres to all, including women, then Hegel's reservation of these spheres for male Europeans can be recognized as a historically specific constraint on freedom, which can be transcended in subsequent epochs. His political analysis can be radicalized then to extend the consciousness of freedom to groups, like women, which Hegel excluded.

Hegel's exclusion of women from political life, from history and from society generates a series of tensions in his political analysis. These tensions can be identified by following through his account of the relations between women and men in *The Philosophy of Right*. The tensions result directly from an ahistorical conception of a difference between women and men, which Hegel conceives as fixed and unchanging, even though it is a part of a historical dynamic, and despite his own rejection of ahistorical theorizing. Identifying these tensions reveals the exclusion of women from politics as disruptive of Hegel's own theory. This makes it possible to claim that the extension of the consciousness of freedom to women is in line with his own project of enquiry. Indeed here the critique of political theory turns into the critique of existing social conditions, in this case the oppression of women. Identifying these weaknesses in Hegel's theory makes it clear that it is the attempt to rationalize the actual exclusion of women from political and cultural life which generates those weaknesses. In order to improve the theory it is necessary to criticize that actual state of affairs. It is the ease of this conversion from theoretical to practical critique in political theory, which makes it liable to censorship. Hegel's work was threatened by the state censor; feminist theory is threatened by attempts to domesticate it, suppressing the disruptive claims of radical feminist analysis in favour of the more acceptable results of liberal feminism.[6] Hegel's changing analysis of the figure of Antigone, in Sophocles' play, brings the difference between the liberal and the radical critique of the disenfranchisement of women sharply in question.[7] The change between the analysis of Antigone offered in *The Phenomenology of Spirit* and in *The Philosophy of Right* suggests alternate accounts of the connection between abstract rights and gender position, and the alternative strategies of liberal reform and radical critique. This paper will move then from identifying the tensions in Hegel's political analysis, to discussing the confrontation between ethical woman and political man in the story of Antigone, and will conclude by pointing the contrast between the radical and the liberal feminist critiques of political theory. There are four main points of tension in Hegel's account of the relation between women and men in *The Philosophy of Right*: in his conception of marriage and legal status; in his conception of education and of educability; in his conception of work and in his conception of property ownership and access to legal process. These four tensions are all connected one to the other, but must be discussed in sequence.

THE PHILOSOPHY OF RIGHT: LEGAL PERSONS AND ETHICAL LIFE

Hegel takes up Rousseau's defence of children's rights over against parental authority from *The Social Contract* (1762). He writes thus in *The Philosophy of Right*:

Children have the same rights to maintenance at the expense of the family's common capital. The rights of the parents to the service as service of their children is based upon and is restricted by the common task of looking after the family generally. Similarly the right of the parents over the wishes of their children is determined by the object in view—discipline and education. The punishment of children does not aim at justice as such; the aim is more subjective and moral in character, i.e. to deter them from exercising a freedom still in the toils of nature and to lift the universal into their consciousness and will. [p. 117]

The contrasting terms 'the wishes of their children' and the 'will' liberated from the 'toils of nature' are, in German, *Willkür* and *Wille*, Kant's terms for the arbitrary will and the rational will, according with the requirements of universal reason. Hegel's account of education therefore seeks to show how a connection might be made between Kant's two conceptions of the will, which Kant leaves unconnected. Hegel seeks to show that through education children reconstruct their arbitrary whims into a capacity to will rational ends.

In the following paragraph, Hegel quotes Rousseau's *Social Contract* almost word for word. Rousseau writes in *The Social Contract*: 'even if man could alienate himself, he could not alienate his children: they are born men and free; their liberty belongs to them and no one but them has the right to dispose of it' (bk 1, sect. 4). Hegel writes in *The Philosophy of Right*: 'Children are potentially free and their life directly embodies nothing save potential freedom. Consequently they are not things and cannot be the property of either their parents or others' (p. 117). Unlike Rousseau, Hegel does not go on to give an account of a differential education process, treating girls and boys differently. In *Émile*, Rousseau takes four chapters to describe the education of a young man, discussing in the fifth and final chapter the devices required to make his chosen wife, Sophie, conform to the following pattern: 'The man should be strong and active; the woman should be weak and passive; the one must have the power and the will. It is enough that the other should offer little resistance. When this principle is admitted, it follows that woman is especially made for man's delight' (bk 5, p. 2).[8] In paragraph 177 of *The Philosophy of Right*, Hegel describes the educational process thus, with no suggestion of different treatment for girls and for boys:

The ethical dissolution of the family consists in this, that once the children have been educated to freedom of personality and have come of age, they become recognised as persons in the eyes of the law and as capable of holding free property of their own and founding families of their own, the sons as heads of new families, and the daughters as wives. [p. 118]

There are conflicting strands in this remark, which produce the first of the tensions in Hegel's political analysis. Hegel seems to suggest that both sons and daughters develop personalities through education, and, on coming of age, become capable of founding new families and holding property. However, it is the sons who become the heads of the new families. Thus a seemingly egalitarian system of education gives rise to an evidently unequal result. The stages by which this occurs can be traced by laying bare the connections between the four points of tension in the analysis.

Marriage for Hegel, as opposed to Kant, is not another form of contractual relation, open to negotiation and modification. It is an absolute relation, involving the surrender by both parties of the individual personalities which they have formed through education. Through that surrender in marriage, the resulting entity, the family, becomes the most basic element in human life. According to Hegel, in *The Philosophy of Right*, the family is both the first ethical relation and, in addition, it constitutes the legal person: 'It is not merely property which a family possesses; as a universal and enduring person, it requires possessions specifically determined as permanent and secure, i.e. it requires capital' (p. 116). This distinction[9] between property and capital is not so important as the claim that the family requires them both, to make it 'a universal and enduring person'. Both wife and husband are thus subsumed in a relation more important than themselves, both surrendering their personalities,[10] but their relations to the resulting legal entity are significantly different. It is the man who becomes the representative of the family in law: 'The family as legal entity in relation to others must be represented by the husband at its head' (p. 116). Hegel states his view of marriage thus:

In essence, marriage is monogamy, because it is personality—immediate, exclusive individuality—which enters into this tie and surrenders itself to it; hence the tie's truth and inwardness (i.e. the subjective form of its substantiality) proceeds only from the mutual and wholehearted surrender of this personality. Personality attains its rights of being conscious of itself in another only in so far as the other is in this identical relation as a person, i.e. as an atomic individual. [p. 115].

Thus it sounds as though two equal people transform their abstract personalities into substantive self-consciousness through the mutual recognition and mutual surrender involved in marriage. This, however, is not the case. Personality according to Hegel is the abstract capacity to exercise and claim rights and recognition, which, when realized, constitutes being a person. This Hegel discusses in the Introduction and first part of *The Philosophy of Right*, in the section on abstract right: 'Personality essentially involves the capacity for rights and constitutes the concept and basis (itself abstract) of the system of abstract and therefore formal right. Hence the imperative of right is "Be a person and respect others as persons" ' (p. 37). Since Hegel's conception of personality is introduced in connection with the legal domain from which women are subsequently barred, women would seem to be excluded from being bearers of personality. Only in the legal domain is mutual respect grounded in objective relations. There would then seem to be no possibility of an objectively grounded mutuality between women and men in marriage. The legal status of marriage, indeed, takes on a peculiarly oppressive character, granted that one of the parties, the woman, is not herself permitted to enter the legal domain in her own right. Thus Hegel himself brings the status and substantiality of marriage into question. Nevertheless, he expects monogamy and lifelong marriage to be the norm. There is then a second tension here between the mutuality and reciprocity in marriage, which Hegel requires to ground the importance of the relation, and the privileges which he seeks to reserve for men.

These two conflicting impulses compel Hegel to distinguish between the kinds of personality attributable to women and to men. Only the personalities of men are such as to permit the evolution of a legal person with rights and duties. Hegel suggests that these differences in kind are the result of natural endowment and are not arbitrarily brought about by a differential educational process. In *The Philosophy of Right* Hegel affirms a fundamental distinction between women and men in the following remark: 'Further marriage results from the free surrender by both sexes of their personality, a personality in every possible way unique in each of the parties' (p. 115). This could be read simply as an attempt to avoid genetic defects from inbreeding, which Hegel does go on to discuss. However, this suggested uniqueness of the surrendered personalities is referring back to a metaphysical difference between women and men, which Hegel introduces on the preceding page. There, he first invokes natural, biological differences and then seeks to derive both rational grounds and rational consequences from them:

The difference in the physical characteristics of the two sexes has a rational basis and consequently acquires an intellectual and ethical significance. This significance is determined by the difference into which the ethical substant-iality, as the concept, internally sunders itself, in order that its vitality may become a concrete unity consequent on this difference. [p. 114]

Hegel is thus providing an alternative account of the ground for the substantiality of marriage. The concept of ethics divides itself into two elements, embodied in women and in men, which then come together again in marriage, forming an indissoluble bond. Individuals may deceive themselves into thinking that their marriages rest on reciprocity and mutual surrender. In objective terms, marriage is grounded, according to Hegel, in the complementarity of the two elements joined together; it is grounded in the difference between the two kinds of personality, not in mutuality and similarity.

Hegel, along with most theorists, apart from Christine Delphy, assumes that natural, biological difference must generate social difference. She puts the assumption thus in her introduction to the recently published English translation of some of her essays: 'the fact that humans reproduce sexually and that males and females look different contains within itself not only the capacity but also the necessity of a social division, albeit the social form varies greatly. The very existence of genders—of different social positions for men and women (or more correctly for females and males)—is thus taken as given and as not requiring explanation' (Delphy, p. 25)). Hegel's rewriting of natural sex difference as social, intellectual and ethical gender difference is thus not unusual. It permits him to assign strongly contrasting social roles and ethical values to women and to men, as completely distinct groups and, as Delphy points out, it permits him to suppose there to be no need for explanation or justification. It is, however, quite clear in whose interests this rewriting lies, and indeed only an androcentric thinker, such as Hegel, could have failed to consider how obvious this is, from the stance of the position assigned to women. Hegel's rewriting runs thus:

Thus one sex is mind in self-diremption into explicit personal self-subsistence and the knowledge and volition of free universality, i.e. the self-consciousness of conceptual thought and the volition of the objective final end. The other sex is mind maintaining itself in unity as knowledge and volition of the substantive, but knowledge and volition in the form of concrete individuality and feeling. In relation to externality, the former is powerful and active, the latter is passive and subjective. [*Philosophy of Right*, p. 114]

The 'other' is of course the female sex; and here Hegel exactly reproduces Rousseau's distinction between women as weak, passive and feeling; men as powerful, active and self-willed.

Hegel supposes that marriage brings about the reunification of two complementary elements of ethical substance. Substance, according to the section on essence in Hegel's *Science of Logic* (1817), is made up of the identity of being and of the flux of accidents within that identity; the immediate identity of being, attributed in ethical substance to the female sex, takes over the character of accidentality, while the flux of accidents attributed to the male sex, is 'the absolute form-unity of accidentality, substance as absolute power' (p. 556). Thus while at first glance the immediate unity of being, the unified mind in the form of concrete individuality and feeling, might seem to be the stronger, preferable mode, it is in fact the split mind, with its flux of accidents, which has the potential to turn into 'absolute power'. This second mode of being is dirempted, or split, into arbitrary individual will, and the universality of goals of rational action. This makes agency possible and gives the bearer the ability to influence the external world. The split mind is then the stronger mode, since it permits agency and influence, movement and self-development, as opposed to the static absence of development in the other mode, attributed to women.

The split mode is attributed to men, who realize their arbitrary individual wills in civil society, while their character as bearers of the universal goals of rational action finds expression through their participation in the state. In civil society, Hegel writes in paragraph 207 of *The Philosophy of Right*: 'A man actualises himself only in becoming something definite, i.e. something specifically particularised: this means restricting himself exclusively to one of the particular spheres of need' (p. 263). The 'other' sex, women, may be posited as immediately self-identical, since for Hegel there is no question but that women are destined to give birth to children, to look after them and to manage the household. Hegel supposes that women never confront choices, nor make decisions. Thus for Hegel there is no split for women between individual inclination and rational choice. He is thus compelled to ignore the need for an explanation of why Antigone chooses to defy her uncle and bury her brother, while her sister Ismene chooses not to. Hegel supposes women to be incapable of self-development. He supposes that women benefit from education, but not from the higher more creative forms. In the addition to paragraph 166, the following clarification of women's educability is to be found: 'Women are capable of education, but they are not made for the activities which demand a universal faculty, such as the more advanced sciences, philosophy and certain forms of artistic production. Women may have happy ideas, taste and elegance, but they cannot attain to the ideal' (p. 263). Thus Hegel is protected against women, who might object to his account. If women hit on the 'happy idea' that there is something unsatisfactory about his assumption that women do not make decisions; or on the idea that the rigidity of the distinction between the sexes is forced; or on the idea that there is something arbitrary and self-interested in assigning the structure with the most possibilities to men, and those with the least to women, the objections can be dismissed in advance as the products of an overly particular understanding, lacking the selfless universality of male idealism.

Hegel outlines the social and political positions reserved for women and for men thus:

It follows then that man has his actual substantive life in the state, in learning and so forth, as well as in labour and struggle with the external world and with himself, so that it is only out of this diremption that he fights his war to self-subsistent unity with himself. In the family, he has a tranquil intuition of this unity and there he lives a subjective and ethical life on the plane of feeling. Woman, on the other hand, has her substantive destiny in the family and to be imbued with family piety is her ethical frame of mind. [*Philosophy of Right*, p. 114]

Thus, men engage in struggle with the external world, in order to overcome the division within themselves, which is the consequence of their split mode of being. They fight a war with themselves in order to achieve self-unity. They fight wars with each other in order to defend the fragile unity of their states. The unity of the state becomes a symbol for the self-divided man's possibility of self-unity. Thus the willingness to fight and die for king and country becomes explicable as the will to retain at the level of the state that unity which has not yet been achieved at the level of the individual. As far as men are concerned, the family is a source for 'a tranquil intuition' of self-unity. Hegel makes no such claim for women's experience of the family. Indeed, he goes straight on from this remark about men's engagement in struggle and warfare to refer to his earlier discussion of Antigone in *The Phenomenology of Spirit*. This discussion suggests that while men may imagine the family to be a tranquil refuge from the struggles and warfare of the world, for women the family is precisely the domain in which we encounter that struggle and labour.[11] Antigone, who follows what she understands to be a divine law, enjoining the burial of her brother, runs into conflict with the human law of her uncle, King Creon, who orders no burial in punishment for her brother's defiance. For Antigone there is no convenient separation of spheres, through which her feelings, her personal ambitions and her sense of abstract right can be mediated through the threefold division of family, civil society and state.

This conflict between women and men in terms of a conflict between divine and human law reappears in more prosaic form in *The Philosophy of Right*, in connection with work and property rights. Work, legal regulation and the public recognition of particular collective interests through guilds and corporations all lie in the sphere of civil society, into which, according to Hegel, women do not enter. Thus Hegel supposes that women do not work; he supposes that no work takes place in the domestic sphere. This is the third point of tension in the analysis. Conversely, women are barred from taking part in legal process and cannot seek legal redress in their own right; women cannot form corporations, to represent a collective interest against the other interests competing in civil society, or against the sphere of the state: in short a collective interest against men. Women are thus prevented from disputing the arrangements, through which women are disadvantaged.

The connections between work, education and political participation, and between work, property and legal participation, make the exclusion of women from work crucial to the mechanisms whereby women are excluded from the public and political spheres. The master–slave dialectic in *The Phenomenology of Spirit*, discussed by Judith Shklar in *Freedom and Independence: A Study in the Political Ideas of Hegel's 'Phenomenology of Mind'*,[12] indicates the importance Hegel attributes to work in the process of realizing freedom in the world. Working, fighting and philosophizing are three of the human activities through which, for Hegel, the process of moving to self-determination away from natural instinct is accomplished. Women are rigorously excluded from all three. Women are thus excluded from the educational benefits which Hegel suggests arise from engaging in them:

The multiplicity of objects and situations which excite interest is the stage on which theoretical education develops. This education consists in possessing not only a multiplicity of ideas and facts, but also a flexibility and rapidity of mind, ability to pass from one idea to another, to grasp complex and general relations and so on. It is the education of the understanding in every way and so also the building up of language. Practical education acquired through working consists first in the habit of simply being busy; next in the strict adaptation of one's activity according not only to the nature of the material worked on, but also and especially the pleasure of other workers; and finally in a habit produced by this discipline of objective activity and universally recognised aptitudes. [*Philosophy of Right*, p. 129]

All these benefits, as far as Hegel is concerned, are reserved for men. In addition, theoretical education, through which the individual acquires the grasp of language required for full participation in legal and political process, is also denied to women. Women are thus even denied the means of articulating discontent with the social order, in which they are subject and oppressed.

Hegel here denies that women might benefit from more advanced education. He refuses to recognize that work takes place in the domestic sphere. He thus refuses to recognize that activities in that sphere make an indispensible contribution to the well-being of the family. When he discusses family property in *The Philosophy of Right*, he construes it as exclusively the concern of the husband as head of household. By juxtaposing the man's role as representative of the family in the legal domain and the man's duty to go out into civil society to work, Hegel conceals the necessity to argue for the proposition that the man should control property:

The family as a legal entity in relation to others must be represented by the husband at its head. Further, it is his prerogative to go out and work for its living, to attend to its needs and to control and administer its capital *(Vermögen)*. This capital is common property so that while no member of the family has property of his own, each has his right in the common stock. This right however may come into collision with the head of the family's right to administration, owing to the fact that the ethical temper of the family is still only at the level of immediacy and so is exposed to partition and contingency. [p. 116]

This right to administer the collective property is converted into a right of alienation, through the ingenious device of suggesting that only the man contributes to its formation and preservation. Hegel gives a detailed account of the way in which the contribution the man makes both to the family's resources and to the resources of the community in general depends on the individual man's particular skills, and in part on chance circumstances:

A particular man's resources, or in other words his opportunity for sharing in the general resources, are conditioned, however, partly by his own unearned principal (his capital) and partly by his skill; this in turn is itself dependent not only on his capital, but also on accidental circumstances, whose multiplicity introduces differences in the development of natural, bodily, and mental characteristics, which were already in themselves dissimilar. In this sphere of particularity, these differences are conspicuous in every direction and on every level, and together with the arbitrariness and accidents which this space contains as well, they have as their inevitable consequence disparities of individual resource and ability. [p. 130]

Thus variations in the fortunes and wealth of families is made to depend solely on the variations in the skill and fortune of the male head of household. By implication, there is no difference between the contributions of women in their various households. Indeed, since women remain in the domestic sphere of immediate self-unity and do not enter the civil society in which differentiation occurs, it is hard to see how Hegel could admit the possibility of difference between women. Women's contribution to the family's well-being is taken to be a constant and therefore, for some unstated reason, to be wholly insignificant.

The family has two forms of possession: property, or *Eigentum*, and competence, or *Vermögen*. The identity of the family as a legal person, represented to other such units in the legal domain by the husband, is based on this ethical moment in the development of this competence for the common good:

It is not merely property (*Eigentum*) which a family possesses; as a universal and enduring person, it requires possessions specifically determined as permanent and secure, i.e. it requires capital (*Vermögen*). The arbitrariness of a single owner's particular needs is the one moment in property taken abstractly; but this moment, together with the selfishness of desire is here transformed into something ethical in the labour and care for a common possession. [p. 116]

Hegel states quite explicitly that 'the introduction of permanent property is linked with the introduction of marriage' (p. 116). Thus those inclined to doubt the justice and value of the one institution are advised by Hegel to doubt the justice and value of the other. While Hegel suggests that the arbitrariness and selfishness of 'a single owner's particular needs and desires' may be converted into an ethical 'labour and care for a common possession', he is also quite clear that the converse is also possible; the common possession can be transformed into an object of the selfish owner's particular desires and needs:

The result of the disintegration of the family is that a man may at will either squander his capital altogether, mainly in accordance with his private caprices, opinions and ends, or else look upon a circle of friends and acquaintances, etc. as if they were his family and make a will embodying a declaration to that effect, with the result that they become his legal heirs. [p. 119]

Thus the supposedly collective possession of the family is collective just so long as the husband, the legal representative, chooses it to be so. Since the wife is, as woman, excluded from the state and from civil society, she cannot resort to law to protect her interest in the property, nor can she campaign to change the system whereby she has no such resort. This is the fourth tension in Hegel's account of the relations between women and men; the four together make that account decidedly unsatisfactory.

NATURAL WOMAN, SOCIAL MAN: THE FIGURE OF ANTIGONE

The tensions in Hegel's analysis are not however confined to the detail of the relations between women and men in communities. They are also evident at the more abstract level, in the relation between natural determinism and self-determination, and in the relation between the natural and the social. The connection between these two more abstract relations and the relations between women and men emerges clearly in the transition from *The Philosophy of Nature* to *The Philosophy of Mind*, the second and third parts of Hegel's systematic presentation of his theories in the *Encyclopaedia of the Philosophical Sciences* (1830). Human beings for Hegel are the highest and most complex form of natural life. They are also the basic element in the realization of reason and freedom in the history of the world. Thus by making women the representative of nature and men the representative of mind, or spirit, Hegel seeks, through his account of marriage and the relations between women and men, to bind together the domains of nature and of spirit. He conceives of these two domains as quite distinct and as structured in quite different ways. The domain of nature is one of cyclical repetition, in which elements lie juxtaposed and disconnected. The domain of spirit is one of cumulative development, in which the elements are mutually dependent and interconnected, one to the other. The less complex relations making up the domain of nature become identifiable and understandable through the use of the richer resources made available in the domain of spirit.

Hegel is keenly aware of the paradoxes arising from attempts to set up a strong opposition between the natural and the social. In his *Lectures on the History of Philosophy* (1833–36), the following ambiguity in Hobbes's conception of nature is identified: 'The expression "nature" has this ambiguity, that the nature of humans is spirit and reason; but their natural condition is another state: that in which humans conduct themselves according to natural instinct' (p. 288). This split between human nature as reason and spirit and human nature as natural instinct subverts appeals to a 'natural order' as an origin for social order, since the appeal is ambivalent between human nature as rational and human nature as instinctual. This opposition between reason and instinct underlies Kant's distinction between the rational will, *Wille*, and the arbitrary individual will, *Willkür*. The full title of Hegel's *The Philosophy of Right* is *Natural Law and the Theory of the State in Outline: Elements of a Philosophy of Law*. The juxtaposition of terms conveys part of the point of the enquiry: neither abstract natural law theory nor an analysis of actual political institutions can be conducted in isolation from the other. The analysis of political institutions must be informed by abstract theory, while abstract natural law theory must be shown to bear on actually existing political institutions. Thus

The Philosophy of Right moves through a discussion of abstract right theory, and of abstract morality, in order to arrive at an analysis of human communities, of public life and of the state.

As far as Hegel is concerned, it is the nature of human beings to convert natural needs into socially constructed desires, to convert natural necessity into a necessity of their own making. Human beings take their natural endowment and construct out of it a 'second nature'. Since human beings play such a focal role in the mediation between the domains of nature and of spirit, between the natural and the social, this ambivalence in the status of human beings, as natural and as self-determining, subverts any attempt to make a complete separation between the natural and the social. As far as Hegel is concerned, for human beings, the natural and the social are not sufficiently distinct for proposals about the founding of one in the other to be either plausible or illuminating. He argues for this substitution of humanly created need for natural necessity thus:

Since in social needs, as the conjunction of immediate natural needs with mental needs arising from ideas, it is needs of the latter type which, because of their universality, make themselves preponderant, this social moment has in it the aspect of liberation, i.e. the strict natural necessity of need is obscured and man is concerned with his own opinion, indeed with an opinion which is universal and with a necessity of his own making alone, instead of with an external necessity, an inner contingency and mere caprice. [*Philosophy of Right*, p. 128]

This conversion of natural necessity into social need is a central feature of Hegel's account of history as the progress of the consciousness of freedom. As this conversion proceeds, so human beings become more free.

Hegel connects this conversion and the increase of human freedom to the liberating effects of work thus;

The idea has been advanced that in respect of his needs, man lived in freedom in the so-called 'state of nature' when his needs were supposed to be confined to what are known as the simple necessities of nature, and when he required for their satisfaction only the means which the accidents of nature directly assured to him. This view takes no account of the moment of liberation intrinsic to work. [p. 128]

The opposition which Hegel seeks to establish between nature and freedom, and the suggestion that nature is in some sense dependent on spirit emerges in what follows: 'to be confined to mere physical needs as such and their direct satisfaction would simply be the condition in which the mental (*Geistigkeit*) is plunged in the natural and so would be one of savagery and unfreedom, while freedom itself is to be found only in the reflection of mind into itself, in mind's distinction from nature, and in the reflex of mind in nature' (p. 128). Freedom thus presupposes a separation of mind from nature, the development of a self-reflexive relation in mind, and the recognition that mind is present in nature, in a way that nature is not present in mind. Hegel goes on to criticize attempts to set up a natural order as a standard by which to criticize the existing social order. He sums up the criticism thus: 'The basis of all these views is the fashionable idea of a state of nature and a natural origin for rights, and the lack of the concept of rationality and freedom' (p. 116). He here parts company with Rousseau. Hegel is similarly severe with respect to the idealism of Kant, which sets up an ideal rational standard, without showing in any way how that rational standard comes to bear on actual social and historical conditions.

Hegel's objection to Kant, developed in many contexts with moral and metaphysical variants, is that Kant deploys categories, without explaining their derivation, in an attempt to describe a reality, to which they bear no relation. Hegel argues that such categories are unhelpful for political analysis and incorrect philosophically. In Hegel's view, categories do not subsist independently of the reality they describe, but interact with it, and indeed play a role in the production of that reality. It is for this reason that Hegel is termed an idealist, and on this basis that Hegel supposes it to be possible to describe reality. Hegel argues that theoretical abstractions must continually be complemented through an analysis of what they have so far failed to address. Thus conceptions of natural law fail to address historical change, and Hegel seeks to complement them with a sense of historical process. Analogously, ahistorical conceptions of 'human nature' and of a fixed and unchanging difference between women and men would seem to require complementation through an analysis of specific social and historical conditions. Hegel criticizes Kant for constructing theoretical abstractions and then convincing himself that they provide an analysis of actual conditions. A case in point for Hegel is Kant's account of 'perpetual peace', of which Hegel writes thus in *The Philosophy of Right*: 'Kant had an idea for securing 'perpetual peace' by a League of Nations to adjust every dispute. It was to be a power recognized by each individual state, and was to arbitrate in all cases of dissension in order to make it impossible for disputants to resort to war in order to settle them' (p. 214). Hegel points out that this idea presupposes what it seeks to guarantee: 'This idea presupposes an accord between states; this would rest on moral or religious or other grounds and considerations, but in any case would always depend ultimately on a particular sovereign will and for that reason would remain infected with contingency' (p. 214). Hegel's distinction between women and men seems to fall under the same censure in presupposing what it seeks to establish: the inappropriateness of permitting women to enter the spheres of public and political life. Moreover, that distinction presents a social relation, which is open to the influence of human beings and is thus alterable, as fixed and unchanging.

Hegel questions the naturalization of legal and social relations by which the changeable and alterable are passed off as fixed and unchanging. Human beings for Hegel are distinguished from other creatures just by this capacity to influence their circumstances and to transform a natural endowment through intellectual endeavour. However, in his discussion of Antigone, in *The Phenomenology of Spirit*, Hegel suggests that Antigone's peculiarity by comparison with the citizens of Thebes is her unquestioning acceptance of the primacy of familial loyalty and of the requirement to respect and bury the dead. Unlike a man, Hegel suggests, she accepts these values as given, instead of questioning them and thereby establishing her own transcendence: 'If I enquire after their origin and confine them to a point whence they arose, then I have transcended them; for now it is I who am universal, and they are the conditioned and limited' (p. 261). For Hegel, it is only men who are thus able to transcend given values, and are thus in a position to generate replacements. On the basis of this difference, Hegel goes on to suggest that there is a difference between the status to be accorded the desires of women and of men:

The difference between the ethical life of the woman and that of the man consists just in this, that in her vocation as an individual and in her pleasure, her interest is centred on the universal and remains alien to the particularity of desire; whereas in the husband these two sides are separated, and since he possesses as a citizen the self-conscious power of universality, he thereby acquires the right of desire, and at the same time preserves his freedom in regard to it. [p. 274–5]

Thus Hegel suggests that, because men are citizens, with an ability to identify with the universal interests of the state, they also have the capacity and the right to form desires and to expect their fulfilment. These two are, as far as Hegel is concerned, interdependent. It is then plainly in the interests of men to prevent women from becoming citizens, for women would thereby also acquire this right and capacity, in direct competition with men.

It is through education, both as informal upbringing and as formal instruction, that the human capacity to question and to transform existing conditions is stimulated and directed. It is through work, theorizing and fighting that Hegel supposes the difficult transition from natural determinism to self-determination to take place. It is thus highly significant that Hegel seeks to exclude women from all three activities. Women's supposed inability to profit from the more advanced forms of education, which Hegel seeks to reserve for men, indicates Hegel's belief that women are not capable of moving from the domain of nature and of determinism to that of self-determination in society. He judges women's nature to be one-sided: natural instinct prevails, untempered by reason and spirit. Women are thus judged to be less than fully human. It is this series of judgements which render women irrelevant to the development of freedom and reason in Hegel's system; to the progress of the consciousness of freedom; to history; and unimportant for political theory. It is this series of judgements which make women hostile to the community, in which that consciousness of freedom supposedly progresses.

In *The Philosophy of Right*, Hegel first of all observes the obvious biological differences between women and men. He then goes on to posit intellectual and ethical differences, as both consequence and cause of those biological differences. He licenses this move through a general theory about the structure of nature as a simplified refraction of the structure of mind, or spirit. He then projects these biological and intellectual differences onto the distinction between the naturally fixed and the socially changeable, reducing women to natural fixity and men to social changeability. He thus draws a distinction in one domain, translates it into another and then projects them both into a third, in order to justify and generate the different roles and expectations which he assigns to women and to men. He can then show that these roles and expectations actually occur in experience, as they must, while the social order is constructed in such a way as to reproduce them. The result is to make changeable social relations appear to be fixed and natural. As a result, he forces both women and men into fixed and unchanging stereotypes, although even in his account the men at least might be expected to change the limits of their activities. He reduces women and men to instances of fixed essences: women are bound to a repetitious cycle of reproduction; men to the unending dynamic of social undertakings. Hegel suggests that, because the natures of women and of men are fixed for all time, the difference between them is also so fixed. There is, however, a tension between supposing the difference between women and men to be fixed, while the relations between them, in society and in history, alter. The alterability of the relations between women and men Hegel cannot deny.

The relations between women and men are governed so far as Hegel is concerned by the division of human society into three spheres: the domestic, the legal and the economic, and the political. Hegel recognizes that introducing a sphere between the domestic and the political is innovatory with respect to Greek political theory. It marks a distinction unknown to Greek theory between a domestic sphere of human reproduction and an economy of material production. Recognizing such a distinction reduces the domain of the household from that of the domestic and economic to that of just the domestic. It therefore reduces the space within which women are confined. The condition of women is thus drastically affected by the introduction of this third term, even though that term is introduced in the domain of high theory to which women do not, according to the theory, have access. Changes in social arrangements have effects on women, even if women are not involved in bringing those changes into being. Thus the supposedly asocial domain of the family is affected by changes in the public and political spheres, bringing into question the firmness of the distinction between them. The domain in which women are confined is thus open to change and therefore the condition of women changes. The relations between women and men must also change as a result of the introduction of the third intermediate sphere. Therefore there are grounds for dismissing both Hegel's insistence on the fixity in women's nature, as opposed to the alterability in that of men, and for dismissing his insistence on this rigid, unchanging difference between women and men.

In *The Philosophy of Right*, Hegel appears to be theorizing the transition from an estate based, agrarian economy, to an industrial, commerce-orientated economy. This transition changes the nature of property relations and alters family consumption patterns, from mainly self-produced, to market purchase. The possibility of alienating estates and acquiring funds with which to undertake commercial ventures clearly changes the relation between families and their property. Property ceases to be held in trust by the present holders from their ancestors for their descendants; the family ceases to be constructed out of many generations. Hegel indeed suggests that the individual family, in early modern society, dissolves when the children grow up and marry, setting up their own families. Similarly, Hegel suggests that the institution of familial authority is disrupted by the inception of civil society. Such dissolution and disruption is inconceivable for the non-nuclear, inter-generational family. Only a nuclear family dissolves at the death of the head of the household.[13] Familial authority can be challenged by that of civil society only when civil society has taken over the role of the family as the primary source for protection and advancement. Thus Hegel writes in *The Philosophy of Right*:

But civil society tears the individual away from his family ties, estranges the members of the family, one from another, and recognises them as self-subsistent persons. Further, for the paternal soil and the eternal inorganic resources of nature from which the individual family derived its livelihood, it substitutes its own soil and subjects the permanent existence of even the entire family to dependence on itself and to contingency. Thus the individual becomes a son of civil society, which has many claims upon him as he has rights against it. [p. 148]

The move from dependence on the paternal soil to dependence on the metaphysical soil of civil society is for Hegel a move in line with the increase of freedom through the replacement of natural necessity by socially constructed needs. It is, however, only the sons of the family who become the sons of civil society. Women have completely dropped out of the analysis.

While Hegel seeks to draw conclusions for all time about women and men, and about the difference between them, the conceptions of the family, and of property, with which he works are historically specific and apply to only one section of the population—those who own property. His proposed separation of spheres and the various arbitrary moves already identified in the analysis of *The Philosophy of Right* thus culminate in an account of a relation between women and men which is both historically and class specific. Hegel fails to show that the processes of history, conceived as the realization of freedom and reason in the world, require and justify the strong assumptions about the difference between women and men which he makes.

He shows only arbitrary discrimination in a particular historical context. He seeks to justify the immobilization of women in a diminishing familial space by lining women up with the landlocked static existence of agrarian economies, with their unchanging natural cycle, and men with the seafaring, dynamic mobility of commerce and industry, with alterable social relations. Women are connected by Hegel to family life and the soil; men to civil society, commerce and the sea: 'The principle of family life is dependence on the soil, on land, on *terra firma*. Similarly the natural element for industry, animating its outward movement, is the sea' (*Philosophy of Right* p. 151). Women are supposed not to reach out beyond themselves; men are engaged in active struggle with the outside world, as a sign of their rationality and capacity for intellectual growth. This encounter with the external world is highly significant in Hegel's system. The transition between *The Philosophy of Nature* and *The Philosophy of Mind* is accomplished precisely through a change in the relation between entities and what is at first conceived as external to them.

In *The Philosophy of Right*, Hegel compares the difference between women and men to that between plants and animals: 'The difference between men and women is like that between animals and plants. Men correspond to animals while women correspond to plants because their development is more placid and the principle that underlies it is the rather vague unity of feeling' (p. 263). This bizarre remark can be explicated with the assistance of the introduction to *The Philosophy of Mind*:

Even in the plant we see a centre, which has overflowed the periphery, a concentration of the difference, a self-development from within outwards, a unity which differentiates itself and from its differentiation produces itself in the bud, something therefore to which attribute an urge *(Trieb)*; but this unity remains incomplete because the plant's process of articulating itself is a coming-forth-from-self of the vegetable subject, each part is the whole plant, a repetition of it, consequently the organs are not held in complete subjection to the unity of the subjecty [p. 9–10]

The animal, by contrast, is forced into opposition to a nature external to itself. This opposition generates an interminable series of conflicts and contradictions, which is cut off only by the death of the individual animal. The animal cannot construct for itself a non-contradictory relation between itself and the world outside itself. For entities in the domain of nature, other entities remain irretrievably other and external: 'The differences into which the notion of nature unfolds itself are more or less mutually independent existences; true, through their original unity they stand in mutual connection, so none can be comprehended without the others; but this connection is in a greater or lesser degree external to them' (p. 9). By contrast, entities in the domain of spirit, or mind, construe and alter the relation between themselves and others, thus making these relations internal and alterable, not external and unchanging:

Therefore, even the most perfect form to which nature raises itself, in animal life, the notion, does not attain to an actuality resembling its soul-like nature, to complete victory over the externality and finitude of existence. This is first achieved in mind, which, just by winning this victory, distinguishes itself from nature, so that this distinguishing is not merely the act of external reflection about the nature of mind. [p. 11]

Hegel thus seeks to distinguish between the processes of differentiation which take place in the domain of nature, and the processes which take place in the domain of spirit. The suggestion is that women remain trapped in the repetitious and undirected processes of natural differentiation, and only men move to the more sophisticated processes of differentiation in the domain of spirit. However, the distinction between nature and spirit is not external to the nature of mind, or spirit, but internal to it. Thus Hegel renders the domain of nature dependent on that of spirit. This result is central to Hegel's account of history as the progress of the consciousness of freedom.

Human beings become more free and more aware of freedom as a result of being able to draw more and more of what lies outside them under their influence, drawing away from natural determinism towards greater self-determination. Hegel supposes that it is men, as embodiments of animality, who are able to do this, through their ability to go out into the world, to change themselves and to recognize what seems to be external as subject to influence. Women, as immobile plant life, remain bound by the constraints of nature, unable to control even their own extremities. Confining women in the family is then for Hegel merely a way of recognizing the difference between the capacities and structures of women and of men, providing women with the sense of self-delimitation which men acquire by trying to realize their aims in the world. Critical reading, however, reveals that this confinement plays a crucial role in keeping women immobile and incapable. By confining women in the family, Hegel reserves change and development, self-improvement and the immortality of fame, for men. He excludes women from social life, from politics, from history and from freedom. The other side of this manoeuvre is that he reserves nature and cyclical repetition for women. This brings with it the dangers associated with detaching men from nature and from reproduction, outlined by Susan Griffin in *Pornography and Silence* (1981). Men become alienated from nature and hostile to the body, to sexuality and to women, with whom they then go on to identify nature, the body and sexuality. Wishing to control their own natures, bodies and sexuality, they therefore seek to control women. Denying their own naturalness and their own bodies, they therefore seek to deny their own mortality. This refusal to recognize human corporeality and mortality makes it easier for men to conceive of sacrificing human life for the sake of abstractions, such as the unity of the state, in which they find consolation for the disunity so graphically presented by Hegel as the human condition. Thus death is put in place of the dangerous naturalness of life. It is then not just women who lose out by being confined in the family sphere, to nature and to reproduction—men lose out too. Women are reduced to mindless mothers and men to heartless killers.

Hegel's political theory is rescued from such a banal reduction by the ambiguous figure of Antigone.[14] In *The Phenomenology of Spirit* Hegel discusses at length Antigone's role in defending the divinely ordained familial virtues of loyalty and respect for the dead, against the arbitrary civil powers of her uncle, Creon. There the emphasis is on the duty of a sister to a brother: Hegel writes, 'The loss of the brother is therefore irreparable to the sister and her duty towards him is the highest' (p. 275). Hegel refers to this discussion in *The Philosophy of Right*, in which he shifts the emphasis, without comment, from the relation between sister and brother to that between wife and husband. He there expounds familial piety as demonstrated in Sophocles's *Antigone*:

as principally the law of the woman, as the law of a substantiality, at once subjective and on the plane of feeling, the law of the inward life, a life which has not yet attained its full actualisation, as the law of the ancient gods, 'the gods of the underworld', as 'an everlasting law, and no man knows at what time it was first put forth. [p. 114]

Having identified this law as the law of woman, Hegel then refers to the opposition set up in the *Phenomenology*: 'This law is there displayed as a law opposed to public law: to the law of the land. This is the supreme opposition in ethics and therefore in tragedy; and it is individualized in the same play in the opposing natures of man and woman' *(Philosophy of Right,* p. 116). Even in the longer discussion in the *Phenomenology,* however, Hegel overlooks features of Antigone's situation which rather suggest that she is the representative of the rule of law, and Creon a law-breaker. She is defying the arbitrary whim of the tyrant king; she dares to set up a universal standard by which to judge his actions. She furthermore pays for her defiance of the public law by being walled up alive, as women are walled up alive in the family in Hegel's theory. She dares to escape that punishment by taking her own life, an act of civil disobedience quite unlike the death of Socrates. She thus becomes a figure of resistance representing freedom as opposed to tyranny, reason as opposed to arbitrary rule, and most of all, resisting the oppression of women by men.

In the *Phenomenology,* Hegel is seduced into recognizing Antigone as an agent, who transforms the ethical terms on which people engage. He accepts that Antigone acted knowingly:

the ethical consciousness is more complete, its guilt more inexcusable, if it knows beforehand the law and the power which it opposes, if it takes them to be violence and wrong, to be ethical merely by accident, and, like Antigone, knowingly commits the crime. The accomplished deed completely alters its point of view, the very performance of it declares what is ethical must be actual. [p. 284]

Even here, then, in a text specially chosen by Hegel to present his views on the ethical difference between women and men, he cannot confine women to the role of the passive delighter of men. On a level of greater abstraction, the opposition between woman as bearer of the ethical order of the family and man as legal person in civil society, cannot be sustained as absolute, since for Hegel these two incomplete parts—ethical life and legality—must be reunified in the state. Hegel seeks to show that just as women and men are two parts of a single unity, which is brought into being through marriage, so ethical life and legality are two parts of a single unity, which is brought into being in particular states. In *The Philosophy of Mind,* Part 3 of his *Encyclopaedia,* he proposes this reunification in the state of family life and civil society; of ethical life and legality; of feeling and will:

The state is the self-conscious ethical substance, the unification of the family principle with that of civil society. The same unity, which is the family as a feeling of love, is its essence, receiving however at the same time through the second principle of conscious and spontaneously active volition the form of conscious universality. [p. 263]

Gillian Rose discusses the complexities of this reconciliation of ethics and law in the state in *Hegel contra Sociology* (1981). Here it is sufficient to note that Hegel fails to question whether he has provided for a reconciliation of the interests of women and of men. Despite this reconciliation at the abstract level, he does not waver in his exclusion of women from the public and political spheres. In *The Philosophy of Right*, he even excludes women from playing a symbolic role in public life; as far as he is concerned, the monarch has a purely symbolic function: 'In a well organized monarchy, the objective aspect belongs to the law alone, and the monarch's part is merely to set to the law the subjective "I will" ' (p. 289). Nevertheless, Hegel earlier takes the trouble to remark on the inappropriateness of letting women rule: 'When women hold the helm of government, the state is at once in jeopardy, because women regulate their actions not by the demands of universality but by arbitrary inclinations and opinions' (p. 264). Women for Hegel are the slaves of feeling and emotion, quite unable to form plans and to take action. Thus the will is for Hegel bound up with being a man, and to permit women to represent the will in the political domain is to disrupt his carefully constructed separation of spheres and capacities.

In *The Philosophy of Right*, Hegel discusses the abstract categories of legal theory and of moral reasoning in advance of his discussion of gender position and of the supposed difference between women and men. Thus female readers need not dissent from his argument until at the beginning of the section on ethical life, where the confinement of women in the family, the lowest form of ethical life, is introduced. Since abstract rights, property, contract and crime, are discussed in advance of the assignation of gender roles, it is possible to suppose that rights and duties are only modified by, and not subject to gender position, and that the assignation of gender roles might be modified in order to permit both men and women to exercise rights and make claims on other people. Similarly, while Hegel attributes very different ethical stances to women and to men, they can both be conceived as having available to them the considerations of abstract morality discussed in the second section, in advance of the differentiation between women and men, introduced at the beginning of the third. This order of presentation suggests a possible reconstruction of Hegel's political analysis, permitting women to take part in public life and in politics, and permitting men to identify with childrearing, if they so desire. It makes it possible to conceive of altering the gender position assigned to women, to permit women to have citizen status. [15] Such a reconstruction must also produce an account of why women have failed either to make such claims in the past or to make good such claims in the past, and will thus tend to reproduce Hegel's cumulative model of the history of the world, as progressive.

The *Phenomenology* presents the issues in a different order. The confrontation between Antigone and Creon, between the law of the ancient gods and the public law of the king's word, is introduced at the point of transition from the analysis of reason, observing nature, achieving rational self-consciousness and becoming purposive, to the discussion of spirit. Hegel reserves until later the discussion of legality and morality. It is at this point that Hegel argues individual reason to be dependent on social and historical context. Rational individuals must at this point be distinguished into female and male. Hegel draws a distinction between the ethical lives of women and of men, and then goes on to discuss abstract morality and legality as pertaining only the ethical lives of men. Thus Hegel excludes women from the following discussion of legality and morality at the same time as he excludes women from the domains of the social and the historical. This doubling of exclusions is more consistent with his questioning, in general, of ahistorical theorizing. For Hegel, ethics and the law occur only in specific social and historical contexts. Thus to be excluded from history and from society is to be excluded from morality and legality. He thus excludes women from playing any part in the realization of reason in history. Only men can enjoy legal status and engage in moral reasoning. Thus the very possibility of exercising rights and the capacity to discuss what rights might be depend in the *Phenomenology* on previously assigned gender position. In order to permit women to engage in these two activities and to become citizens, Hegel's system of assigning gender position has to be brought into question. A radical critique of male privilege and theoretical special pleading is made necessary.

It becomes necessary to ask why such systems of gender privilege are so frequently proposed without argument by theorists such as Hegel. If those systems are just and reasonable, then of course conclusive arguments for the privilege might be sought; but if it is plain that the exclusion of women from public and political life is arbitrary and unjust, then it becomes urgent to ask why for so long theorists, whose justice and wisdom is not generally in doubt, should have erred so consistently on this issue. The radical feminist answer to this question is succinct: it is not in men's interests to permit women to participate in public life, and it is not in their interests to discuss their own will to exclude women; therefore, male theorists exercise themselves to produce false justifications for that exclusion, sometimes at the cost of internal consistency, and make efforts to deflect criticism of those false justifications. Thus, in response to Hegel declaring women to be the enemy of the political community, radical feminists declare political theory and its theorists to be the enemy of women. The rigorousness with which Hegel attempts to secure the exclusion of women from public and political life makes that exclusion all the more susceptible to Hegel's own strategy of inversion, as outlined in the section on the inverted world, in the *Phenomenology*.[16] All the properties attributed to one side of the opposition must be attributed to the other side of the opposition, and the inverse, to see more clearly the implications of the proposed theory. The resulting confinement of men to the family, and the reservation to women of the positing of value, of law, philosophy and state service looks like a radical feminist utopia, bringing into question existing gender roles. Hegel's work then can be used to show that it is Hegel, and political theory, not women, who are the enemy of the progress of reason and history in the world, since it is they who, against reason and justice, deny justice and reason to women.

NOTES

I should like to thank Lyndal Roper, David Norbrook, Susan Mendus, Ellen Kennedy and especially Patricia Duncker for criticism and support in the course of writing this paper; Charles Taylor and Michael Theunissen for encouraging me to take Hegel on in the first place.

1.   Jean Bethke Elshtain, *Public Man, Private Woman* (Princeton University Press, 1981). Her overall aim is to strengthen the private, familial sphere, as a defence against the bad effects of the public sphere. In her concluding chapter, she writes, 'To affirm a vision of the private-familial sphere as having its own dignity and purpose is to insist that particular experiences and spheres of social relations exude their own values and purposes, and have ends not attainable by, or within, other spheres. To assert the continued necessity of such relations and a particular notion of their reconstructed vitality is to recognize that we are all impoverished if all of life falls under a single set of terms' (p. 334–35). Also, Bethke Elshtain (p. 333) seems to suggest that the values of the 'private-familial sphere' can subvert the inadequate values of the public sphere. In either case, she refuses to accept the argument that the values of the private sphere are in fact produced in the public sphere. For her discussion of Hegel's political philosophy, see Part 1, Chapter 4 'Politics and social transformation. Rousseau, Hegel and Marx on the Public and the Private', particularly pp. 170–83.

2.   Carol B. Landes, 'Hegel's conception of the family', in *The Family in Political Thought* (Harvester Press, 1982) ed. Jean Bethke Elshtain, pp. 125—145.

3.   *Ibid*, p. 125.

4.   See Christine Delphy, *Close to Home: A Materialist Analysis of Women's Oppression*, trans. Diana Leonard (Hutchinson, 1984): 'I use the term 'class' to refer to the division between men and women' (p. 25). Shulamith Firestone begins her famous radical feminist analysis *The Dialectic of Sex* (1970) in the following way: 'Sex class is so deep as to be invisible.'.

5.   Susan Moller Okin begins her challenging survey, *Women in Western Political Thought* (Virago, 1980), with the following claim: 'It must be recognized at once that the great tradition of political philosophy consists, generally speaking, of writings by men, for men and about men' (p. 5).

6.   Feminists working within the academy who ignore or ridicule the critiques of radical feminists lose the invigorating effects of a feminist theory less constrained by the considerations of tact and tactics, over against established disciplines, syllabi and colleagues.

7.   Gillian Rose, in *Dialectic of Nihilism* (Blackwell, 1984), also identifies the disruptiveness of the figure of Antigone in Hegel's analysis: 'the suffering of Antigone, sister and citizen, stands out as the question of the relationship between philosophy, justice and individual identity' (p. 6). As far as Hegel is concerned, of course, Antigone is sister, but not citizen.

8.   For an eighteenth century critique of Rousseau's educational programme, see Mary Wollstonecraft: *A Vindication of the Rights of Woman* (1792).

9.   For a useful discussion of ambiguities in Knox's translation of these terms, see Landes' article in Elshtain (ed.), p. 130.

10.   Moller Okin suggests in a footnote (p. 341, n. 5) that the man's surrender of personality is 'more symbolic than real'. While her suspicion is well-founded, this formulation of it misconstrues Hegel's conception of personality. For Hegel, personality is an abstraction, which, when embedded in a system of mutually recognized rights and duties, is transformed into the substantial state of being a person.

11.   Moller Okin remarks, 'Since women are not perceived as having any distinct life or interests at all, it is not difficult for Hegel to perceive the family as a place from which all discord and conflict of interest is absent, and where love and altruism reign supreme' (p. 285). Once the woman's stance is made central, however, this apparent absence of discord and conflict of interest is brought in question.

12.   This perceptive book is curiously silent on questions of concern to feminists, both liberal and radical.

13.   See Shulamith Firestone *The Dialectic of Sex,* Chapter 4: 'Down with Childhood' for a discussion of the invention of childhood and the transformation of the intergenerational family from a 'legal heredity line' into a 'conjugal unity' (p. 75).

14.   For an alternative criticism of interpreting Hegel's political philosophy reductively, stressing the anthropological writings and moral relativism of the Lectures on the Philosophy of World History, see Susan Easton, 'Functionalism and feminism in Hegel's political thought', *Radical Philosophy* 38. She writes, 'his work reveals an awareness of the cultural mediation of gender roles, which presents a challenge to reductionist theories' (p. 4).

15.   A serious obstacle to the liberal feminist reconstruction of Hegel's argument is the connection between bearing arms, being a soldier and being a citizen. While the frontier between military and non-military life becomes increasingly ill-defined, and the necessity for muscle in the performance of a soldier's duty weakens, there nevertheless remains a strong resistance to the participation of women in the armed forces on equal terms with men. As in the case of the ordination of women, one of the threatened groups resisting change is made up of the wives of the men who are soldiers and clergymen. Such a division between the interests of women is to be expected, according to radical feminist analysis. For a discussion of the resistance to women serving on equal terms in the armed forces, see Cynthia Enloe, *Does Khaki Become You? The Militarisation of Women's Lives* (Pluto 1983).

16.   See the section 'Force and Understanding', in Part 3 of the section on 'Consciousness' (pp. 79—104).

HEGEL: SELECTED WORKS

The Phenomenology of Spirit, trans. A.V. Miller (Oxford University Press, 1977)

The Science of Logic, trans. A.V. Miller (Allen and Unwin, 1969)

The Philosophy of Right, trans. T.M. Knox (Oxford University Press, 1952)

The Philosophy of Mind being Part 3 of *The Encyclopaedia of the Philosophical Sciences,* trans. W. Wallace and A.V. Miller (Oxford University Press, 1971)

Lectures on the Philosophy of World History: Introduction, trans. Nisbet; Intro. by Duncan Forbes (Cambridge University Press, 1975)

Lectures on the History of Philosophy (Suhrkamp Werke Bd. 20, 1971)

6 Utilitarianism and Feminism

Lea Campos Boralevi

Utilitarianism is not only compatible with feminism: historical feminism was, it is argued here, produced by classical utilitarianism. The relationship between them can be traced along three dimensions. First, utilitarianism was a positivist and empirical philosophy that ignored a question which had inflamed argument for centuries: do women have souls? In doing so it excluded one important intellectual justification for the subjection of women. Second, the principle of utility assumed a fundamental equality in the structure of human psychology. Women as well as men, according to this theory, have interests which should be taken into consideration. Finally, the psychological axioms of utilitarianism provided the intellectual and ideological background of feminism and offered a general view of human nature and social life compatible with the political goals of historical feminism.

THE MORAL NEWTONIANS

The key concepts and terms employed by utilitarianism are 'pain' and 'pleasure'. These are fundamental units constituting the happiness of individuals and of communities of individuals whose interests must be calculated on the criterion of the greatest happiness of the greatest number. Quantities of individual and general happiness are added and subtracted by means of the *felicific calculus*, which constitutes the fundamental operation of *moral arithmetic*. These concepts and terms enjoyed wide circulation in eighteenth-century Europe, for a variety of reasons which cannot be considered in detail here. Briefly, utilitarianism exerted what has rightly been called

159

'epistemological appeal'.[1] In fact, it should be remembered that many enlightened thinkers attempted to remedy Descartes' greatest 'failure' and to realize the old dream of transforming the study of ethics into a science. Through their practical applications, the natural sciences had given new power to the human capacity to transform the surrounding world so that it might satisfy human needs. In a time when mankind had just started to explore these new possibilities, without being yet touched by doubts concerning their destination and utilization, the highest goal was (and is still) the assimilation of moral sciences (what we would nowadays call social sciences) to the natural sciences' model, with special reference to the Newtonian model which had profoundly impressed public opinion of that time.

The attempt to do for the moral sciences what Newton had done for the natural sciences was expressed in different contexts by a great number of philosophers from David Hartley and Hume, to Adam Smith and even Immanuel Kant. It characterised a whole era.

From this point of view, the 'epistemological appeal' of utilitarianism can be explained, first of all, by the possibility it offered of gathering *all* the phenomena of the moral world under a single principle—*the principle of utility*—an enterprise which seemed to provide a direct analogy with Newtonian physics, which reduced all physical phenomena to the single *principle of gravitation*. Utility became thus the great, unifying 'scientific' principle under which all human behaviour could be studied.

Second, Newtonian physics had shown that the existence of rational and universal laws governing nature could only be discovered by observation and experiment, and that religious and metaphysical speculation played no part in the description of empirical reality. Most philosophers of the Enlightenment believed that the study of man could become a new kind of natural science, based on empirical experiment and observation.[2] The principle of utility thus allowed its users to create a new science of man and of society, starting from sensible experience—that is, from sensations of *pain* and *pleasure*, and from 'matters of fact' which were empirically verifiable, such as 'benefit and mischief'—rather than grounding ethical and anthropological assertions on hypostasized, abstract principles.[3]

Third, the newly discovered possibility of measuring pain and pleasure opened the way to the introduction into ethics of quantification which, at that time no less than in our own, was held to be the principal guarantee of its scientific claims. The mathematically based system of ethics was called *moral arithmetic*, and it claimed to be able to compute the different amounts of pleasure and of happiness experienced by men in differing circumstances. From Francis Hutcheson[4] to Hartley, from Beccaria and Helvetius to Jeremy Bentham (who coined the term 'felicific calculus') these moral Newtonians[5] shared the conviction that a mathematical calculus, associated with an 'experimental method', relying only on 'facts' testified by experience, could be applied to the study of 'morals': 'what counts as human happiness was thought to be...a scientifically establishable domain of facts'.[6] This need for quantification also gave birth to one of the most widespread formulations of the principle of utility—the formula of *the greatest happiness of the greatest number*[7].

In comparison with other theories of that time, utilitarianism seemed able not only to guarantee a descriptive approach but also to support a normative principle—a guide to human actions. In other words, utilitarian theories did not only explain why men perform certain acts, it also showed, or at least purported to show, which acts should be performed and which not. By analogy with the natural sciences, which allowed men to enlarge their dominion over Nature in Baconian terms, the new moral sciences should have opened up a new era of social progress: 'Correspondent to *discovery* and *improvement* in the natural world, is *reformation* in the moral', Bentham affirms triumphantly in the Preface to his *Fragment on Government.*[8]

On these methodological premises, the principle of utility allowed ethics, law and politics to be founded on earthly happiness. It made possible therefore the liberation of law and politics from the 'moral prejudices' of natural law, and the liberation of ethics from the domain of religion, with its goal of non-earthly happiness. These arguments provide the link that always binds morals to legislation and administration (politics and economics) in all utilitarian doctrines. Utilitarians were not 'philosophers meditating upon Being and non-Being, but men actively engaged in framing political platforms and carrying on popular agitations'.[9] Man as a social being is the centre of their attention, because happiness—this kind of happiness—cannot be achieved outside of a mutual dependence of men upon each other, in a constant interdependence of ethics and politics, which will cause them never to dissociate moral meditation from political and social action.

Utilitarianism places morals and legislation on the same footing, since both are founded on the principle of utility, and their existence denies any possible superiority to morals or to natural law. Furthermore, natural law is not only denied superiority over positive law, but it is also deprived of its validity from a moral point of view, since it ignores the fundamental units of 'scientific morality'; that is, the 'physical' concepts of pleasure and pain. On these grounds Bentham and Godwin, following Hume, could reject any kind of 'original contract'. For Bentham, indeed, obedience to the sovereign is not founded on the formality of a promise, but on the substantial calculation of 'benefit and mischief' (that is 'of pleasure and pain') deriving from obedience and from resistance respectively.[10] So, whereas each person is engaged in seeking his own happiness, and is the best judge of his own interests, the function of government is to achieve the most general goals, of which individuals alone are not capable, and above all to ensure the greatest happiness of the greatest number, even for those who are not able to pursue their own interests, or for those who do not know them.

Law—positive law—is the great instrument of power. The greatest happiness of the greatest number can be achieved only through good—that is, 'scientific'—legislation, based on a scientific knowledge of man and society, and directed towards the attainment of the greatest happiness. Already for Helvetius, the legislator is a pedagogue, a moralist, as morals and legislation are 'une seule et même science'.[11] Thus, having rejected all psychological theories based on nativism, Helvetius, Bentham and most of the other utilitarians believed in a social conditioning that could be accomplished through education (for children) and legislation (for adults). The true legislator in fact must not only limit himself to codifying already existing habits, his main task is to show the way to be followed in accordance with the principle of utility. For this reason the reform of legislation was of the greatest importance in all the utilitarians' eyes. And for this reason Bentham spent most of his life writing new codes and defining the principles on which all future codes should be reformed. For this reason, finally, the philosophical radicals fought their greatest battles for the reform of existing legislation.

UTILITY AND EQUALITY

The new image of man presented by classical utilitarians, and the reforms of society they proposed, concerned women directly. The principle of utility, used as a fundamental means of explaining human behaviour, had to be applied to the whole of mankind. According to Newtonian physics, the validity of a principle was directly connected with its *generality*. Just as the principle of gravitation was applicable, and was to be applied, to all physical bodies, so the principle of utility had to be applied to all human beings, including women, children and slaves. Women constitute 'One Half the Human Race'[12] and could not be excluded without seriously jeopardizing the validity of such a principle. Since women could experience 'pain and pleasure', there was no reason to doubt that they could also 'maximize pleasure and minimize pain'.

As a point of departure at least, therefore, utilitarianism is egalitarian in so far as it postulates a fundamental equality of psychological structure in all human beings.[13] Women could not only experience pains and pleasures, they also had 'interests' which had to be taken into consideration. Whether women had souls or not, or whether they were less intelligent or less rational than men was not relevant, at least as far as the consideration of their interest was concerned.

Jeremy Bentham, trying to extend his system of 'universal benevolence', went even further, and claimed that:

The French have already discovered that the blackness of the skin is no reason why a human being should be abandoned without redress to the caprice of a tormentor. It may come one day to be recognized, that the number of the legs, the villosity of the skin, or the termination of the *os sacrum*, are reasons equally insufficient for abandoning a sensitive being to the same fate. . .the question is not, Can they *reason*? nor, Can they *talk*? but, Can they *suffer*?[14]

Suffering and happiness, or pain and pleasure, are the only 'objective' data on which moral sciences—including 'morals' and 'legislation'—could be founded. If these fundamental, 'objective' units of data served even the cause of animals for Bentham, this was all the more evident with women, who incontestably belonged to mankind. If there were good reasons for protecting animals from wanton maltreatment, there were a hundred more reasons for asking for a change in the condition of women, which was, in J. S. Mill's famous words, a state of *subjection*, due to the 'tyranny' of the male sex over the 'softer sex'.[15] The adoption of the principle of the greatest happiness of the greatest number thus also entailed the calculation of the happiness of that half of the population which is female. Such a calculation necessarily implied that a woman's happiness was held to count as much as and not less than the happiness of any man in a given society.[16]

The way in which women's happiness was thought to be obtained differed slightly from one utilitarian thinker to the other, but utilitarians were all fundamentally and positively concerned with the happiness of women. This concern was not only different from Ancient Greek and Roman thinkers, in whose societies autonomous legal personality was given to the *pater familias*, a man with his family, including children, women, slaves and servants. It was also different from modern philosophers, such as Locke and Rousseau, who tried to give an autonomous personality to single *individuals* excluding women, or better, including women's interests in those of the men to whom they were closely related—fathers, brothers, or husbands. In this light, the famous formula 'everyone to count for one, and no more than one' can be read as the *manifesto* of utilitarian feminism: *everyone*—each man and each woman—has *his/her own interests*, which are not necessarily compatible with those of others, and therefore have to be taken into consideration as single units of the general happiness of any society. Utilitarianism brings women 'to count for one'—not as fractions of one.

For this reason Bentham—whom I consider to be the father of historical feminism—always spoke out clearly in favour of the autonomy that was to be guaranteed to women's legal personality, and against all existing laws which denied it: the statute book of the *Pays de Vaud*, in which 'the testimony of two women or girls shall be equal and neither more nor less than equal to that of a man'[17] is certainly archaic, but it was in principle no worse than the existing English legislation, which excluded the evidence of a wife against her husband (and *vice versa*) before a tribunal court. The 'implacable dissension' and the disruption of 'the peace of families' were simple pretexts offered by legislators: 'The reason that presents itself as more likely to have been the original one, is the grimgribber, nonsensical reason—that of the identity of two persons thus connected'.[18] For this reason only could such a law be conceived, by analogy with that which excluded the testimony of a party to the cause, for or against himself.

Besides its implications for legal procedure, the conception of woman's autonomous legal personality had two main consequences: divorce and the vote. Divorce and women's enfranchisement belong respectively in the private and public spheres, and are founded on the presupposition that women have their own interests, which can be incompatible with men's. Divorce and the vote recognize and protect the interests of women outside and independent of their relationship with men.

The social reforms which were proposed by the utilitarian thinkers therefore entailed fundamental changes in the conditions of women. Legislation had to be reformed in the name of utility and of the greatest happiness of the greatest number, including women in that number: legislation therefore had to be reformed towards a more favourable consideration of women's interests. To use Bentham's words, the 'reformation of the moral world' had to bring about an improvement in women's conditions. From a more general point of view, the emancipation of women from their slavery would have eliminated a cause of suffering and a hindrance to the enjoyment of happiness for half the human race, thus augmenting the general amount of happiness in society.

John Stuart Mill also used this purely Benthamite argument, illustrating the added happiness deriving to society from the difference between 'a life of subjection to the will of others, and a life of rational freedom'.[19] His main point was more 'Millian', however, though still in the path of utilitarianism: the emancipation of women would have contributed to the 'improvement of society' as a whole, by 'doubling the mass of mental faculties available for the higher service of humanity',[20] by creating the stimulus of female competition and by creating at home 'a school of sympathy in equality which would have developed in children the true virtue of human beings, fitness to live together as equals'.[21]

Furthermore, according to utilitarianism, earthly happiness could no longer be given up or postponed in the name of a future, non-earthly happiness. No matter what religion and traditional morals say, women should enjoy the same quantity of earthly happiness as men:

On the ground of the greatest happiness principle...The happiness and interest of a person of the female sex, constitutes as large a portion of the universal happiness and interest, as does that of a person of the male sex. No reason can be assigned, why a person of the one sex, should as such, have less happiness than a person of the other sex. Nor, therefore, whatsoever be the external means of happiness why a female should have a less portion of those same means...If the possession of a share in the constitutive power[22] be a means of securing such equal share of the external means of happiness, the reason in favour of it, is therefore at least as strong in the case of the female sex, as in the case of the male.[23]

In other words women's enfranchisement does not only provide them with legal and moral autonomous personality but also bestows on them an 'equal share of the external means of happiness'—political power. By promising or refusing their vote, women can force legislators to show more consideration for their interests.

Women's natural inferiority is only a pretext, 'a reason alleged' for justifying the 'tyranny which has been exerted by the male sex over the female'. Were it not a pretext, but a true cause, women's natural inferiority would have resulted in different legislation, favouring rather than discriminating against the weaker sex:

> If there be any difference, it ought to be in favour of the weakest—in favour of the females, who have more wants, fewer means of acquisition, and are less able to make use of the means they have. But the strongest have had all the preference. Why? Because the strongest have made the laws.[24]

The principle of utility is not only the criterion on which future legislation ought to be built, but is also the criterion for all existing legislation. From Helvetius to Bentham, down to Godwin and J.S. Mill, utilitarians asserted the fundamental importance of social conditioning. Social inequality, Helvetius argued, is not due to natural causes, but to social ones: 'c'est donc uniquement dans la morale qu'on doit chercher la veritable cause de l'inegalite des esprits'.[25] As far as women are concerned, social conditioning has two direct consequences: first, women's supposed inferiority is wholly or mostly due to the conditions in which existing legislation keeps women, and to the kind of education which is given to them:

> In certain nations, women, whether married or not, have been placed in a state of perpetual wardship: this has been evidently founded on the notion of a decided inferiority in points of intellects on the part of the female sex, analogous to that which is the result of infancy or insanity on the part of the male. This is not the only instance in which tyranny has taken advantage of its own wrong, alleging as a reason for the domination it exercises, an imbecility, which, as far as it has been real, has been produced by the abuse of that very power which it is brought to justify.[26]

Some sixty years later on, John Stuart Mill asked, 'But was there ever any domination which did not appear natural to those who possessed it?'[27] Nature has been used simply to legitimize custom: 'So true is it that unnatural generally means only uncustomary, and that everything which is usual appears natural'.[28] Social and natural causes, Mill's argument continues, are not so easily separable:

> I deny that any one knows or can know, the nature of the two sexes, as long as they have only been seen in their present relation to one another. If men had ever been found in society without women. . ., or if there had ever been a society. . .in which the women were not under the control of men, something

might have been positively known about the mental and moral differences which may be inherent in the nature of each.[29]

In any case, the undoubted natural differences between the sexes do not justify the oppression of the 'weaker'.

Second, given that 'the inequality of the sexes results from social and modifiable, not physiological and immutable causes',[30] this inequality can be diminished and even eliminated by means of appropriate legislation and education.

The sharp distinction between 'nature' and 'society', and the claim for the autonomy of the latter from the former, which is a common feature of utilitarianism, entail a reconsideration of the relationship between the two sexes that points towards feminism. The differences between the sexes are not natural and everlasting, but social and therefore changeable by a reform of society. As far as truly natural differences are concerned, they must have no influence on social conditions; in any case, they ought to be compensated, and not magnified by society. 'Nature' was invoked not only by theories which preceded or were contemporary with the first formulations of utilitarianism in eighteen-century Europe, but also by the Romantic reactions to Enlightenment, and also by positivism, through the pre-eminence of biology. In this respect it is interesting to note that it was Auguste Comte who railed against John Stuart Mill about the 'natural' inferiority of women, which Comte argued was demonstrable both 'anatomically and physiologically'.[31] The removal of relationships between the two sexes from the realm of 'nature' and their introduction into the realm of 'society', which has and can be reformed and changed, gives an historical dimension to the whole question.

Even Jeremy Bentham, who is generally believed to be the most *ahistoric* of all utilitarians, places the relationship between men and women in a historic context:

Laying aside generosity and good-breeding, which are the tardy and uncertain fruits of long-established laws, it is evident that there can be no certain means of deciding it [the competition between the two sexes] but physical power: which indeed is the very means by which family, as well as other competitions, must have been decided long before any such office as that of legislator had existence... As between man and wife... The only reason that applies to this case is, the necessity of putting an end to competition... This affords a reason for giving a power to one or other of the parties: but it affords none for giving the power to the one rather than to the other.[32]

In a civilized society, and even more so in a utilitarian society, the relationship between men and women can no longer be grounded on the criterion of physical superiority characteristic of preceding stages of civilization.

Even James Mill, who was undoubtedly the least 'feminist' of all the utilitarians—as we shall see below—took 'the condition of women' to be 'one of the most decisive criteria of the stage of society at which [a nation has] arrived':

In proportion as society...advances into that state of civilization, in which...the qualities of the mind are ranked above the qualities of the body, the condition of the weaker sex is gradually improved, till they associate at last on equal terms with the men, and fill the place of voluntary and useful co-partners.[33]

Exactly as women were not *by nature* subjected to men, so they were not necessarily *by nature* intellectually inferior. No doubt the emancipation of women passed not only through their enfranchisement but also through their education—equal education, since as Helvetius says: 'Les femmes, par l'éducation qu'on leur donne, doivent acquérir plus de frivolité et de graces, que de force et justesse dans les idées'.[34] By social conditioning, Bentham argued, even 'moral biases' can be changed, or at least enhanced because 'chastity, modesty and delicacy, for instance, are prized more than courage in a woman: courage, more than any of those qualities, in a man'.[35]

If, therefore, women are so often found on the wrong side, this is due to a lack of education, which perpetuates men's tyranny over them; 'the female sex is banished from the dominion of utility' because 'for the benefit of the ruling few, as the bodies of some men, so the minds of all women are castrated. Pretended ignorance and insincerity forced on them, by knowledge alone are they disgraced', with very few exceptions.[36] In a softer, more 'progressive' way, J.S. Mill illustrates this same conception, using the metaphor of the tree that has been reared with one half in a vapour bath and the other in the snow, 'forced repression in some directions, unnatural stimulation in others'.[37] University College, still 'one of the greatest institutions for higher secular learning', the first English University which was open to all students, without distinction of class, religion or sex, the first university open to women, was founded by Benthamites, philosophic radicals, such as Joseph Hume, Henry Brougham, Francis Place and James Mill himself.

Because natural differences, in so far as they really exist, must be compensated, not magnified by society, education becomes not only a means of women's emancipation but also a rectification of their oppression. If women's emancipation is part of a project for the general reform of society, *compensatory discrimination* is part of a pragmatism which takes into account existing situations and tries to cope with them in the short run, tries to alleviate the suffering produced by oppression. Utilitarianism is egalitarian in so far as it postulates the original equality of psychological structure of those who belong to mankind and in so far as it thus demands *equal consideration*. But equal consideration does not automatically entail *equality of treatment*; on the contrary, it might demand *compensatory discrimination*.[38] Thus Bentham asked for particularly severe punishments for those who have done violence to women,[39] special measures to be taken by judges in order to preserve 'female dignity and modesty' in tribunal courts, when such cases are debated,[40] on account of the observation of women's inferior physical strength and greater psychological sensibility.

Again, taking into account the inequality of conditions in existing society, and the double standard afforded by public opinion to sexual behaviour in the two sexes, Bentham, who had written pages of brilliant and stringent polemic in favour of divorce,[41] was strongly against legal separation. Separation does 'not imply the permission to either of the parties to remarry'—which, given actual inequality, would impose 'restraint upon the weaker sex', leaving free the stronger.

From this point of view, *equal* consideration for different people, or for people in *different* conditions, leads to different treatment: to treat the 'injured wife and her tyrant' in the same way would only favour the stronger: such an 'apparent equality covers great real inequality'.[42]

UTILITARIANISM AND THE LIMITS OF HISTORICAL FEMINISM

For all these reasons the ideological background of feminism can be said to have been derived from the fundamental philosophical axioms of utilitarianism. The important point is not that most utilitarians were feminists, nor that men like John Stuart Mill or William Godwin married and loved women like Harriet Taylor or Mary Wollstonecraft: it was not a question of personal inclination and biography, but a much more deeply rooted conviction which moved these men towards a relationship with this kind of woman. Nor did these women convert their men to feminism: William Godwin had already published his *Enquiry Concerning Political Justice* (1793) before his relationship with Mary Wollstonecraft began (she had published her *Vindication of the Rights of Women* in 1792). John Stuart Mill, who was certainly very much influenced by Bentham's thought, had already written a strongly polemical article against the 'male chauvinism' of the *Edinburgh Review* as early as 1824, and had enjoyed the friendship of William Thompson, the author of the *Appeal*, since 1825, five years before he first met Harriet Taylor.

It might be objected that, first, not all the utilitarians were in fact feminists, and, second, utilitarianism was not the only political theory which was compatible with or sympathetic towards feminism. As far as the first objection is concerned, the first example which comes to mind is James Mill's position on women. The polemics which accompanied and followed the publication of his *Essay on Government* (1820) are instructive in this respect. In this essay Mill advocated universal suffrage, but excluded women on the grounds that 'all those individuals whose interests are indisputably included in those of other individuals may be struck off with inconvenience' and that women were included in this category, since 'the interests of almost all of whom [women] is involved either in that of their fathers or in that of their husbands'.[43]

The answer from the philosophical radical group, and particularly from the younger members of it, was sharply critical. As John Stuart Mill recalls in his *Autobiography*, these younger radicals—among whom he counted himself—reacted to Mill's *Essay* pointing out that:

the interest of women is included in that of men exactly as much and no more, as the interest of subjects is included in that of kings; and that every reason which exists for giving the suffrage to anybody, demands that it should not be withheld from women. This was also the general opinion of the younger proselytes: and it is pleasant to be able to say that Mr Bentham, on this important point, was wholly on our side.[44]

In truth Bentham expressed his open and clear dissent from James Mill's exclusionist position, whose object he believed was 'to place all females under the absolute dominion of all males'.[45] As I have shown elsewhere, Bentham consistently spoke in favour of women's enfranchisement, at least in point of principle, although he tended to play down this issue in his later works, fearing that his opponents' scorn for women was also extended to the claim for universal male suffrage.[46]

Such debate was particularly important, since it touched the central issue of the relationship between utilitarianism and feminism, and claimed that consistency between them was not only possible but necessary. The appeal to Bentham meant not only the recognition of Bentham's authority with respect to James Mill—one of the most outstanding personages of that group—but also the illustration of the possible and necessary alliance of utilitarianism and feminism.

This same position was also taken up by William Thompson, who was in touch with the philosophical radicals and Bentham and, later on, with J.S. Mill as well. But Thompson disagreed with the utilitarians on fundamental aspects of the woman question and was, as will be shown below, more under the influence of Robert Owen's utopian socialist views:

Thus cavalierly are dealt with by this philosopher of humanity, the interests of one half of the human species! Not so Mr Bentham, whose disciple he is: the philosophy of that enlightened and benevolent man, embraces in its grasp every sentient human being, and acknowledges the claim of every rational adult, without distinction of sex or colour, to equal political rights. Is the authority of the disciple above that of the master?[47]

Thompson attacks Mill's exclusionist position from an 'internal' point of view; that is, testing the consistency of such a position against the fundamental axioms of utilitarianism: the result is even more disruptive than that mentioned in J.S. Mill's *Autobiography*. In his *Appeal of One Half the Human Race, Women, against the Pretension of the Other Half, Men, to Retain Them in Political, and Thence in Civil and Domestic Slavery, in Reply to a Paragraph of Mr Mill's Celebrated "Article on Government"*, Thompson asks whether 'in point of fact and necessity' any identity of interest exists between women and men.[48] In any case, Mill's assumption is, first, that 'the grand governing law of human nature' says that all human beings are self-interested and, second, that each one is the best judge of his own interests. If—as Mill's *Essay* suggests—one half the human race is allowed to judge about the interests of the other half, men will judge in their own interest, and not that of women. To obtain a different result, Mill supposedly exempts all men from this grand governing law of human nature; but 'This exception of one half from the influence of the general rule, is certainly a pretty large exception. . .In any other hands, so large an exception would. . .destroy the rule'.[49] Four years later, Thomas Babington Macaulay—who was then the spokesman of the Whigs in British Parliament—used Thompson's argument on the incompatibility between James Mill's exclusionist position and utilitarianism, but employed it to demonstrate the opposite conclusion.[50] Macaulay started from Mill's exclusion of women from the franchise—which he found right and reasonable—and used its logical inconsistency with utilitarian postulates to demonstrate that the latter were wrong:

Except in a few happy and highly civilized communities, they [women] are strictly in a state of personal slavery. . .Mr Mill is not legislating for England or the United States; but for mankind. Is the interest of a Turk the same with that of the girls who compose his harem?. . .The interest of a respectable Englishman may be said, without any impropriety, to be identical with that of his wife. But why is it so? Because human nature is *not* what Mr Mill conceives it to be;. . . because there is a pleasure in being loved and esteemed. . .

That they do not pass such a law, though they have the power to pass it. . . proves that the desire to possess unlimited power of inflicting pain is not inseparable from Human nature. . . The identity of interest between the two sexes. . .arises from the Englishman's pleasure of being loved, and of communicating happiness.[51]

This debate is interesting because it shows that contemporary thinkers—both within and adverse to the utilitarian circle—already faced the question of the theoretical compatibility of utilitarianism and feminism. They concluded that the two were compatible.

Historical evidence supports the compatibility of utilitarianism and feminism, which has been elaborated from a theoretical point of view in the first part of this essay, and lends further weight to the assertion that the historical feminist movement derived its ideological background from classical utilitarianism. This does not mean, however, that all utilitarians were in fact ardent feminists: in the case of James Mill, for example, this conclusion would certainly be unjustified. But, as I have shown elsewhere, even Jeremy Bentham's feminism was not altogether free of shadows and inconsistencies.[53]

This does not mean either that only utilitarianism contained feminist elements; these were also present in the political thought of other contemporary social theorists—Owen, Fourier, and Saint-Simon. But historical feminism, the movement which fought for women's rights, was not the child of those other theories, but of utilitarianism.

My point here is that this affinity was not only the fruit of spatio-temporal contiguity, since historical feminism developed in nineteenth-century Great Britain, in the same *milieux* as that of the philosophical radicals, but had much deeper theoretical roots. An argument in support of this view can also be found in a demonstration *e contrario*, starting from the limits of utilitarian feminism, or better, from what utilitarian feminism was not. Classical utilitarianism believed that the reform of society towards a more favourable consideration of women's interests—changing women's conditions, and thus bettering the whole society—was to be carried out through legislation and education. Utilitarians considered the woman question from a legal, historical, social and political, even moral point of view, without ever caring about its economic aspects. Only a few utilitarian thinkers paid attention to the economic dimension of that question, and none of them ever believed that women's condition in society could be changed only by subverting the economic order of society.[54] This was the great ideological distance which separated utilitarian feminism from the feminist elements present in other political theories of that time.

Owen and Fourier, for example, shared with utilitarians the belief that *evil*—in this case the subjection of women—was not due to *nature* but to *society*, and that therefore women's liberation could be realized by changing society. But their analyses identified the origin of women's condition in the economic structure of society (not only in legislation, as for utilitarians); that is, in the patriarchal *regime* of private property. The social change they advocated would have subverted the economic order of society and replaced it by another kind of society based on different principles. Even William Thompson, who had criticized James Mill from an internal, utilitarian point of view, came under other influences, most importantly the work of Robert Owen and of Anne Wheeler, who was in touch with all the socialist feminists of the day. Thus, although he criticizes James Mill from 'within', Thompson goes much beyond the scope of classical utilitarianism in preaching the abolition of property and the creation of communities based on co-operation, and in labelling political economy the ideology of dominating classes.[55]

Historical feminism, indeed, restricted itself to women's right to vote and to equal education, without touching the economic structure of Victorian society. It might be argued that this was done only for strategic reasons—so as not to appear *too* revolutionary. Nevertheless, the limits (or merits) of historical feminism were not 'strategic' but the direct ideological consequence of the limits (or merits) of classical utilitarianism.

NOTES

1. C. Taylor, 'The diversity of goods' *Utilitarianism and Beyond,* ed. A. Sen and B. Williams, (Cambridge,1982), p. 129.

2. For example, the subtitle of D. Hume's *Treatise on Human Nature* (1738) is 'Being an attempt to introduce the experimental method of reasoning into moral subjects'. Cf. my article 'Jeremy Bentham e l'utilitarismo come scienze sociale', *Il pensiero politico,* 12 (1979), 2. 361–71.

3.   'Nature has placed mankind under the governance of two sovereign masters, *pain* and *pleasure*. . .On the one hand the chain of causes and effects, are fastened to their throne. . .The *Principle of utility* recognises this subjection, and assumes it for the foundation of that system, the object of which is to rear the fabric of felicity by the hands of reason and of law'. By these words, Bentham solemnly initiated his *Introduction to the Principles of Morals and Legislation* p. 11 heavily referring and almost copying C.A. Helvetius, *De l'Esprit* (1758), Disc. 3, Ch. 9, *Oeuvres Complètes* (Paris 1795)

4.   The invention of 'moral arithmetic' is generally attributed to F. Hutcheson, in his *Enquiry into the Origin of Our Ideas of Beauty and Virtue*, 1725; see esp. II Treat., Sect. 3, para. 11.

5.   This term was first used by Elie Halevy in his standard work on utilitarianism, I, p. 4.

6.   Taylor, p. 130.

7.   The way in which this formula passed from Hutcheson to Beccaria, down to Bentham has been masterfully reconstructed by R. Shackleton, 'The greatest happiness of the greatest number: the history of Bentham's phrase', in *Studies on Voltaire and the Eighteenth Century*, ed. T. Besterman, XC, 1972, pp. 1462–64; but see now J.R. Dinwiddy, 'Bentham on private ethics and the principle of utility', *Revue Internationale de Philosophie* (1982), pp. 271–309.

8.   J. Bentham, Preface to *A Fragment on Government* (1776), in *Complete Works*, ed. H.L.A. Hart and J.H. Burns, London, 1977, p. 393.

9.   L. Stephen, *The English Utilitarians* (3 vols., New York, 1900) vol. 1, p. 2; cf. W.L. Davidson, *The Utilitarians from Bentham to Mill* (1915; Oxford, 1944), pp. 10, 16–17.

10.   Bentham, *A Fragment on Government*, pp. 444, 484; cf. W. Godwin, *Enquiry Concerning Political Justice* (1793), ed. by I. Kramnick (London, 1976), pp. 212, 216–17, 234.

11.   Helvetius, Disc. 2, Ch. 24; vol. 3, p. 141.

12.   It was not by chance that William Thompson entitled his work, *Appeal of One Half the Human Race, Women, against the Pretension of the Other Half, Men, to Retain Them in Political, and Thence in Civil and Domestic Slavery, in Reply to a Paragraph of Mr Mill's Celebrated "Article on Government"'* (London, 1825).

13.   E. Griffin-Collart, *Égalité et Justice dans l'Utilitarisme; Bentham, J.S. Mill, Sidgwick* (Brussels, 1974), pp. 31–2, 115; cf. also H.L.A. Hart, *Essays on Bentham* (London, 1982), pp. 97–8.

14.   Bentham, *An Introduction to the Principles of Morals and Legislation*, pp. 282–3.

15.   J.S. Mill, *On Liberty, Representative Government, and The Subjection of Women* (London, 1912); cf. J. Bentham, Ms. in Univ. College, London (hereafter referred to as UC) CLXX, 144: 'As to the custom which has prevailed so generally to the disadvantage of the softer sex, it has tyranny for its efficient cause, and prejudice for its sole justification.';compare this Ms. of 1789 with another Ms. of 1817, in which Bentham speaks of the 'tyranny of

the stronger sex', UC CLI, 336–7. For the relationship between prejudice on the one side, and oppression and tyranny on the other, see Lea Campos Boralevi, *Bentham and the Oppressed*, Publications of the European University Institute, (Berlin and New York, 1984), pp. 10, 176–7.

16.   D. Lyons, *In the Interest of the Governed: A Study in Bentham's Philosophy of Utility and Law* (Oxford, 1973), pp. 27–31.

17.   J. Bentham, *Treatise on Judicial Evidence* (Edinburgh, 1825), p. 210.

18.   Bentham, *The Rationale of Judicial Evidence*, in *Works*, ed. J. Bowring (11 vols., Edinburgh and London, 1838–43), vol. 8, p. 485 (hereafter referred to as '*Works*').

19.   J.S. Mill, *The Subjection of Women* (Oxford University Press, 1975) p. 542; for an analysis, see S. Moller Okin, *Women in Western Political Thought* (Princeton, 1979), Ch. IV.

20.   J.S. Mill *The Subjection of Women* p. 525.

21.   *Ibid.*, p. 479.

22.   By 'constitutive power' Bentham means the power to elect; that is, the right to active vote.

23.   Bentham, *Constitutional Code*, in *Works*, vol. 9, p. 108.

24.   Bentham, *Principles of the Civil Code*, in *Works*, vol. 1, p. 335; in the chapter devoted to 'Women' of the book *Bentham and the Oppressed*, pp. 5–36, I have used the comparison between this paragraph and another (taken from *Constitutional Code*, p. 108) in order to show the continuity of thought and of Bentham's attitude towards women over fifty or more years. Compare also the following: 'Add to which, in point of motives, that legislators seem all to have been of the male sex, down to the days of Catherine', in *Introduction*, p. 238, and cf. n. 17.

25.   Helvetius, Disc. 3, Ch. 27; vol. 2, p. 220.

26.   Bentham, *Introduction*, p. 245. The other instance to which Bentham refers is that of slaves and of Negroes; for the relationships between these different oppressed groups, see Boralevi, *Bentham and the Oppressed*, pp. 6, 9–10, 144, 180.

27.   J.S. Mill, *The Subjection of Women*, p. 440.

28.   *Ibid.*, p. 441. The Conception of this 'nature' as far as women are concerned changes in different countries and times: in the Orient they are 'by nature' voluptuous, in England, 'by nature' cold; but compare the remarkable resemblance between Mill's and Bentham's arguments in J. Bentham, *UC*, LXXIX, 'Offences', pp. 479, 480: 'The truth is that by the epithet *unnatural*. . .the only matters of which it affords any indication. . .is the existence of a sentiment of disapprobation, accompanied with passion'.

29.   *Ibid.*, p. 451.

30.   Helvetius, Disc. 2, Ch. 20; vol. I, p. 359.

31.   A. Comte, *Lettres d'Auguste Comte à J.S. Mill* (1841–46), Paris, 1877, p. 175, quoted in Okin, pp. 216–21.

32.   Bentham, *Introduction*, pp. 237–8.

33.   James Mill, *The History of British India* (London, 1817), vol 1, pp. 293–4. T. Ball, in his article on 'Utilitarianism, feminism, and the franchise: James Mill and his critics', *History of Political Thought* 1 (1980), 1: 94–5,

108–9, shows the direct influence of James Mill's *History*, at least on this point, on his son, John Stuart Mill, who repeated this same concept in *The Subjection of Women*, p. 38.

34.   Helvetius, vol. 1, p. 359.

35.   Bentham, *Introduction,* p. 64.

36.   J. Bentham, *A Table of the Springs of Action*, (together with *Deontology* and *The Article on Utilitarianism),* in *Complete Works*, ed. A. Goldworth, (Oxford, 1983), 'Marginals', p. 54.

37.   J.S. Mill, *The Subjection of Women*, p. 451. For the strong influence of Bentham on him, cf. with Bentham's passage from the *Introduction* the following: 'It is considered meritorious in a man to be independent. . .In a woman, helplessness. . .is the most admired of attributes. A man is despised, if he be not courageous. In a woman, it is esteemed amiable to be a coward'. *Westminster Review* 1 (April, 1824), 526.

38.   From this point of view, Bentham was always strongly opposed to the *Declaration des droits de l'homme*, which 'stopped' at formal equality; cf. his *Anarchical Fallacies*, in *Works*, vol. 2, pp. 499–502.

39.   Bentham, *Specimen of a Penal Code*, in *Works*, vol. 1, p. 164–7.

40.   Bentham, *Principles of Judicial Procedure, Works,* vol. 2, p. 114.

41.   Bentham, *Principles of the Civil Code*, vol. 1, p. 353. For Mill's position and its relation with Harriet Taylor's ideas, see Okin, pp. 226–9.

42.   Bentham *Principles of the Civil Code*, vol. 1, p. 353.

43.   James Mill, *Essay on Government* (Edinburgh, 1820), ed. C.V. Shields (Indianapolis, 1977), pp. 73–4.

44.   J.S. Mill, *Autobiography* (London, 1940), pp 87–8.

45.   J. Bentham, *UC*, XXXIV, 302–3, published in *Bentham's Political Thought*, ed. Bhiku Parekh (London, 1973), App.B, pp. 311–12; it is worth noting that the date of this manuscript (April 1824) is the same as that of the cited article by J.S. Mill in the *Westminster Review* (see n. 39).

46.   Boralevi, *Bentham and the Oppressed*, pp. 15–19.

47.   Thompson, *Appeal*, pp. 9–10.

48.   *Ibid*, p. 25.

49.   *Ibid*, p. 7.

50.   T.B. Macaulay, 'Mill on government', in *Works* (London, 1848), vol 7, p. 354 ff; see T. Ball's article, pp. 112–14.

51.   Macaulay, 'Mill on government', pp. 354–55.

52.   This is, however, T., Ball's argument in his cited article. For an exchange of views between Ball and the Author, see *The Bentham Newsletter* (1980), 4: 25–48.

53.   Boralevi, *Bentham on the Oppressed*, pp. 5–36.

54.   On the contrary, they were eager to show that women's enfranchisement would not have attacked the principle of private property and that it would not have been dangerous for the order of society.

55.   W. Thompson, pp. 10–12.

7 Nietzsche: Women as Untermensch

Ellen Kennedy

Perhaps the whole of philosophy exists as empty spaces in the head of an old woman.

Menschliches Allzumenschliches

To go wrong on the fundamental problem of 'man and woman', to deny the most abysmal antagonism between them and the necessity of an eternally hostile tension, to dream perhaps of equal rights, equal education, equal claims and obligations, that is a *typical* sign of shallowness.

Jenseits von Gut und Böse

Can women be just at all, since they are so used to loving, to feeling either for or against something immediately?

Menschliches Allzumenschliches

No philosopher is more controversial than Friedrich Nietzsche. For some he seems, as Giles Deleuze remarks, 'to celebrate the death of philosophy as the highest philosophy' in a bizarre mishmash of ontology and anthropology, atheism and theology, while for others Nietzsche's radical rejection of 'the triumphal march of the theoretical' is the only honest starting place for philosophy. So unsettling for the philosophical trade is Nietzsche's method and argument that the question 'Is Nietzsche a philosopher?' doesn't seem far fetched.[1]

In political philosophy Nietzsche's place is, if anything, even more uncertain. As a contributor to modern thought about politics, society and the state, Nietzsche hangs suspended between general ignorance of him—he seldom appears in a standard course on the history of political thought or political theory—and the worst of all political reputations as the philosophical forerunner of National Socialism. With few exceptions, literature on Nietzsche between 1933 and 1950 concentrated on the relationship between his philosophy and Nazi ideology and practice, and even (in the case of German philosophers during this period) assumed an immediate connection between them. Elizabeth Förster-Nietzsche encouraged this view, and the politically authoritative interpretations of Nietzsche presented by Alfred Bäumler made Nietzsche's philosophy the philosophical cornerstone of fascist thought in Germany.[2] From the other side, too, this view of Nietzsche was reinforced by Georg Lukács's influential commentaries, which condemned Nietzsche as 'the founder of irrationalism in the imperialistic age, the ideologist of a declining and brutal ruling class, a philosopher who when he wrote about power half a century beforehand, meant Hitler fascism and the moral ideology of "the American century" '.[3] Allied propaganda during the war contributed to this interpretation of Nietzsche by popularizing it, and as Rudolf Kuenzli has pointed out, headlines such as 'Hitler's War Urge Blamed on Insane Philosopher' were not uncommon.[4] However crude both sides now seem, even philosophically serious commentators such as Karl Jaspers and Georges Bataille recognized that the question of his relationship to Nazism was one that could not simply be ignored, or left in the hands of ideologists.[5]

This intermediate phase of Nietzsche scholarship, then, was highly political, unlike the most recent view of him. The contemporary paradigm of Nietzsche studies was established by Walter Kaufmann's *Nietzsche: Philosopher, Psychologist, Antichrist* (1950) which even in its title repudiates the earlier 'political' Nietzsche.[6] Kaufmann's central thesis rejects the politically charged Nietzsche by claiming that Nietzsche's conception of power is not political but psychological. Although the will to power is basic to Nietzsche's thought, his *Übermensch*, Kaufmann contended, is neither a racial 'aryan' nor a political Nazi, but a quite different figure: 'the man who has overcome himself'.[7] Further, Kaufmann argued, 'the powerful. . .have no need to prove their might either to themselves or to others by oppressing or hurting others; if they do hurt others, they do so incidentally in the process of using their power creatively; they hurt others 'without thinking of it'. Only the weak man 'wishes to hurt and to see the signs of suffering'.[8]

The view of Nietzsche offered here sees him as a political philosopher of the first order. Power, not just as self-knowledge or as self-realization, but in a sense familiar to every student of politics—as power over others—was the central preoccupation of Nietzsche's philosophy. His work is concerned with its exercise at every level: in the purportedly private relations between individuals, in the emerging capitalist values of Imperial Germany and, most importantly for Nietzsche as political thinker, power in the cultural and social structures of the modern state.

Nietzsche's preoccupation with power in this sense is particularly evident in his cultural critique of state and society in Imperial Germany, which serves as an example of bourgeois society in general, and in Nietzsche's view of women's cultural and political role within it. The referent of Nietzsche's *Unzeitgemasse Betrachtungen* (1873–76) was a Germany only recently unified and bursting with national pride. Its cultural values, Nietzsche asserted, elevated philistinism to new heights and made the lowest common denominator of popular sentiment, nationalism, into a public value.[9] The analysis of human types within this society (his implicit question about politics and society was always, 'What kind of people does this culture bring forth?') led Nietzsche to a radical challenge of existing moral and social beliefs. Just as his philosophical analysis challenged the first premises of Kant's philosophy, Nietzsche's cultural and political analysis pushed through the socially accepted boundaries of good and evil and sought to transvalue all values in bourgeois society. Except, that is, where women are concerned: here Nietzsche's views accord with those of the 'narrow-minded bourgeois' who was his primary philosophical and cultural target. In this respect at least, Nietzsche's reflections on German society were perfectly in step with his times, as the contemporary reception of his cultural–philosophical thought demonstrates.

YOU ARE GOING TO VISIT WOMEN? DON'T FORGET YOUR WHIP!

For the first Nietzsche generations, he was a *Frauenfeind* (male chauvinist) without par. Writing in 1898, the German feminist Hedwig Dohm characterized Nietzsche's comments on women as a 'Gedanken-Trödelmarkt' (intellectual flea-market) where 'the dregs and sediment of centuries of half-thoughts which have crept around the corners and wrinkles of the human brain for countless generations occasionally come to light'.[10] Here Nietzsche's philosophy is no occasion for a divine 'family reunion' 'much less a twilight of the gods'.[11] So widespread was this image of Nietzsche—he did after all provide German with its classic expression of male chauvinism in the *Zarathustra* quotation above—that Elizabeth Förster-Nietzsche wrote a book to set the record straight, *Nietzsche und die Frauen seiner Zeit* (1935), and the only full length treatment of the subject Henry (*sic*) Braun's *Nietzsche und die Frauen* (1931, 1974) was also written under the influence of this popular image of Nietzsche as a misogynist.[12]

It would be misleading, however, to present the anti-feminist passages in Nietzsche's works as though his views on women's social and political role were exceptional. On the contrary, they belong, as Hans Vaihinger's *Nietzsche als Philosoph* (1902) pointed out, to a set of antagonistic positions which characterize Nietzsche's philosophy and which can be explained in terms of its fundamental principle, 'the will to power'.[13] None of Nietzsche's 'anti' positions which Vaihinger identified were systematically developed in one place. Rather they are 'scattered in thousands of aphorisms, apparently without connection' throughout Nietzsche's published and unpublished works,[14] united to one another, as negations of the will to power. Nietzsche's anti-feminism is consistent with his opposition to democracy, socialism, Christianity, 'intellectualism', 'pessimism' and his 'anti-morality', all tendencies that deny the basically 'healthy' will to power which all living things have, each of them in one way or another its antagonist. In every one of these, Nietzsche argues, women have played a major role in the transmission of values hostile to the will to power.

This is clearly so in the case of Christianity—which, according to Nietzsche, was a 'slave morality' that replaced the superior moralities of Ancient Rome and Greece. Although the critique of Christianity appears throughout Nietzsche's work, it was first introduced in *Zur Genologie der Moral* (1887) and expanded in *Der Antichrist* (1895). In the first, Nietzsche gives a geneological account of the emergence of Christianity among the Roman slaves; 'this slave religion' and slave morality, Vaihinger notes, 'naturally prized those virtues which were useful for slaves: pity, love, caution. It condemned recklessness, selfishness, cruelty and invented abusive words for the relevant natural virtues of uncorrupted men: courage, energy, ambition, will to power'.[15] Each of the positions Nietzsche opposed—democracy, socialism, pessimism, intellectualism, feminism—appear in his works as weaknesses, movements or attitudes which erode the will to power by taming its natural force; in short, by civilizing natural man.

As the weaker sex, Nietzsche argues, women have always had the most to gain from 'civilization' and Christianity, and women's role as helpmate of priests, teacher of the Christian virtues, tamer of the natural wildness in man encourages the degeneration of the will to power. All the virtues which Nietzsche's philosophy will 'transvalue'—pity, love, caution—are in a particular way 'feminine' and life-denying.

That Nietzsche praises the *natural* will to power, but based his anti-feminist views on women's purely natural function of childbearing is only a seeming contradiction. When his arguments against the emancipation of women are considered in combination with his views on women's negative moral function and social place, the paradox disappears.

THE WOMAN WHO UNLEARNS FEAR SURRENDERS HER MOST WOMANLY INSTINCTS

The revolution in Nietzsche scholarship, initiated by Walter Kaufmann, detached Nietzsche from two major preoccupations of the early and intermediate phases of interpretation: the influence of Schopenhauer and of Darwinistic biology. Only if Nietzsche's works can be presented as having abandoned the former and having nothing to do with the latter can 'the will to power' be understood in the way Kaufmann does, as strength which takes no pleasure in oppression. In this revision Kaufmann overlooked the role fear plays in Nietzsche's account of the origins of morality, an aspect that was central to the sober reading of Nietzsche, especially the social and political implications of his thought, which one finds in an early study by the great German social philosopher, Ferdinand Tönnies.

In *Der Nietzsche-Kultus* (1897) Tönnies noted that in *Jenseits von Gut und Böse*, 'pride is not the origin of one, revenge the origin of another morality, but fear is the mother of all morality, and at the same time, mother of that reservoir of all experienced fear, the Herd-Instinct'.[16] Moreover, Tönnies emphazised the role Nietzsche's philosophy accords to women in the origin of morality and its continued function in social life. Here Nietzsche took over Schopenhauers's view of women as naturally piteous, and made this responsible for the moderation of morals in the later phases of a culture. None of this was positive. In Nietzsche's view it led to the disappearance of 'soldierly-virtues' through a gradual 'femininization' of morals. Nietzsche's assertion of a general moral 'decline' was accompanied, Tönnies saw, by a corresponding attack on modernity—the democratization of politics, the appearance of socialism, industrialization and the emergence of mass society— none of which could be separated from the other. If those moral values Nietzsche prized most were to be revitalized, then, as Tönnies reads him, a eugenic programme of breeding and selection would be necessary.[17]

The specifically biological aspect of this reading of Nietzsche will be taken up below. First let us turn to the issue of Schopenhauer's influence on Nietzsche and the similarities between them.

In a coincidence of views, both modern and earlier Nietzsche scholarship agrees on the importance of Schopenhauer for understanding Nietzsche's view of women, and most see the comparison in Nietzsche's favour. Elizabeth Förster-Nietzsche's defence of her brother's views on women and feminism rests on a comparison of the two philosophers, as does Frederick Copleston's remark that Schopenhauer's judgement of women was 'very harsh indeed'.[18] For Hans Vaihinger, too, a comparison of Nietzsche with Schopenhauer could only work to the benefit of the former: 'one would be mistaken, were one to look for such crude invective against women in Nietzsche's as in Schopenhauer's works'.[19] Most of the comparisons are based on Schopenhauer's *Parerga und Paralipomena* (1851), where, in a chapter 'Über die Weiber', he dismisses women as an 'undersized, narrow-shouldered, broad-hipped, and short-legged race...the number two of the human race'.[20] Schopenhauer offered woman's childbearing faculty as the central explanation here for her irrationality, lack of foresight and inability to appreciate any of the arts; she is, on Schopenhauer's account of it, 'her life long, a child'[21] and 'herself childish, silly and short-sighted, in a word—a kind of middle-stage between the child and the man'.[22]

By contrast with Schopenhauer, Vaihinger believes, Nietzsche 'has words of the most profound reverence for that which he found to be the most profound true vocation of woman'.[23] A careful reading of those passages in which Nietzsche discusses women produces rather a different view. Woman's 'true vocation' is not and cannot be separated from his assessment of women's place on the scale of a will to power that runs downwards from masters to slaves.

The outline of Nietzsche's view of women appeared first in *Menschliches Allzumenschliches* (1878) and remained constant throughout his other works. Bits and pieces were added, but the melody remained unchanged. In a chapter of *Menschliches Allzumenschliches*, 'Weib und Kind', Nietzsche asserted that 'Women want to serve and find their happiness in this';[24] from that it follows that women lack the will to power which superior human beings have and that women's innervation is the source of cultural degeneracy. A creature whose basic nature is subservient cannot lead, dominate, create—cannot be an *Übermensch*.

There is, of course, an interpretation of this and other similar passages in Nietzsche's work according to which women's lot and fate by nature is not oppressive. This was Elizabeth Förster-Nietzsche's view and, with important differences, Hans Vaihinger's as well. It emphasizes that women, as the weaker sex, need protection and Elizabeth Förster-Nietzsche stresses her brother's 'fatherly solicitude...for the female sex:

Of course fathers can also be strict, when their charge sets off on the false track. He saw this false track at that time in the beginning of women's emancipation, which he suspected would prove very damaging for the female sex...He wanted to a certain extent to keep the female in its naturalness, because he desired a strengthening of the fullness for the human species. But to that belongs above all things, beautiful, strong and healthy mothers.[25]

The emphasis on 'beautiful, strong and healthy mothers' is pure invention, tinged with Elizabeth Förster-Nietzsche's sympathy for the mother-aesthetic of National Socialism; but the rest of her description is accurate, though incomplete. How far did Nietzsche's social thought go in keeping 'the female in its naturalness?'

AT BOTTOM, THE EMANCIPATED ARE ANARCHISTS IN THE WORLD OF THE 'ETERNALLY FEMININE'

Opposition to women's emancipation was partly, as Tönnies noted, an extension of Nietzsche's political and cultural critique. Liberated women were in this area no different from democrats and socialists. All of these social and political types were instruments of 'the herd mentality' that was at the heart of contemporary cultural decay. But the metaphor of sickness and health that is constant in Nietzsche's work reveals another element of Nietzsche's anti-feminism and misogyny.

For Nietzsche feminism was part of a modern sickness, a symptom which only woman's return to her 'natural function' would cure. Since natural woman wants to serve man and will be happy in her servitude, the movement to free women from this primary role as mothers appears in his philosophy as sick and unnatural:

'Emancipation of women'—that is the instinctive hatred of the abortive (*missraten*) woman, who is incapable of giving birth, against the woman who has turned out well (*wohlgeraten*)—the fight against the 'man' is always a mere pretext, tactic. By raising themselves higher, as 'woman in herself', as the 'higher woman', as a female 'idealist', they want to lower the level of the general rank of woman; and there is no surer means for that than higher education, slacks and political voting-cattle rights. At bottom, the emancipated are anarchists in the world of the 'eternally feminine', the underprivileged whose most fundamental instinct is revenge.[26]

Although women's emancipation appears here as a plot by sick and unhealthy women against healthy and happy ones, this view is in fact characteristic of Nietzsche's presentation of women as a whole. 'What a dangerous, creeping, subterranean little beast of prey she is!', he writes in *Ecce Homo*:

A little woman who pursues her revenge would run over fate itself. Woman is indescribably more evil than man; also cleverer: good nature is in a woman a form of degeneration . . . The Fight for equal rights is actually a symptom of a disease: every physician knows that. Woman, the more she is a woman, resists rights in general hand and foot: after all, in the state of nature, the eternal war between the sexes gives her by far first rank . . . Love—in it means, war; at bottom, the deadly hatred of the sexes. Has my answer been heard to the question of how one *cures* a woman— 'redeems' her? One gives her a child.[27]

Although aimed primarily at women's sexuality, Nietzsche's views here merely echo his description of the slave revolt which founded Christianity. Women scheme like slaves to weaken their master's power, using all their wiles, but especially their sexuality, in a relation to men that is one of 'abysmal antagonism' and 'eternally hostile tension'; at a certain point in 'the war between the sexes', man subdues woman in an age-old way: he makes her pregnant.

In a section of *Der Wille zur Macht*, 'Why the weak conquer', Nietzsche summarizes the development of moral philosophy and women's role within it.[28] Although *Wille zur Macht* was never published in his life-time, this paragraph was written sometime between March and June 1888, in the last year of Nietzsche's relative good health. It too elaborates the metaphor of sickness and health, and begins with an allusion to themes which Nietzsche dealt with at length in *Jenseits von Gut und Böse* (1886) and *Zur Geneologie der Moral* (1887): the origin of morality and law, and the geneology of revolts which overthrew the master morality of ancient Greece and Rome and established the slave morality of Christianity. Under it, the sick and the weak have power over the healthy and strong; they have fascination on their side: 'the sick are more interesting than the healthy'. In the passages that make up this section, Nietzsche enumerates a scale of sick and weak types: the fool and the saint; women; 'morbid elements; the neurotic-psychiatric and criminal'; finally the social hodge-podge, a product of the Revolution, the establishment of equal rights and the 'superstition of "equal man" '. Of all these types—the negative images in his philosophy—only women are determined by their biology. Moral characteristics are derived from natural ones in a manner characteristic of Nietzsche's view:

Finally: woman! One-half of mankind is weak, typically sick, changeable, inconstant—woman needs strength in order to cleave to it; she needs a religion of weakness that glorifies being weak, loving, and being humble as divine: or better, she makes the strong weak—she rules when she succeeds in overcoming the strong. Woman has always conspired with the types of decadence, the priests, against the 'powerful', the men. Woman brings the children to the cult of piety, pity, love: the mother represents altruism convincingly.[29]

The crucial aspect of Nietzsche's argument here is its production of a dichotomy: on one side, the powerful and strong, men; on the other, the weak and subversive, women. In the larger context of the rest of this paragraph, women as an element that undermines strength, are woven into Nietzsche's negative community of priests, democrats, the mob and liberals—mediocrities who only gain at the expense of the powerful. Finally, in the last section ('Reflection') Nietzsche rejects the notion that 'this whole victory of values' (he means Christianity and democracy, but also the middle classes who live by trade and who are necessarily 'mediocre' and liberal) could be 'anti-biological'; 'one must try' he continues, 'to explain it in terms of an interest life has in preserving the type "man" even through this method of the dominance of the weak and underprivileged'.[30] Another aspect of women's negation of the will to power was integrated into this view of the female sex as morally and biologically subversive. Nietzsche's criticism of Kant and his rejection of Western philosophy since Socrates, begins with an attack on its origins in 'the theoretical'. It ends with the prediction that philosophy will finish as 'empty spaces in the head of an old woman'. Although Socrates plays a key role in Nietzsche's history of intellectualism, a special role is assigned to Xanthippe, his wife. 'Actually, she drove him deeper into his real calling', Nietzsche writes, 'in that she made house and home foreign and unbearable for him: she taught him to go into the back streets and live where one could gossip and be useless, she made him the great alley philosopher'.[31] Here, too, then, women destroyed and frustrated the will to power:

they 'intrigue silently against the higher souls of their men'. Women drive out the spirit of adventure in every free-spirit, and even at the moment of death 'if fate gives the free-spirit a poisonous cup to sip', women torment him: 'they scream and mourn and even disturb the sunset peace of the thinker, as they did in the Athenian prison. "Oh Criton, tell someone to send these women away!" '.[32]

LIFE ITSELF RECOGNIZES NO SOLIDARITY, NO 'EQUAL RIGHTS'

Nietzsche's moral philosophy, with its central conception of the will to power, directs his political thought. It is the criterion of judgement for his views of the state as an existing reality and it serves, too, as the genesis of an idealized conception. His principal aim in each was to avoid the moral result of the 'herd mentality': mediocrity, weakness, submission, and to foster the appearance of a race of men superior to that produced by Christian values and bourgeois society. Given his reading of woman's moral character and her role as the carrier of values which weaken the will to power, it is hardly surprising that Nietzsche was one of the most bitter opponents of women's emancipation. But his reasons for excluding women from an ideal state at once reveal the weakness of his philosophical system and the nature of his political vision. Both conceptions of the state are set out in *Wille zur Macht* where Nietzsche's discussion begins with an account of morality in existing societies. In the scale of justifications—economic, aesthetic, political, physiological—for a division of labour in society and its concomitant identities of class and individual self, the political makes specific reference to power relations. As 'the art of enduring the tremendous tension between differing degrees of power' politics both justifies the norms of society's moral code and puts them into practice.[33] A creature of this art, the state then appears as an institutionalization of these differences in power. It restrains the will to power, holds freedom in check through law and punishment, and is aided in this function by the institutional carriers of moral values necessary for the acceptance of this social discipline.

This view of the state as the agent of social discipline offers a radical insight into the necessary links between public pieties and legitimate force. On the one hand, the state tames man, just as Christianity tames him; but the state also appears to Nietzsche as a higher force that transcends the boundaries of 'morality'. It is 'organized immorality'—it does indeed exist to do what 'morality' forbids the individual to do. Internally, the state is 'police, penal law, classes, commerce, family', all contradictions of the Christian morality of brotherly love. Externally, the state is 'will to power, to war, to conquest, to revenge'.[34] It follows from this view of the empirical state and its cultural substructure that the political institutions of democracy (political parties, elections and voting, rights of all sorts, both political and social, the law and its enforcement) are condemned for the same reason that Nietzsche condemns existing states. They all serve to destroy the will to power and to encourage the herd mentality.

Nietzsche's adamant rejection of the claims for women's emancipation appears within this view of democracy as one example of his general opposition to the claim of 'equal rights', not just by feminists but by various social groups and classes throughout the nineteenth century. Primarily concerned with Germany's cultural development, Nietzsche's critique of existing states starts at a moral conclusion and works back to the evidence for it. For example, every line on the socialists and democrats of his time castigates them, but what he knew of German socialist demands and concerns—women's emancip- ation, enfranchisement of the working class, capital and labour relations in modern economics—was taken from John Stuart Mill. In fact, much of Nietzsche's argument against the democratic political and social movements of his time can be read as a reply to and critique of the fundamental assumptions of Mill's liberalism.[35] Given his substantialist conception of power as a certain kind of freedom, defined negatively as a suppressed and controlled instinct in existing states, Nietzsche's political philosophy must reject the liberal–democratic notion of equality and its ethic as well:

with its unconscious instinct for education and breeding, [ethics] has hitherto aimed at holding the desire for power in check: it disparages the tyrannical individual and with its glorification of social welfare and patriotism, emphasises the power–instinct of the herd.[36]

Nietzsche's discussion here approaches one of the central questions of traditional political philosophy, and does so in the course of a powerful polemic against much of the mass-produced 'individualism' of modern societies. But the question, 'What authorizes political power?' is never asked in a way that would lead to the formulation of telling conceptions of authority and legitimacy. Instead, Nietzsche's concern with the state aims haphazardly at issues that are either crudely *realpolitisch*, and thus exclude normative statement, or they are social–psychological, an aspect of his thought that makes him a very modern thinker, but still avoids the essence of justification. The question, 'How does it happen that the state will do a host of things that the individual would never countenance?', for example, foreshadows Max Weber's definition of political power as the anticipation of being obeyed, and his definition of the state in terms of its rationalization of functions, a rationalization that enhances state power. But while the forms of modern politics were the basis of democratization for Weber, they are in Nietzsche's thought the means to inculcate the herd mentality.[37]

The vision of a better state is not developed by Nietzsche, and only its outlines are visible in *Wille zur Macht*. Negatively defined, Nietzsche's ideal state would avoid all those social and political practices which serve to support empirical states and through which the power relations within them are expressed. An ideal state, if we try for a moment to imagine it more concretely, would have no politics on the lines we in the liberal democracies know today: there would be no political parties or interest groups; no legislative bodies and no laws or courts to interpret them. There would be no set of rights guaranteed under a constitution and of course no political agitation to secure those rights or to alter their interpretation. In the ideal state, citizenship would not mean the legal definition of individual rights and their enjoyment, but power. Would power in this state, regardless of its actual exercise in existing states mean, as Walter Kaufmann claims, self-realization rather than power over others? Would power here really mean the end of 'power' as we know it in the exercise of domination, control and force, subtle and explicit? On the basis of Nietzsche's élitist conception of an Übermensch—a human type morally superior to the type produced by Christianity and bourgeois society—that view seems, when we set it into the context of everything western political philosophy tells us about political life, hardly likely. Moreover, Nietzsche's élite race of Übermenschen would be an 'open' product of education and excellence, but is defined in explicitly biological terms. Woman's gender excludes her from ever participating in a state of this kind. Women would always be subversive in the enjoyment of power transvalued. In his critique of existing states Nietzsche's view of women's roles and appropriate place is more complicated and offers two further perspectives. One is a vigorous opposition to the emancipation of women on the grounds of a principle of natural equality, the same principle which defines the élitist vision of an ideal state. The other is based on Nietzsche's theory of civil society, which sees women as men's property without rights of their own and not entitled to them, and on a practical objection to women's participation in the state.

The main line of practical argument offered is that things are bad enough already in society and in the state, but women would only make things worse. *Menschliches Allzumenschliches* (1878) clearly states this position in a paragraph on 'The Emancipation of Women'. Nietzsche asks 'whether women can be just at all, since they are so accustomed to loving, to being immediately for or against something?' Because they are so much more interested in persons than in things, when they do take an interest in things and issues (Sache), they carry their 'personalized' way of loving and hating, of taking sides for or against, with them. The result is that women are 'Parteiganger' (partisans) and corrupt the pure working of things; thus entrusting women with politics or with the arts and sciences (he mentions especially history) poses no small danger because 'What is more uncommon than a woman who knows what science (Wissenschaft) is?'[38]

In a further paragraph Nietzsche comments, in opposition to the education of women, that 'one could in a few centuries make whatever one wants to out of women in the three or four civilized European countries, even men, though of course, not in their gender'. But even if women were educated, the result would be terrible:

This would be the time [while women were being educated] in which rage would constitute men's real feelings, rage that every art and science were flooded by an outrageous dilettantism, forgotten and neglected, philosophy talked to death in stupid chatter, politics even more fantastic and partisan than ever, society in complete dissolution, while the guardians of the old customs (Sitte) would have become laughable to themselves and would yearn for success in every area other than morals.[39]

The reader might be forgiven at this point when she asks herself why, given this castigation of existing morality, Nietzsche doesn't just let these educated women get on with tearing down the facade. Why not let the subversive subvert it all, anyway? The answer again is blindingly simple, if you start with a certain view of women and never, but never let go, however radical your scepticism about everything else might be. Given the chance to participate, women would not actually destroy things; they would reinforce it all, the whole structure of law and ethics and the state as the authoritative interpreter of values. Again, a quote from *Menschliches Allzumenschliches*.

As much as women honour their men, they honour the powers and notions which are acknowledged by society even more: for centuries they have given way to the dominant, bowed with their hands folded over their breasts, and they disapprove of any challenge to public authority.[40]

Women are thus excluded from participation in both Nietzsche's conceptions of the state, though for different reasons in each: from the ideal state because our nature denies and tames the source of morality, the 'will to power', and from the really-existing state because women's participation here would only deepen the cultural crisis. Both these exclusions point to a not inconsiderable failure in Nietzsche's philosophical system as a whole and in his cultural critique. Instead of pursuing the radical analysis of morality and politics which characterizes his view of every other specific issue, when it comes to women—the most effective carrier of those values he attacks in existing states—Nietzsche really does have nothing more to offer (as Heidwig Dohm noticed a century ago) than the common prejudices of his age and sex. On this point, perhaps the most crucial in his thought, Nietzsche betrays his own philosophical intentions.

HOW TO PHILOSOPHIZE WITH A HAMMER

The core of Nietzsche's philosophy criticized Kant's division of the world into noumenal and phenomenal and the accompanying elaboration of pure and practical reason. For Kant the rational world guided by truth was necessary because if a logically perfect and *a priori* true world were not conceivable, science and morals would also be impossible; both would be reduced to preferences, prejudices and partial visions of the world. This noumenal world, Kant argued, was human reason; its structures gave epistemology and ethics their coherence. Nietzsche's project a century later aimed at the destruction of that philosophical system, first in its epistemological certainties and, second, in the legitimacy of the moral customs which it sanctioned. Nietzsche's questions are destructive reversals of Kant's, which force men to give an account of themselves. Through geneology Nietzsche tried to discover not just the history of moral ideas and philosophical truth, but their meaning in time and place and their transformation into a 'mythological basis of action'. The result, as Tracy Strong's careful exposition demonstrates, is that there can be no permanent facts and no synthetic *a priori*; reason is always, for Nietzsche, reason about. All acts of intellect are creative.[41]

For the moral and political philosopher Nietzsche's deconstruction of Kantian philosophy raises important questions. The first concerns the consequences of what Strong calls 'a perverse necrophilia', the will to truth. If there is no world to be known and no structure of knowing that is unquestionable, then 'the desire to found knowledge on truth must result in the gradual undermining of that which might serve as a basis for truth'.[42] Erosion of the basis of science through its own activity—pushing the barriers of 'ignorance' further back—must gradually erode the distinction between the knower and the objects of knowledge.

At this level all knowledge will be conjectural in a particular way:

I maintain the phenomenality of the inner world too: everything of which we become conscious is arranged, simplified, schematized, interpreted through and through—the actual process of 'perception', the causal connection between thoughts, feelings, desires, between subject and object are hidden from us—and are perhaps only imaginary. The 'apparent *inner* world' is governed by just the same forms and procedures as the 'outer' world. We never encounter 'facts'... 'Causality' eludes us... 'Thinking' as epistemologists conceive it simply does not occur... both the deed and the doer are fictions.[43]

On this basis the cultural problematic is that much more intense. Knowledge in *this* society of *that* thing will become equivalent to knowledge in *that* society of *this* thing: the criteria of distinction, in the Kantian sense, have disappeared. In its place Nietzsche inserts a conception of *Lebensform* (form of life, or life-forms) according to which 'a form of life is a form of truth'.

Although Strong tries to save Nietzsche from interpretation as holding 'a *simplistic* relativistic notion that somehow, autre temps autres moeurs'[44] (my emphasis), can they save him from his own ultimately relativistic world view? Would they do him justice were they to succeed? Nietzsche's destruction of the basis for cultural graduations—which his contemporaries would have arranged on a scale ranging from civilized to barbaric—is exactly the radicalism of Nietzsche's philosophy. A superficial interpretation of Nietzsche's position which understands knowledge as something that can be changed at will because it is all illusion is certainly false. The social and moral function of knowledge is too vital an aspect of Nietzsche's philosophy to allow that perspective:

The valuation 'I believe this and that is so' as the essence of 'truth'. In Valuations are expressed conditions of preservation and growth... Trust in reason and its categories, in dialectic, therefore the valuation of logic, proves only their usefulness for life proved by experience—not that something is true... What is needed is that something must be held to be true—not that something is true. 'The real and apparent world'—I have traced this antithesis back to value preservations. We have projected the conditions of our preservation as predicates of being in general. Because we have to be stable in our beliefs if we are to prosper, we have made the 'real' world a world not of change and becoming, but one of being.[45]

When these two aspects of Nietzsche's thought are brought together—a radical critique of cultures and the peculiar specificity of knowing anything at all—questions about the political implications of Nietzsche's philosophy force themselves into the foreground. The first aspect of Nietzsche's thought focuses on the power of discourse in every language, and language itself as a vehicle and expression of social power; second, it tries to reveal the power which objects in the world have over their observer-creator. Finally, each of these perspectives imply questions about rights or access in respect of them, and from both these perspectives Nietzsche's philosophy demonstrates a remarkable continuity with his predecessors on the subject of women. Like Kant, Nietzsche excludes women as knowers, but in even more violent language: 'When a woman has scholarly inclinations there is usually something wrong with her sexually'.[46] And in respect of the second element of Nietzsche's thought, here too conservatism rather than a radical break marks out his horizon. In a philosophical world from which all facts have disappeared, 'woman' remains as one, an object seen and known, a thing in a world out there.

CONCLUSION

Nietzsche's predecessors in the history of Western political thought almost unanimously opposed the participation of women in politics and the life of the state. Exceptions to this view are rare, and the reader might well ask—so consistent is the history of misogyny in philosophy—how these few came to hold the view they did. In Nietzsche's case, it is not an unfair conclusion to say that on the question of women, his refusal of us was as radical and thorough-going as it was consistent with the inherited prejudice of centuries of philosophers before him. Women cannot be citizens of either state: the really-existing or the ideal. The one would only deepen Europe's cultural crises, while the other is a contradiction in terms. The grounds for women's exclusion in both cases are the same. Other philosophers regarded women as ineligible for citizenship because women are not, on their account, rational beings. For Nietzsche the reasons are rather different, and it is as though, having finally managed to gain acceptance in the set of potential citizens (=human beings), the rules are suddenly changed against us. Instead of intellect, what now counts is will. And while Nietzsche is prepared, unlike Schopenhauer, to grant that women are rational beings, and are actually more rational than men, this isn't quite the right thing to be. Women have passion too, and more than men; but again, this isn't quite right either. What is it then? The answer lies, again, in *Menschliches Allzumenschliches*, where the line of argument is set out in stages: women have reason, but it doesn't count; women have passion, but the wrong kind; men have less reason and less passion than women—but mysteriously, their combination of both is just the right one.[47]

The reader who reads Nietzsche's sections on women as though he really meant what he wrote—they are neither ironical, nor simple mistakes about what constitutes being a human being, but intentional exclusion and subordination of women—will, I think, come to reject the new Nietzsche Walter Kaufmann found in the early 1950s. Kaufmann's central claim, as the introduction noted, was that Nietzsche's conception of a will to power had been misunderstood in the second, political phase of its interpretation; the strong don't wish to hurt, but the weak do. Reading Nietzsche's texts 'neutrally' allowed Kaufmann to depict the philosopher as a psychologist. But when the passages dealing with women are read as gender specific, and those dealing with men and *Übermenschen* too, Kaufmann's interpretation becomes rather strained. For it is women who are weak, but also women who are caring and loving, while men—the stronger sex—are not. Although the *Übermensch* is one who has 'overcome himself', Nietzsche's texts depict him as one overcoming a succession of 'weaker' types, but above all women: first mothers, then as lovers, finally 'woman' as a cultural gestalt.

Both the ground for women's subordination in women's biology and Nietzsche's coherently masculine state of adventurers and warriors are founded on a Darwinistically derived master-sex. In light of this the preoccupation with Nietzsche as anti- or philo- Semitic seems rather antiquated: his ideal state is not 'Teutonic', nor is Nietzsche a racialist in the earlier sense. But he is, in our sense of it, the founder of peculiarly modern patriarchy and the inventor of one of the crassest and most subtle misogynies: 'The enormous expectation in sexual love and the sense of shame in this expectation spoils all perspective for women from the start'.[48]

NOTES

Unless otherwise indicated, all references to Nietzsche's work are taken from *Werke, Kritische Gesamtausgabe*, ed. Giorgio Colli and Mazzino Montinari (Berlin, de Gruyter, 1967).

1. Giles Deleuze, *Nietzsche und die Philosophie* (German trans. of *Nietzsche et la philosophie,* 1962 (München, Roger and Bernhard, 1976)); Arthur C. Danto, *Nietzsche as Philosopher* (New York: Macmillan, 1965).
2. Alfred Bäumler edited Nietzsche's works for the Kröner edition, Dünndruck Gesamtausgabe, (6 vols., Leipsig, Kröner, 1930) and produced the afterwords for the current Kröner edition. He wrote among other postscripts books and articles on the subject: 'Nietzsche und der National-sozialismus' (1934), in *Studien zur deutschen Geistesgeschichte* (Berlin, Junker and Dünnhaupt, 1937); *Nietzsche der Philosoph und Politiker* (Leipzig, Reclam, 1931). For a very competent discussion of Bäumler's interpretation and its political context, see Rudolf R. Kuenzli, 'The Nazi appropriation of Nietzsche', *Nietzsche-Studien* 12 (1983), 428—435.
3. Georg Lukács, 'Die Zerstörung der Vernunft' (1954), in Jörg Salaquarda (ed.), *Nietzsche* (Darmstadt, Wissenschaftliche Buchgesellschaft, 1980), p. 88. On the influence of Bäumler and Lukács, cf. Mazzino Montinari 'Nietzsche zwischen Alfred Bäumler und Georg Lukács', *Basis* 9 (1979), 188–223.
4. Kuenzli, 'The Nazi appropriation of Nietzsche', p. 429.
5. Georges Bataille, *Sur Nietzsche* (Paris, Gallimard, 1945) and Karl Jaspers, *Nietzsche: Einführung in das Verständnis seines Philosophierens* (Berlin and Leipzig, de Gruyter, 1936).
6. Walter Kaufmann, *Nietzsche: Philosopher, Psychologist, Antichrist,* (Princeton NJ, Princeton University Press, 1950,[1] 1974[4]). On Kaufmann's interpretation and the current controversy over Kaufmann's interpretation, see 'The political uses and abuses of Nietzsche', Session at the Modern Languages Association (1980) reprinted in *Nietzsche-Studien* 12 (1983), 428 ff. Kuenzli's paper appeared first here; but see also Walter H. Sokel, 'Political uses and abuses of Nietzsche in Walter Kaufmann's image of

Nietzsche', *Nietzsche-Studien* 12 (1983), 436–42, and the earlier critique by Kurt Rudolf Fischer, 'Nazism as a Nietzschean experiment', *Nietzsche-Studien* 6 (1977), 116–22.

7. Kaufmann, p. 310.

8. *Ibid.,* p. 194.

9. Each of the four 'untimely meditations' attacks aspects of contemporary German taste and cultural values via a critique of their expression in public attitudes toward leading cultural–political figures (David Strauss, Schopenhauer, Richard Wagner). The first section already makes clear Nietzsche's immediate referent: expansive German nationalism after the Prussian victory over France in 1871. Of all the evil consequences that have followed the recent war with France, Nietzsche writes, the worst is the universal belief that 'German culture too was victorious'. (Nietzsche, *Unzeitgemasse Betrachtungen,* 'David Strauss, der Bekenner und der Schriftsteller', section 1, quoted from the translation by R.J. Hollingdale, *Untimely Meditations,* Cambridge University Press, 1983, p. 3).

10. Hedwig Dohm, 'Nietzsche und die Frauen', *Die Zukunft* 25 (1898), p. 534. Hedwig Dohm was a leading feminist at the turn of the century in Germany, the author of many books on women's social and intellectual position, among them: *Die Wissenschaftliche Emanzipation der Frau* (1874); *Der Frauen Natur und Recht* (1876); and *Die Antifeministen* (1902). It is very likely that Elizabeth Förster-Nietzsche's references to feminists and their 'false' *(sic)* interpretation of her brother was inspired by Dohm. Elizabeth Förster-Nietzsche, *Nietzsche und die Frauen seiner Zeit* (München, Beck, 1935) pp. 5 ff; here Elizabeth Förster-Nietzsche claims that her brother planned to write a book on women, *Das Weib,* 'in which he would treat the woman-problem scientifically and with certainty' (p. 155). A list of chapter headings is all that came of the intention, and these are reproduced in her book (p. 156). A number of aphorisms strewn throughout Nietzsche's works 'certainly would have belonged to the contents of this book' Förster-Nietzsche comments, but the contents alone do not give an indication of what he would have said. In lieu of this, she quotes Hans Vaihinger, *Nietzsche als Philosoph,* at length (cf. 157–61). I have not been able to verify the existence of the contents of a planned book on women.

11. Dohm, 'Nietzsche und die Frauen', p. 535.

12. Henry Walter Braun, *Nietzsche und die Frauen* (Bonn, Bouvier Verlag, 1978). On the relationship between Lou Andreas-Solomé and Nietzsche—brief, confused and unhappy that it was—see the very different views of Elizabeth Förster-Nietzsche, *Nietzsche und die Frauen,* pp. 108 ff. and Lou Andreas-Solomé, *Lebensrückblick. Grundriss einiger Lebenserinnerungen,* (Frankfurt/M., Insel Verlag,) pp. 75ff., and Andreas-Solomé, *Friedrich Nietzsche in seinen Werken* (Wien, Konegen, 1911). A picture of her, whip in hand, driving a pony cart pulled by Nietzsche and Paul Ree produces a special irony in light of *Zarathustra* advice from the old woman. The humiliation of this failure in love certainly contributed to Nietzsche's views on women. See Ronald Hayman, *Nietzsche: A Critical Life* (London, Weidenfeld and Nicolson, 1980) which also reproduces the photograph of Andreas-Solomé, Paul Ree and Nietzsche.

13. Hans Vaihinger, *Nietzsche als Philosoph* (Berlin, Reuter und Richard, 1916) 'Das eigentümliche Grundprinzip Nietzsche's'.

14. *Ibid.,* p. 24.

15. *Ibid.,* p. 34.

16. Ferdinand Tönnies, *Der Nietzsche-Kultus, Eine Kritik* (Leipzig, Reisland, 1897), pp. 78–9.

17. *Ibid.,* pp. 108 ff.

18. Fredrick Copleston, *Arthur Schopenhauer: Philosopher of Pessimism* (London, Search Press, 1946), p. 39.

19. Vaihinger, p. 79.

20. Arthur Schopenhauer, 'Pererga und Paralipomena', in *Sämtliche Werke* ed. von Löhneysen, (Darmstadt, Wissenschaftliche Buchgesellschaft, 1976), vol. 5, sect. 369.

21. *Ibid.,* Sect. 366.

22. *Ibid.,* Sect. 364.

23. Vaihinger, p. 79.

24. Nietzsche, *Menschliches, Allzumenschliches,* sect. 432.

25. Förster-Nietzsche, p. 159.

26. Nietzsche, *Ecce Homo* (Kaufmann trans.) p. 267.

27. *Ibid.,* pp. 266–7.

28. Nietzsche, *The Will to Power,* sect. 864.

29. *Ibid.,* sect. 460.

30. *Ibid.,* sect. 460.

31. Nietzsche, *Menschliches, Allzumenschliches,* sect. 433.

32. *Ibid.,* sect. 434, cf. Andreas-Solomé, *Nietzsche in seinen Werken.*

33. Nietzsche, *The Will to Power,* sect. 719.

34. *Ibid.,* sect. 717.

35. Nietzsche's library contained not just the complete works in German translation, but also a single volume with Mill's and Harriet Taylors' essays on women's subjugation and enfranchisement. 'He studied the volume on women's emancipation, the worker question and socialism so carefully', Karl Brose comments, 'that exact citations appear in his work.' Karl Brose, 'Nietzsche's Verhaltnis zu John Stuart Mill', *Nietzsche-Studien,* 3, 1974, 152–4.

36. Nietzsche, *The Will to Power,* sect. 720.

37. *Ibid.,* sect. 717.

38. Quotations in this paragraph are from *Menschliches Allzumenschliches,* sects. 416 and 419.

39. *Ibid.,* sect. 425.

40. *Ibid.,* sect. 435.

41. Tracy B. Strong, *Friedrich Nietzsche and the Politics of Transfiguration* (Berkeley, University of California Press, 1975), 42 ff.

42. *Ibid.,* 76.

43. Nietzsche, *The Will to Power.*

44. Strong. pp. 44–5.

45. Nietzsche, *The Will to Power,* sect. 507.

46. Friedrich Nietzsche, *Beyond Good and Evil: Prelude to a Philosophy of the Future,* trans. with commentary by Walter Kaufmann, New York,

Vintage Books, 1966, sect. 144.

47. Nietzsche, *Menschliches Allzumenschliches* 'Weib und Kind'.

48. Nietzsche, *Beyond Good and Evil,* sect. 114.

Bibliography

GENERAL BIBLIOGRAPHY

Bethke Elshtain, Jean. *Public Man and Private Woman: Women in Social and Political Thought,* (Princeton, NJ, Princeton University Press, 1981)

Bethke Elshtain, Jean (ed.). *The Family in Political Thought* (Brighton, Harvester Press, 1982)

Butler, M. 'Early Liberal Roots of Feminism: John Locke and the Attack on Patriarchy', *American Political Science Review* 72 (1978)

Clark, L. and Lange, L. *The Sexism of Social and Political Theory: Women and Reproduction from Plato to Nietzsche* (Toronto, 1979)

Delphy, Christine. *Close to Home: A Materialist Analysis of Women's Oppression* (London, Hutchinson, 1984)

Eisenstein, Zillah. *The Radical Future of Liberal Feminism* (New York, 1981)

Enloe, Cynthia. *Does Khaki Become You? The Militarisation of women's lives* (London, Pluto, 1983)

Firestone, Shulamith. *The Dialectic of Sex: The Case for Feminist Revolution* (London, Women's Press, 1979)

Flora, C.B. and Lynn, N.B. 'Women and political socialization: considerations of the impact of motherhood', in J. Jaquette, (ed.) *Women in Politics,* (New York, Wiley, 1974)

Gould, C.C. and Wartofsky, M.W. (ed.). *Women and Philosophy: Toward a Theory of Liberation,* (New York, Capricorn, 1976)

Jennings, M.K. and Parah, B.C. 'Ideology, gender and political action: a cross-national survey' *British Journal of Political Science,* 10 (1980)

Lloyd, Genevieve. 'The Man of Reason. "Male" and "Female" ', in *Western Philosophy* (London, 1984)

Lyndon Shanley, Mary. 'Marriage contract and social contract in seventeenth-century English political thought', *Western Political Quarterly* 32 (1979)

Maclean, Ian. *The Renaissance Notion of Woman: A Study in the Fortunes of Scholasticism and Medical Science in European Intellectual Life* (Cambridge, Cambridge University Press, 1980)

McLuhan, M. *Understanding Media* (London, Routledge and Kegan Paul, 1964)

Meld Shell, Susan. *The Rights of Reason* (Toronto, University of Toronto Press, 1980)

Midgley, Mary and Hughes, Judith. *Women's Choices* (London, Weidenfeld and Nicolson, 1983)

Moller Okin, Susan. *Women in Western Political Thought* (Princeton, Princeton University Press, 1979)

Pateman, Carole. ' "The Disorder of Women", Women, Love and the Sense of Justice', *Ethics* 91 (1980)

Pateman, Carole. 'Feminist Critiques of the Public/Private Dichotomy', in S.J. Benn and G.F. Gaus (ed.), *Public and Private in Social Life* (London, Croom Helm; New York, St Martin's Press, 1983)

Pateman, Carole. 'Women and Consent', *Political Theory* 8 (1980) 2

Pomper, G. *Voters Choice* (New York, Dodd Mead, 1975)

Randall, V. *Women and Politics* (London, Macmillan, 1982)

Richards, J.R. *The Sceptical Feminist* (Penguin Books, 1982)

Rose, Gillian. *Dialectic of Nihilism,* (Oxford, Blackwell, 1984)

Verba, S., Nie, N.H. and Kim, J.O. *Participation and Political Equality: A Seven-Nation Comparison* (Cambridge, Cambridge University Press, 1978)

Welch, S. 'Women as Political Animals? A Test of Some Explanations for Male–Female Political Participation Differences, *American Journal of Political Science,* 21 (1977)

KANT: BIBLIOGRAPHY

I. Texts and Editions

Anthropology from a Pragmatic Point of View, trans. M. Gregor (The Hague, Martinus Nijhoff, 1974)

The Metaphysical Elements of Justice, trans. John Ladd (Indianapolis, Bobbs-Merrill, 1965)

Metaphysic of Morals and *Theory and Practice,* in G.H. Reiss (ed.), *Kant's Political Writings* (Cambridge, Cambridge University Press, 1970)

Philosophical Correspondence, 1759-99, ed. Arnulf Zweig (Chicago, University of Chicago, 1967)

II. Secondary Sources
Cohen, Morris R. 'A Critique of Kant's Philosophy of Law', in G.T. Whitney and D.F. Bowers (eds.), *The Heritage of Kant* (New York Russell and Russell, 1962)

Williams, Howard. *Kant's Political Philosophy* (Oxford, Blackwell, 1983)

Aris, Rheinhold. *History of Political Thought in Germany 1789-1815* (London, Frank Cass and Co., 1965)

ADAM SMITH: BIBLIOGRAPHY

I. Texts and Editions
An Inquiry into the Nature and Causes of Nations, ed. R.H. Campbell, A.S. Skinner, and W.B. Todd (2 vols., (Oxford, Oxford University Press, 1979)

The Theory of Moral Sentiments, ed. D.D. Raphael and A.L. Macfie, (Oxford, Oxford University Press, 1976)

II. Secondary Sources
Bryson, G. *Man and Society: The Scottish Inquiry of the Eighteenth Century* (Princeton, NJ, Princeton University Press, 1945)

Campbell, T.D. *Adam Smith's Science of Morals,* (London, 1971)

Chitnis, A. *The Scottish Enlightenment: A Social History* (London, 1976)

Cropsey, J. *Polity and Economy: An Interpretation of the Principles of Adam Smith* (The Hague, 1957)

Forbes, D. *Hume's Philosophical Politics* (Cambridge, 1975)

Haakonssen, K. *The Science of a Legislator: The Natural Jurisprudence of David Hume and Adam Smith* (Cambridge, 1981)

Hont, I. and Ignatieff, M. (eds.) *Wealth and Virtue: The Shaping of Political Economy in the Scottish Enlightenment* (Cambridge, 1983)

Hutcheson, Francis. *Short Introduction to Moral Philosophy... Containing the Elements of Ethics and the Law of Nature,* trans. from the Latin (Glasgow, 1750)

Krieger, L. *The Politics of Discretion* (Chicago, 1965)

Lindgren, J. Ralph. *The Social Philosophy of Adam Smith*, (The Hague, 1973)

Macintyre, Alasdair. *After Virtue: A Study in Moral Theory*, (London, 1981)

Meek, R. *Social Science and the Ignoble Savage*, (Cambridge, 1976)

Pocock, J.G.A. *The Machiavellian Moment: Florentine Political Thought and the Atlantic Republican Tradition* (Princeton, NJ, 1975)

Pocock, J.G.A. *Politics, Language and Time* (London, 1972)

Pocock, J.G.A. 'Virtue, Rights and Manners. A Model for Historians of Political Thought', *Political Theory* 9 (1981)

Reisman, D.A. *Adam Smith's Sociological Economics* (London, 1976)

Rendall, Jane. *The Origins of the Scottish Enlightenment, 1707–1776* (London, 1978)

Robbins, Caroline. *The Eighteenth Century Commonwealthsman*, (Cambridge, Mass., 1959)

Rosenberg, N. 'Adam Smith's Consumer Tastes and Economic Growth', in: *Journal of Political Economy* 76 (1968)

Schneider, L. *The Scottish Moralists on Human Nature and Society* (Chicago, 1967)

Scott, W.R. *Francis Hutcheson: His Life, Teaching and Position in the History of Philosophy*, (1900; repr. New York, 1966)

Skinner, A. *A System of Social Science: Papers relating to Adam Smith* (Oxford, 1979)

Stein, P. *Legal Evolution* (Cambridge, 1980)

Stewart, Dugald. 'Account of the Life and Writings of Adam Smith LL.D. from the Transactions of the Royal Society of Edinburgh . . .', repr. in *Adam Smith: Essays on Philosophical Subjects*, ed. W.P.D. Wightman (Oxford, 1980)

Taylor, W.L. 'Gershom Carmichael: A Neglected Figure in British Political Economy', in *South African Journal of Economics* 13 (1955)

Tribe, Keith. *Land, Labour and Economic Discourse* (London, 1978)

Tuck, R. *Natural Rights Theories: Their Origins and Development* (Cambridge, 1981)

Winch, Donald. *Adam Smith's Politics: An Essay in Historiographic Revision* (Cambridge, 1978)

Wodrow, Robert. *Analecta: Or Materials for a History of Remarkable Providences; Mostly Relating to Scotch Ministers and Christians*, (4 vols., Glasgow, 1843)

Wodrow, Robert. *Reflections upon Laughter, and the Fable of the Bees* (Glasgow, 1750)

JEAN-JACQUES ROUSSEAU: BIBLIOGRAPHY

I. Texts and Editions

Consideration on the Government of Poland; Rousseau's Political Writings, trans. F. Watkins (Edinburgh, Nelson, 1953)

Oeuvres Complètes de Jean-Jacques Rousseau (Paris, Bibliothèque de la Pléiade, 1959–69)

Politics and the Arts: Letter to M. d'Alembert on the Theatre, trans. A. Bloom (Glencoe, Free Press, 1960)

The Social Contract, trans. by M. Cranston (Harmondsworth, Penguin, 1968)

The Social Contract and Discourses, trans. G.D.H. Cole (London, Dent, 1913)

II. Secondary Sources

Arendt, Hannah. *Eichmann in Jerusalem* (London, Faber, 1963)

Arendt, Hannah. *The Human Condition* (Garden City, Doubleday, 1959)

Berman, M. *The Politics of Authenticity* (London, Allen and Unwin, 1971)

Canovan, M. 'The Limits of Seriousness: Rousseau and the Interpretation of Political Theory', in *European Studies Review* 2 (1972)

Ellenburg, S. *Rousseau's Political Philosophy: An Interpretation from Within* (Ithaca and London, Cornell University Press, 1976)

Derathé, R. *Jean-Jacques Rousseau et la Science Politique de son Temps* (Paris, Presses Universitaires de France, 1950)

Fralin, R. *Rousseau and Representation* (New York, Columbia University Press, 1978)

Gellner, E. *Nations and Nationalism* (Oxford, Blackwell, 1983)

Groethuysen, B. *Jean-Jacques Rousseau* (Paris, Gallimard, 1949)

Masters, Roger D. *The Political Philosophy of Rousseau* (Princeton, NJ, Princeton University Press, 1968)

Millar, James. *Rousseau: Dreamer of Democracy* (Yale, Yale University Press, 1984)

Schwartz, J. *The Sexual Politics of Jean-Jacques Rousseau* (Chicago, University of Chicago Press, 1984)

Shklar, J.N. *Men and Citizens: A Study of Rousseau's Social*

Theory (Cambridge, Cambridge University Press, 1969)

Talmon, J.L. *The Origins of Totalitarian Democracy* (London, Secker and Warburg, 1952)

Wexler, V. ' "Made for Man's Delight": Rousseau as antifeminist', in *American Historical Review* 81 (1976)

HUMBOLDT AND THE ROMANTICS: BIBLIOGRAPHY

I. Texts and Editions

Behrens, K. (ed.). *Frauenbriefe der Romantik* (Frankfurt, Insel Verlag, 1981)

Hippel, T.G. von. *Über die bürgerliche Verbesserung der Weiber* (1793), (Frankfurt, Syndicat 1977)

Humboldt, Wilhelm von. *Werke* (Stuttgart, Cotta, 1960)

The Poems and Ballads of Schiller, trans. Sir Edward Bulwer Lytton (London and New York, Frederick Warne and Co., 1887)

Schlegel, Caroline. Letter of 27 December 1799, quoted in Gisela Dischner, *Friedrich Schlegels Lucinde und Materialien zu einer Theorie des Müssiggangs,* (Hildesheim, Gerstenberg Verlag, 1980)

Schlegel, Friedrich. 'Gespräch über die Poesie' (1799), in *Kritische Schriften,* ed. W. Rasch, (München, Carl Hanser Verlag, 1956)

Schlegel, Friedrich. *Theorie der Weiblichkeit,* ed. W. Mennighaus, (Frankfurt, Insel Verlag, 1983)

Schleiermacher, Friedrich. *Vertraute Briefe über Schlegels Lucinde* (Frankfurt M, Insel Verlag, 1964)

II. Secondary Sources

Burrow, J.W. *Introduction to Wilhelm von Humboldt, The Limits of State Action* (Cambridge, Cambridge University Press, 1969)

Condorcet, M. 'On the Admission of Women to the Rights of Citizenship' (1790), in *Selected Writings,* ed. K.M. Baker (Indianapolis, Bobbs-Merrill Company Inc., 1976)

Dischner, Gisela. *Caroline und der Jenaer Kreis. Ein Leben zwischen bürgerlicher Vereinzelung und romantischer Geselligkeit* (Berlin, Wagenbach, 1979)

Dischner, Caroline. *Friedrich Schlegels Lucinde und Materialien zu einer Theorie des Müssiggangs,* (Hildesheim, Gerstenberg Verlag, 1980)

Giese, F. *Der romantische Charakter*

Huebner, R. *A History of Germanic Private Law,* trans. F.S. Philbrick (London, John Murray, 1918)

Kelly, Petra. *Fighting for Hope,* trans. M. Howarth (London, Chatto and Windus, 1984)

Klessmann, E. *Caroline. Das Leben der Caroline Michaelis— Böhmer—Schlegel—Schelling, 1763–1809* (München, Deutscher Taschenbuch Verlag, 1979)

Kluckhohn, Paul. *Die Auffassung der Liebe in der Literatur des 18. Jahrhunderts und in der deutschen Romantik,* (Tübingen, 1966)

Lovejoy, A. 'The Meaning of "Romantic" in Early German Romanticism', in A. Lovejoy, *Essays in the History of Ideas* (Baltimore and London, Johns Hopkins Press, 1948)

Marcuse, Ludwig. *Obszön. Geschichte einer Entrüstung,* (München, 1962)

Mill, John Stuart. *On Liberty* (London, Dent, 1972)

Sweet, P.R. *Wilhelm von Humboldt: A Biography,* vol. I, (1978)

Vogel, Ursula. 'Liberty is Beautiful: von Humboldt's Gift to Liberalism', in *History of Political Thought* 3 (Jan. 1982)

Wellek, R. *A History of Modern Criticism 1750-1950,* vol. 2., *The Romantic Age* (Cambridge, Cambridge University Press, 1981)

Wollstonecraft, Mary. *A Vindication of the Rights of Woman,* ed. M. Kramnick (Harmondsworth, Penguin, 1975)

HEGEL: BIBLIOGRAPHY

I. Texts and Editions

The Phenomenology of Spirit, trans. A.V. Miller (Oxford, Oxford University Press, 1977)

The Science of Logic, trans. A.V. Miller (London, Allen and Unwin 1969)

The Philosophy of Right, trans. T.M. Knox (Oxford, Oxford University Press, 1952)

The Philosophy of Mind, being Part 3 of *The Encyclopaedia of the Philosophical Sciences,* trans. W. Wallace and A.V. Miller (Oxford, Oxford University Press, 1971)

Lectures on the Philosophy of World History: Introduction, trans. Nisbet; Intro. by Duncan Forbes (Cambridge, Cambridge University Press, 1975)

Lectures on the History of Philosophy (Suhrkamp Werke Bd. 20, 1971)

II. Secondary Sources
Easton, Susan. 'Functionalism and feminism in Hegel's political thought', *Radical Philosophy* 38.

FRIEDRICH NIETZSCHE: BIBLIOGRAPHY

I. Texts and Editions
German: *Werke,* Kritische Gesamtausgabe, ed. Giorgio Colli and Mazzino Montinari (Berlin, de Gruyter, 1967)
Werke, Kröner edition, Dünndruck Gesamtausgabe, ed. Alfred Bäumler (Leipzig, Kröner, 1930)
Beyond Good and Evil: Prelude to a Philosophy of the Future, trans. with commentary by Walter Kaufmann, (New York, Vintage Books, 1966)
The Will to Power, trans. Walter Kaufmann and R.J. Hollingdale, (New York, Vintage Books, 1968)

II. Secondary Sources
Andreas-Solomé, Lou. *Friedrich Nietzsche in seinen Werken* (Wien, Konegen, 1911)
Andreas-Solomé, Lou. *Lebensrückblick. Grundriss einiger Lebenserinnerungen* (Frankfurt/M., Insel Verlag, 1911)
Bäumler, Alfred. *Nietzsche der Philosoph und Politiker* (Leipzig, Reclam 1931)
Bäumler, Alfred. 'Nietzsche und der Nationalsozialismus', in *Studien zur deutschen Geistesgeschichte* (Berlin, Junker und Dünnhaupt, 1937)
Bataille, Georges. *Sur Nietzsche* (Paris, Gallimard, 1945)
Berthold, A. *Bücher und Wege zu Büchern* (Stuttgart, Spemann, 1900)
Braun, Henry Walter. *Nietzsche und die Frauen* (Bonn, Bouvier Verlag, 1978)
Brose, Karl. 'Nietzsches Verhältnis zu John Stuart Mill', *Nietzsche-Studien* 3 (1974) 152–74
Copleston, Fredrick. *Arthur Schopenhauer: Philosopher of Pessimism* (London: Search Press, 1946)
Danto, Arthur C. *Nietzsche as Philospher,* (New York, Macmillan, 1965)
Deleuze, Giles. *Nietzsche und die Philosophie,* (German trans. of *Nietzsche et la philosophie,* 1962, (München, Roger and Bernhard, 1976)
Dohm, Hedwig. *Die Antifeministen,* (Berlin F. Dümmerverlag, 1902)

Dohm, Hedwig. *Der Frauen Natur und Recht,* (Berlin, Wedekind und Schwieger, 1876)

Dohm, Hedwig. 'Nietzsche und die Frauen', *Die Zukunft* 25 (1898)

Dohm, Hedwig. *Die Wissenschaftliche Emanzipation der Frau* (Berlin, Wedekind und Schwieger, 1874)

Fischer, Kurt Rudolf. 'Nazism as a Nietzschean Experiment', *Nietzsche-Studien* 6 (1977) 116–122

Förster-Nietzsche, Elizabeth. *Nietzsche und die Frauen seiner Zeit* (München, Beck, 1935)

Hayman, Ronald. *Nietzsche: A Critical Life* (London, Weidenfeld and Nicolson, 1980)

Jaspers, Karl. *Nietzsche: Einführung in das Verständnis seines Philosophierens* (Berlin and Leipzig, de Gruyter, 1936)

Kaufmann, Walter. *Nietzsche: Philosopher, Psychologist, Antichrist,* (Princeton, NJ, Princeton University Press, 1950, 1974)

Kuenzli, Rudolf E. 'The Nazi Appropriation of Nietzsche', *Nietzsche-Studien* 12 (1983), 428–35

Lukács, Georg. 'Die Zerstörung der Vernunft' (1954), in: *Jörg Salaquarda, Nietzsche,* (Darmstadt, Wissenschaftliche Buchgesellschaft, 1980)

Modern Languages Association. *The Political Uses and Abuses of Nietzsche, 1980* rep. in *Nietzsche-Studien* 12 (1983), 428 ff.

Montinari, Mazzino. 'Nietzsche zwischen Alfred Bäumler und Georg Lukács', *Basis* 9 (1979), 188–223

Schopenhauer, Arthur. 'Pererga und Paralipomena' in *Sämtliche Werke,* ed. von Löhneysen, (Darmstadt: Wissenschaftliche Buchgesellschaft, 1976), sect. 369

Sokel, Walter H. 'Political Uses and Abuses of Nietzsche in Walzer Kaufmann's Image of Nietzsche', *Nietzsche-Studien,* 12 (1983)

Strong, Tracy B. *Friedrich Nietzsche and the Politics of Transfiguration* (Berkeley, University of California Press, 1975)

Tönnies, Ferdinand. *Der Nietzsche-Kultus. Eine Kritik* (Leipzig, Reisland, 1897)

Vaihinger, Hans. *Nietzsche als Philosph,* (Berlin, Reuter und Richard, 1916)

Index

Absolutism, 6, 7
Accidentality, 134–5
Active/passive citizenship, 25–30, 34
Animal life, 149–51, 164
Antigone, analysis by Hegel, 129, 135, 136–7, 144, 151–2
Aris, Rheinhold, 22, 39
Authority, 2–3
Autonomy, 80–4, 91, 165

Bataille, Georges, 180
Bäumler, Alfred, 180
Bentham, Jeremy, 9, 161, 162, 163–5, 168, 170, 172
Bildung, 109–10, 118–20
Bodin, Jean, 3
Boralevi, Lea, 9–10
Braun, Henry, 182
Brougham, Henry, 170

Caird, E. 40
Canovan, Margaret, 5–7, 9, 12, 13
Carmichael, Gershom, 47, 49–51
Chastity, 60
    see also Fidelity
Children, 48, 50, 55, 69, 93, 130–1
    see also Motherhood
Christianity, 66, 182–3

Citizenship, 2, 3, 44, 56, 196–7
    active/passive, 25–30, 34
    Greek model, 6, 8
    juristic, 80–1, 91
    Kant on, 23–30
    Rousseau on, 78–101
    Spartan, 81–4, 89
City state, 45, 84
Classical republicanism, 45, 52, 56
Cohen, M.R., 22–3, 36
Communal living, 107
Comte, Auguste, 168
Condorcet, M., 17, 121
Consanguinity, 49, 67–8
Contractual relationships, 46–9, 54
Copleston, Frederick, 184

Declaration of Independence, 1, 17
Declaration of Rights of Man (France), 1
Delphy, Christine, 128, 134
Deleuze, Giles, 179
Democracy, 190–1
Desires, 145
Differences between sexes, 109–10, 111–17, 133–6, 145, 146, 149, 167–70
Divorce, 48–9, 51, 54, 65, 67, 111, 165, 170

211

Dohm, Hedwig, 182, 193
Domesticity, 8–9, 93, 146–7
  Rousseau on, 85–90
  as woman's world, 117–20
Dupin, Madame, 85

Education, 61, 69–70, 83,
    130–1, 135, 137–8, 145,
    169, 170
Elshtain, Jean Bethke, 90, 127
Emotion, 16
Equality, 1
  of citizenship, 94–7
  Kant on, 33–4
  in marriage, 54
  natural, 33–4, 39
  and utility, 163–70
Ethics, 133, 152–4

Family, 135–40, 147–8
  see also Children,
  Domesticity, Marriage,
  Public/private distinction
Fascism and Nietzsche, 180
Fear, 183–4
Female values, 15–17
Femininity, 111–14
Feminism, 14–19
  and Rousseau, 90–100
  and utilitarianism, 159–75
Fidelity, 63–4
  see also Chastity
Fletcher, Andrew, 45
Förster-Nietzsche, Elizabeth,
    180, 182, 184, 185
Fourier, 174, 175
Freedom, 2, 80–4, 91
  and nature, 143, 150
French Revolution, 22, 108,
    121

Gellner, Ernest, 98

Generosity, 58–9
Gierke, Otto von, 2
Goodwin, William, 162, 171
Governmental power, 2
Grotius, Hugo, 46
Griffin, Susan, 151

Haakonssen, Knud, 67–8
Hampshire, Stuart, 16
Hegel, 9, 12, 127–56
  analysis of Antigone, 129,
    135, 136–7, 144, 151–2
  tensions in political analysis,
    128–30, 131, 137, 140
Helvetius, 162, 167, 169
Historical position of women,
    64–6, 68
Hobbes, Thomas, 3, 141
Hodge, Joanna, 7–8, 11, 12,
    13
Humboldt, Wilhelm von,
    110–12
Hughes, Judith, 21, 37
Hume, David, 60
Hume, Joseph, 170
Hutcheson, Francis, 47, 51–7,
    71

Independence, 24–30
  see also Autonomy
Individual freedom, 2, 80–4,
    91
Individualism, 39–41, 191
Institutions, 141

Jaspers, Karl, 180
Jealousy, 63–4
Jurisprudence, natural, 45–6,
    50, 62
Juristic citizenship, 80–1, 91

Kant, Immanuel, 9, 10, 12,

21–41, 130
  on citizenship, 23–30
  Hegel on, 143–4
  on marriage, 30–6
  Nietzsche on, 194–5
Kaufmann, Walter, 180, 183, 191, 197
Kelly, Petra, 122
Knowledge, 194–6
Kuenzli, Rudolf, 180

Ladd, John, 23–4, 38
Landes, Carol B., 127
Law, 151–5, 162
  see also Legislation
Legislation, 14, 64, 165
  and morals, 162
  see also Law
Liberalism, 91–2
Locke, John, 50, 53, 92
Love, 60, 96–7, 115–17, 121
Lukàcs, Georg, 180

Macauley, T.B., 173
Machiavelli, 45
Macintyre, Alasdair, 71–2
Male values, 15
Marriage
  Carmichael on, 49–51
  Hegel on, 131–3
  Humboldt on, 110–11
  Hutcheson on, 52–6
  Kant on, 30–6
  Pufendorf on, 47–51
  Smith on, 59–72
Marxism, 18–19
McLuhan, Marshall, 101
Menschlichkeit, 113–15
Midgley, Mary, 21, 37
Mill, James, 169, 170, 171, 172–5

Mill, John Stuart, 4, 9, 12, 17, 41, 116, 164, 166–9, 171–2, 190
Molesworth, Viscount, 45
Monarchy, 3
Montesquieu, 45
Moral arithmetic, 159, 161
Moral faculty, 52
Morality, 7
  see also Ethics
Motherby, Elizabeth, 38
Motherhood, 13, 97, 112, 185–6
  see also Children
Moyle, Walter, 45

Natural
  equality, 33–4, 39
  jurisprudence, 45–6, 50
  law, 46–8
  sciences, 160, 161
Nature
  and society, 168–70
  and spirit, 141–3, 150
  of women, 10–13, 34–7, 86–9, 116, 153
Newtonian scientific model, 160–1
Nietzsche, F., 8–11, 13, 15, 179–98

Okin, Susan, 87
Owen, Robert, 172, 174, 175

Pateman, Carole, 93, 96
Patriarchy, 87
Peace, 144
Personality, 132–3
Place, Francis, 170
Plato, 85, 88
Pocock, J.G.A., 45, 71

Politics
  importance of, 120–2
  interest in, 96–7
  realm of, 15–18
  rejection of, 16–17
  western theories of, 128,
    155
  see also Public/private
    distinction
Polygamy, 48, 51, 66, 67
Power, 2, 89, 166, 180–1
  see also Will to power
Property, 66, 67, 137, 138–40,
  147–8
Public/private distinction,
  5–10, 14, 17–18, 44–5,
  54–6, 71, 80–1, 91–2,
  98–9
  dehumanizing effect of, 99
Pufendorf, Samuel von, 46–54,
  66, 71

Reason, 35–6, 197
Relevance of political
  philosophies, 4–5
Rendall, Jane, 6–8
Republicanism, 45, 52, 56
Rights
  of children, 130–1
  of individual, 44–5, 62
Romanticism, 15, 17, 106–22
Rome, 65, 67
Rose, Gillian, 153
Rousseau, J-J., 4, 6, 8, 10, 11,
  12, 22, 78–101, 130–1

Saint-Simon, H. de, 174
Sappho, 113
Schiller, Friedrich, 106–7, 110
Schlegel, A.W., 8, 11, 106–10,
  112–22
  Lucinde, 115–16, 119–20
Schlegel, Caroline, 108

Schleiermacher, F., 117–18,
  119
Schopenhauer, A., 183, 184–5
Self-interest, 58
Self-realization, 109, 111, 191
Sensuality, 110, 115–16
Sex
  Hutcheson on, 52–3
  Kant on, 31–2
  Schlegel on, 115–17
Sexual differences, 109–10,
  111–17, 133–6, 145,
  146, 149, 167–70
Sexuality, 151
Shklar, Judith, 79, 137
Smith, Adam, 6, 8, 10, 44–5,
  56–72
Social conditioning, 167
Social contract, 80
Social roles, 98, 136, 146–8
Socialism, 9
Socialization, 82, 84, 96
Society and nature, 141–3, 150
Sovereign, individual and state,
  2
Spartan citizenship, 81–4, 89
Spirit and nature, 141–3, 150
State, the, 189–92
Stereotypes, 146
Strong, Tracy, 194
Suffrage, 2, 29, 165
Sympathy, 57–63

Taylor, Harriet, 171
Tensions
  in Hegel, 128–30, 131, 137,
    140
  in Kant, 22–3, 38–9
Theology, natural, 50
Thompson, William, 171,
  172–3, 175
Tönnies, Ferdinand, 184, 186
Totalitarianism, 6, 83

Übermensch, 180, 185, 192
Utilitarianism, 9–10, 12, 159–75

Vaihinger, Hans, 182, 183,
 184–5
Values, male and female, 15–17
Veit, Dorothea, 108
Virtue, 55–6, 58–60, 62
Vogel, Ursula, 8, 15, 17
von Herbert, Maria, 38
von Pufendorf, Samuel, 46–54,
 66, 71
Vote, 165, 166
 see also Suffrage

Weber, Max, 84, 191
Wheeler, Anne, 175
Will to power, 182–3, 185–90

Will to truth, 194
Williams, Howard, 22, 38
Wolff, R.P., 99–100
Wolgast, Elizabeth, 40
Wollstonecraft, Mary, 4, 17,
 121–2, 171
Women
 historical position, 64–6, 68
 likened to plants, 149–51
 nature of, 10–13, 34–7,
  86–9, 116, 153
 poor, 69
 recurring themes in
  philosophies on, 3–4
 as subversive, 187–9, 193
Work, 137–9, 142, 145

Xanthippe, 188

UNIVERSITY OF WOLVERHAMPTON
LIBRARY